Air Band Radio Handbook

Patrick Stephens Limited, a member of the Haynes Publishing Group, has published authoritative, quality books for enthusiasts for more than 25 years. During that time the company has established a reputation as one of the world's leading publishers of books on aviation, maritime, military, model-making, motor cycling, motoring, motor racing, railway and railway modelling subjects. Readers or authors with suggestions for books they would like to see published are invited to write to: The Editorial Director, Patrick Stephens Limited, Sparkford, Nr Yeovil, Somerset BA22 7JJ.

Air Band Radio Handbook

4th edition

David J. Smith

Patrick Stephens Limited

First published in 1986
Second edition 1987
Reprinted (with revisions) July 1988
Third edition February 1990
Reprinted (with revisions) July 1990
Reprinted August 1991
Fourth edition October 1992

A Catalogue record for this book
is available from the British Library

Library of Congress catalog card no. 92–73814

ISBN 1 85260 430 1

*Patrick Stephens Limited is part of the
Haynes Publishing Group P.L.C., Sparkford,
Nr Yeovil, Somerset, BA22 7JJ.*

Printed in Great Britain by
J.H. Haynes & Co. Ltd.

Contents

Introduction

Prior to 1963 enthusiasts had to rely on their own eyesight, aided by binoculars and telescopes, to identify aircraft. A minor revolution occurred in that year when the first radios covering the VHF air band (then 108 – 136 MHz) were put on the market. The messages between pilots and ground controllers could now be overheard by anyone who cared to buy one. More important, the majority of aircraft flying over could be identified by their registration or serial number.

These early sets were neither cheap nor very portable but over the years the trend towards miniaturisation has brought us pocket-sized sets from many manufacturers. Also, if one is prepared to part with several hundred pounds, there are magnificent receivers which scan the entire band automatically, or can be pre-set to receive only those local frequencies which may be of interest.

A great many people have bought air band radios, however, and found the jargon they hear almost incomprehensible. It is easy to pick out callsigns but most VHF listeners I have talked to would like to build up a better picture of what is going on and to unravel the 'mysteries' of Air Traffic Control. This book aims to do just that.

Similarly, people embarking upon a course of flying lessons for a Private Pilot's Licence would find it useful to acquire an air band radio and listen to how the professionals do their R/T. My experience shows that to the majority of trainee pilots learning how to use the radio is almost as big a hurdle as mastering their aircraft. Nothing brands one as an amateur so much as the long, rambling transmissions which controllers have to face on numberless occasions on a busy frequency! Some people may have been flying for years with a lot of skill but they let themselves down by poor R/T technique.

The terse messages, so confusing at first hearing, follow a definite pattern known as 'standard phraseology'. This verbal shorthand is designed to impart the maximum amount of unambiguous information in the shortest possible time. Since English is the international language of Air Traffic Control it must be understood easily by those with a different native tongue. With careful listening, and the aid of the examples in this book, the R/T exchanges on the air band will soon become both logical and familiar.

It must be emphasised that in the extremely complex world of Air Traffic Control procedures are changing all the time; new air lanes may be brought into use, others replaced or re-routed. Similarly new beacons and reporting points are always being introduced. Frequencies tend to stay the same for years, although with the current introduction of closer spacing between them there may be some upheavals in the future. The fact that radio navigation charts are updated every month or so shows just how frequently changes are liable to occur.

Since the third edition of this book was published in 1990 the long air traffic delays which hit the headlines around that time have largely been eradicated. This was chiefly the result of a co-ordinated effort throughout Europe to organise Air Traffic Flow Management and improve communications between the agencies involved. The downturn in worldwide air traffic in the aftermath of the Gulf War has also granted some breathing space.

The introduction of the Centralised Control Function (CCF) continues on schedule, December 1995 being the target date for completion. It is designed to smooth and integrate the flows of traffic into and out of London's airports by using a network of separate 'tunnels' of airspace. Planned for March 1993 is the move of the CCF Approach functions for Heathrow and Gatwick to a new operations room at the London Air Traffic Control Centre. A week later the CCF TMA function will come into service. Although the CCF will remain at West Drayton, near Heathrow, the rest of the London ATCC will relocate to an entirely new site near Fareham in Hampshire. At present referred to by the acronym NERC, the New En Route Centre is due to become fully operational in 1996 ready to take British ATC into the 21st century.

Acknowledgements

For their help in the preparation of this book I would like to thank the Civil Aviation Authority, British Airways Aerad, Lowe Electronics at Matlock, The Airband Shop in Stockport, Raycom Communications, Waters and Stanton Electronics, Nevada Communications, and Andy Rackham, who co-runs Air Supply near Leeds & Bradford Airport (both proprietors are air traffic controllers and thus ideally placed to give guidance to enthusiasts!). I am particularly grateful to Ron Bishop of the Ulster Aviation Society for supplying much helpful advice and allowing me to draw freely on the material he has written about air band listening for the Society's magazine *Ulster Air Mail*. Other friends who have helped include Keith Crowden, John Locker, Gary Nuttall, Dave Mobbs, Margaret and Adrian Thompson, and Ken Rodgers. The magazine of the Merseyside Branch of Air-Britain, *North West Air News*, proved an invaluable source of information, particularly its 'Commscan' column and Andrew Hulme's 'Airline News'.

Abbreviations and Q-Codes

ADF	Automatic Direction Finder	EAT	Expected Approach Time
ADR	Advisory Route	ETA	Estimated Time of Arrival
ADT	Approved Departure Time		
AFIS*	Aerodrome Flight Information Service	ETD	Estimated Time of Departure
AGL	Above Ground Level	FIR	Flight Information Region
AIS	Aeronautical Information Service		
ATCC	Air Traffic Control Centre	GMC	Ground Movement Control
ATD	Actual Time of Departure	GMP	Ground Movement Planning
ATIS*	Automatic Terminal Information Service	GPWS	Ground Proximity Warning System
BAA	British Airports Authority	HF	High Frequency
CAA	Civil Aviation Authority	ICAO*	International Civil Aviation Organisation
CAAFU*	Civil Aviation Authority Flying Unit	IFR	Instrument Flight Rules
CHAPI*	Compact Helicopter Approach Path Indicator	ILS	Instrument Landing System
		IMC	Instrument Meteorological Conditions
D/F	Direction Finding	INS	Inertial Navigation System
DFR	Departure Flow Regulation		
DFTI	Distance From Touchdown Indicator	IRVR	Instrumented Runway Visual Range
		LATCC*	London Air Traffic Control Centre
DME	Distance Measuring Equipment	LITAS*	Low Intensity Two Colour Approach Slope Indicators

MATZ*	Military Aerodrome Traffic Zone	RIV	Rapid Intervention Vehicle
MDH	Minimum Descent Height	R/T	Radio Telephony
MEDA	Military Emergency Diversion Aerodrome	RTTY*	Radio Teletype (pronounced Ritty)
METRO*	US military met office (pronounced Mee-tro)	RVR	Runway Visual Range
		SAR	Search and Rescue
MLS	Microwave landing system	SID*	Standard Instrument Departure
MOR	Mandatory Occurrence Report	SOTA	Shannon Oceanic Transition Area
NDB	Non-Directional Beacon	SRA	Surveillance Radar Approach
OAT	Operational air traffic *or* outside air temperature	SSB	Single Side Band
		SSR	Secondary Surveillance Radar
OCH	Obstacle Clearance Height	STAR*	Standard (Instrument) Arrival Route
PAPIS*	Precision Approach Path Indicator System	STOL*	Short take off and landing
PAR	Precision Approach Radar	TAF*	Terminal Aerodrome Forecast
PPR	Prior Permission Required	TCAS*	Traffic Alert and Collision Avoidance System (Tee-kass)
QAR	Quick Access Recorder		
QDM	Magnetic track to the airfield with nil wind	TMA	Terminal Control Area (formerly Terminal Manoeuvring Area)
QFE	Barometric pressure setting at aerodrome level		
		UHF	Ultra High Frequency
		USB	Upper Side Band
QGH	Controlled descent through cloud	UTC	Universal Time Consultant
QNH	Barometric pressure at sea level	VASI*	Visual Approach Slope Indicator
QSY	Change frequency	VDF	VHF Direction Finder
QTE	True bearing from the airfield	VHF	Very High Frequency
		VMC	Visual Meteorological Conditions
RAS	Radar Advisory Service		
RCC	Rescue Co-ordination Centre	VOR	VHF Omni-Directional Range
RIS	Radar Information Service		

* The abbreviations marked with an asterisk are normally spoken as a complete word.

Chapter 1

Listening

What you can hear, and in turn relate to aircraft you see flying overhead, obviously depends on the position of your location relative to airports and air lanes. Since VHF radio waves follow approximate lines of sight, the higher the aircraft, the farther away you can hear messages from it. Transmitter power is also a factor but, generally speaking, high flying aircraft can be received up to 200 miles away. As a rule of thumb, frequencies below 123 MHz are allocated to tower and approach units and those above 123 MHz to Air Traffic Control Centres (ATCCs), although there are exceptions to this.

Ground stations may be screened by hills, buildings and other obstructions, so you may not be able to pick up the replies from a tower or approach unit if you live more than ten miles away from it. The coverage for the ATCCs at London and Prestwick and the Sub-Centre at Manchester is very much better, however, there being few places in the flatter parts of the British Isles out of range of one or more of the powerful transmitters. This is because they are sited at some distance from their associated ground stations, usually on high ground. There may, however, be some 'blind spots' in reception for no apparent reason.

The first thing to do is to establish which ground stations are within range and which can help you to identify aircraft flying in your local area. If you are fortunate enough to own a scanning receiver you can set up the appropriate frequencies and monitor them when required. With experience you will soon know which station an aircraft is likely to be 'working', its height being a good clue as to whether it is talking to the local airfield, ATCC, radar unit etc. Unfortunately in an area such as the Midlands there are so many ATC units capable of giving a radar service that it may be difficult to discover to which a transit aircraft is talking. A flight below airways in the South Midlands, for example, might be in contact with Upper Heyford, Bedford or Brize

Norton Radar units or simply the London Flight Information frequency. Of course, the pilot might not be talking to anyone, nor does he need to if he keeps clear of aerodrome traffic zones and other restricted airspace.

If you have the good fortune to live beneath an airway and, even better, close to one of its reporting points, the relevant airways frequency can be selected and you can sit back and wait for something interesting to appear. Alas, rare aircraft seem to have a tendency to fly over when there is a solid cloud layer and only a tantalising drone or rumble can be heard! Unfortunately, it is not just a simple case of listening in, running outside at the right moment and rapidly filling up one's notebooks. Aircraft do not always use their registrations or serial numbers as callsigns, the trend in commercial flying is for more and more companies to use a callsign totally unrelated to what is painted on the aircraft. The airlines have been doing this for years but the practice has now spread even to taxi aircraft.

The answers to any questions which may arise from this practise, for the most part, are to be found in the network of enthusiasts' magazines which keep most airfields under surveillance and publish detailed lists of visitors, usually tabulated by callsign as well as registration letters. The information is normally acquired by courtesy of the airport management or ATC, the ranks of which are riddled with enthusiast 'moles'. Some private airfields, such as those run by British Aerospace, which operate military aircraft are understandably less co-operative, but there is often a local spotter who makes notes and passes them on! Since most transatlantic flights from north-west Europe have to cross Britain at some point even those anonymous airliners on contrails can be identified as there are several publications available which match the callsign and registration of most of them.

Identifying military aircraft is very difficult as few use the actual serial number, USAF transports being one of the few exceptions. Military airfields generally use UHF frequencies to talk to their own aircraft, but UHF receivers, hitherto virtually unobtainable, are now on the market. Unfortunately, the call signs of first line aircraft are changed frequently for security reasons.

Bearing in mind that air traffic has its rush hours too, certain times of the day can be particularly rewarding for air band listeners. For example, the Heathrow peak period for arriving traffic is mid-morning, reflected in the increased landing fees at this time. Late afternoon, particularly on Fridays, sees an even larger volume of traffic in the congested United Kingdom airways system as the entire

British executive fleet seems intent upon making for home!

For insomniacs there is plenty going on even in the smallest hours of the night as aircraft flying the mail wend their way towards Liverpool and East Midlands five nights a week from all points of the compass and fan out again some time later. Heathrow has a virtual ban on traffic after midnight because of noise restrictions, but Luton, Manchester, Glasgow and others send load after load of holiday-makers to the Mediterranean and beyond, particularly on summer weekends. Mixed in are the cargo aircraft, most of them scheduled, but occasionally including an extra service rushing some urgently needed parts for the motor industry.

Finally, a note about the law relating to air band listening. In a word, **it is illegal for the unlicensed! It is also a myth that listening is permitted if one does not impart the information to another person. Judging by the number of radios one hears blasting out across public viewing areas at airports, it would appear that officialdom turns a blind eye to what is essentially a harmless activity. The law may be changed one day but in the meantime do not telephone the newspapers if you overhear a hijack or some other emergency in progress. This sort of thing could end the authorities' tacit acceptance of air band listening.**

In 1965 there was some trouble caused by cheap super-regenerative receivers which actually re-transmitted the received signal. The resulting carrier wave interfered with air to ground communications and air band radios were banned on Manchester Airport's public viewing galleries, unless the owner had a dispensation from the telecommunications section which offered a free testing service. This seems to have been the only time when air band radios have ever been controlled in this country and there is no evidence that it was done at any other British airport.

However, since modern air band receivers are totally passive, there is no chance of spurious transmissions jamming the air waves. Trouble may loom in another area because many advanced scanners are able to monitor cellular telephone conversations. British Telecom and its competitors have complained about this to the Department of Trade and Industry but no action has so far been taken to control the sale of scanning receivers. Listening to police messages is another illegal activity, and there have been a number of recent cases involving heavy fines and confiscated scanners. Merely having these frequencies in the receiver's memory is considered proof of guilt.

Right *View from the air traffic control tower at Southampton Eastleigh Airport* (Airports UK).

Chapter 2

ATC terminology

The majority of air band listeners use their radio as a means of logging aircraft registrations but there are others for whom this is of no more than academic interest. Their listening pleasure is derived from learning how aircraft are controlled and the way the ATC system operates. Those in the second category will soon begin to grasp the principles, and will want to find out more, whilst those in the first will recognise that a basic knowledge of them will assist in tracking the aircraft in which they are interested.

Before I embark upon a more detailed description of ATC I should like first to cast some light on the jargon words which seem to puzzle the new air band listener. The most obvious are the terms QNH, QFE and Flight Level. The first two are codes rather than abbreviations and refer to the current atmospheric pressure at sea level and aerodrome level respectively. When the value in millibars is set on the aircraft's altimeter the instrument will indicate the distance above the appropriate datum. The term QFE Threshold refers, by the way, to the barometric pressure converted to that at the end of a runway.

Above a point known as the transition altitude, normally between 3,000 ft and 6,000 ft in the United Kingdom, a standard setting of 1013.2 millibars is used, producing what is termed a Flight Level (abbreviated to FL). This ensures that all aircraft, particularly within controlled airspace, are flying on the same altimeter setting and can thus easily be separated vertically by the required amount. This obviates the necessity of continually adjusting the altimeter to allow for local pressure variations over the route, any error being common to all aircraft in the system. FL 70 is roughly equivalent to 7,000 ft, FL 230 to 23,000 ft and so on.

Times are given in the form of two figures; for example 14, pronouced one-four, indicates 14 minutes past the hour, four-two 42 minutes past the hour and so on. The standard ATC time in the United

Kingdom, and indeed in the entire aviation world, is Universal Time Constant known as UTC. In the winter it is the same as local or *Alpha* time in the United Kingdom but British Summer Time is one hour ahead of it. This use of UTC ensures that there is no confusion with Flight Plans on aircraft transmitting time zones.

The word *squawk* is often heard, particularly in route clearances, along with a four figure code. This is set on the aircraft's transponder, a device which responds to automatic interrogations from a ground station by sending a return signal in coded form. The information appears on the radar screen as a label giving callsign, height and destination, adjacent to the appropriate aircraft position symbol. (The word *blip* is now somewhat outmoded, the image on the screen on modern airways radars being produced electronically via a computer. The centre sweep familiar in films is now only seen on approach radars at the smaller airports.)

The term *clearance* or *cleared* is a legal one meaning that the aircraft may proceed under certain explicit conditions and that it will not be impeded by other traffic. It has, in the past, been somewhat over-used by controllers in circumstances where its use was unnecessary so the authorities have narrowed it down considerably. It is now confined mainly to route clearances and runway occupancy for take-off and landing, thus avoiding any possible confusion with the meaning.

Directions are given in degrees magnetic so that if an aircraft is heading 360° it is flying due north, 090° due east and so on. Note the difference between heading and actual path over the ground (track). If there is a strong cross-wind an aircraft may be pointing (heading) in a particular direction but travelling over the ground in a considerably different direction. There is an analogy here with rowing a small boat across a fast-flowing river, although you may be aiming for a point on the opposite bank, the current will also be deflecting you sideways. Simple right and left are used for direction changes, as in the instruction 'Turn right heading 340', port and starboard being long outmoded in aviation.

Speed is expressed in knots, one knot being equal to one nautical mile per hour. The exception to this is on transatlantic and similar long-haul flights where a Mach Number is employed, speed being expressed as a ratio of the speed of sound. Jet transports cruise at around Mach 0.8 and Concorde at Mach 2, twice the speed of sound.

Distances are measured in nautical miles (approx 2,025 yd). References to DME, as in 'Report 8 DME Wallasey', relate to the Distance Measuring Equipment carried aboard aircraft. This receives radio transmissions from ground beacons and enables the distance to or from the particular position to be presented automatically to the pilot as a continuous read-out in miles and tenths. In some systems, the 'time to go' to the beacon can also be displayed to the pilot.

Runways are designated by two numbers derived from the heading in degrees magnetic. The main runway at Manchester, for example, is 06/24. This is rounded up from the actual direction of 057/237° magnetic and the end zero omitted. Similarly a heading of 054/234 would be presented as 05/23. Other familiar examples are 09 Right/ 27 Left and 09 Left/27 Right at Heathrow and 08/26 at Gatwick.

Somewhat confusing to the layman are the terms VFR, IFR, VMC and IMC, so I shall explain them at some length because they are of paramount importance in ATC. Flight conditions are divided thus:

(a) Visual Flight Rules (VFR) which apply under Visual Meteorological Conditions (VMC);

(b) Instrument Flight Rules (IFR) which apply under Instrument Meteorological Conditions (IMC).

The minima for VFR flight are quite complicated but can be summarised as follows. At or below 3,000 feet AMSL at an indicated air speed of 140 knots or less, an aircraft must remain in sight of ground or water and clear of cloud in a flight visibility of at least 1,500 metres. If the indicated air speed (IAS) is more than 140 kt up to a limit of 250 kt, the flight visibility must be at least 6 km. Above 3,000 ft up to FL100 the minima are 5 km visibility and at least 1,500 metres horizontally, or 1,000 ft vertically clear of cloud. At FL100 and above, the speed limit no longer applies and the visibility minimum is increased to 8 km.

Since it is his or her responsibility to keep clear of other traffic, the pilot must maintain a good look-out. Furthermore, under certain conditions, climbs or descents maintaining VMC may be authorised for aircraft flying under IFR so as to expedite traffic, it is then the pilot's responsibility to avoid other traffic. In R/T transmissions the terms VFR or Victor Fox are used freely. Similarly, VMC may be referred to as Victor Mike. The phrase 'VMC on top' means that the aircraft is flying in VMC conditions above a cloud layer.

IFR comes into force when the visibility requirements described above cannot be met, and at all times during the hours of darkness. It is then mandatory for aircraft to be flown on instruments by a suitably qualified pilot. It must also carry a minimum scale of navigational and other equipment. Within controlled airspace, responsibility for separation from other aircraft is in the hands of ground controllers.

Outside controlled airspace, pilots flying above the transition altitude of 3,000 ft must reset their altimeters to the standard setting of 1,013 millibars and fly in accordance with what is known as the quadrantal rule. This is intended to ensure that aircraft on converging headings at levels below 24,500 ft remain clear of each other by at least 500 ft, as the following table explains:

Magnetic track	*Cruising level*
Less than 90°	Odd thousands of feet
90° but less than 180°	Odd thousands of feet plus 500 ft
180° but less than 270°	Even thousands of feet
270° but less than 360°	Even thousands of feet plus 500 ft

Above 24, 500 ft the semi-circular rule applies:

Magnetic track	*Cruising level*
Less than 180°	25,000 ft
	27,000 ft
	29,000 ft or higher levels at intervals of 4,000 ft
180° but less than 360°	26,000 ft
	28,000 ft
	31,000 ft or higher levels at intervals of 4,000 ft

A final variation on the IFR/VFR theme is Special VFR, an authorisation by ATC for a pilot to fly within a control zone, even though he is unable to comply with IFR and in certain airspace where provision is made for such flights. Depending on the visibility, amount of cloud and its height and the limitations of the pilot's licence, a Special VFR clearance may be requested and issued.

Standard separation is provided between all Special VFR flights, and between such flights and other aircraft operating IFR. In practice much use is made of geographical features to keep Special VFR traffic apart, routeing along opposite banks of an estuary for instance. When flying on this type of clearance a pilot must comply with ATC instructions and remain at all times in flight conditions which enable him to determine his flight path and to keep clear of obstructions. It is implicit in all Special VFR clearances that the aircraft stays clear of cloud and in sight of the surface. ATC almost always imposes a height limitation which will require the pilot to fly either at or below a specific level. A typical clearance at Liverpool, for example, is 'GYE is cleared to the zone boundary via Chester, Special VFR not above 1,500 ft Liverpool QNH 1002.'

The phrase 'Rule 21 Airspace' is heard from time-to-time on R/T; it simply means that in certain airspace such as airways and Control Zones IFR applies all the time, regardless of actual weather conditions. It refers to the Rules of the Air and Air Traffic Control contained in the UK Air Navigation Order. The term 'Class A Airspace' is replacing it.

Phonetic alphabet

The use of phonetics on radio to overcome the problems of confusing similar sounding letters like 'B' and 'P' or 'M' and 'N' dates back to the First World War when it was essential that such information as map references were passed accurately by aircraft spotting for the artillery. The phonetic alphabet of the time began A-Ack, B-Beer and has left us with such enduring phrases as 'Ack-Ack' for anti-aircraft fire. I am not certain when this alphabet was superseded but by the time of the Second World War it was as follows:

A — Able	J — Jig	S — Sugar
B — Baker	K — King	T — Tare
C — Charlie	L — Love	U — Uncle
D — Dog	M — Mike	V — Victor
E — Easy	N — Nan	W — William
F — Fox	O — Oboe	X — X-Ray
G — George	P — Peter	Y — Yoke
H — How	Q — Queen	Z — Zebra
I — Item	R — Roger	

In the fifties, by international agreement, the British wartime code was replaced by a new alphabet designed to be more easily pronounced by aircrew whose native language was other than English. Some of the original phonetics were retained but a number of words known throughout the world were now employed. The resulting alphabet was almost identical to that in use today, the exceptions being M — Metro, N — Nectar and X — Extra.

The new offering sparked off some ribald comment that its originators seemed to have spent a lot of time hanging around in bars and dancehalls, such was the emphasis on these admirable pursuits! The alphabet was overhauled once more in 1956 and remains in use to this day. My only subjective criticism is that Juliet and Zulu can be confused, admittedly not very often, when used by certain foreign nationals against a background of engine noise. Papa is another weak point. Correctly it should be pronounced Pah-*Pah* but this is more difficult to say and most pilots and controllers pronounce it with equal emphasis on the two syllables.

Certain universally accepted codes and abbreviations, such as QNH, QFE, ILS, SRA, QDM are not put into phonetics but said as written. There is also a standard way of pronouncing numbers and the word decimal, as used in radio frequencies, is supposed to be said as 'dayseemal' although this rarely happens in practice. (I once heard an Irish pilot who, after the controller used the word 'tree' to him for three, accused him of 'takin' da micky'!)

Current phonetic alphabet

A — Alfa	J — Juliet	S — Sierra
B — Bravo	K — Kilo	T — Tango
C — Charlie	L — Lima	U — Uniform
D — Delta	M — Mike	V — Victor
E — Echo	N — November	W — Whiskey
F — Foxtrot	O — Oscar	X — X-Ray
G — Golf	P — Papa	Y — Yankee
H — Hotel	Q — Quebec	Z — Zulu
I — India	R — Romeo	

Transmission of numbers

0 — Zero	4 — Fower	8 — Ait
1 — Wun	5 — Fife	9 — Niner
2 — Too	6 — Six	Thousand — Tousand
3 — Tree	7 — Seven	

Examples of number transmissions are: 10 — Wun Zero; 583 — Fife Ait Tree; 2,500 — Too Fife Zero Zero; 3,000 — Tree Tousand. Frequences are passed in the form: 118.1 — Wun Wun Ait Day-see-mal Wun; 120.375 — Wun Too Zero Day-see-mal Tree Seven (the final digit being omitted).

Q-Code

A further note concerns the Q-Code, now obsolete in aviation, apart from certain enduring terms like QGH, QNH and QFE. This was an expansion of the Q-Code already in use by the merchant marine and it became possible to exchange information on practically all subjects that might be needed in aviation communications. These three letter groups could be sent by Wireless Telegraphy (W/T) in morse with great speed and overcame any inherent language difficulties. For example, an operator would send the code 'QDM' to a ground station, which meant 'What is my magnetic course to steer with zero wind to reach you?' The ground operator would transmit 'QDM' and the appropriate figure.

Standard words and Phrases used in R/T communications

Word/Phrase	Meaning
Acknowledge	Let me know that you have received and understood this message.
Affirm	Yes.
Approved	Permission for proposed action granted.
Break	Indicates the separation between messages.
Cancel	Annul the previously transmitted clearance.
Check	Examine a system or procedure (no answer is normally expected).
Cleared	Authorised to proceed under the conditions specified.
Confirm	Have I correctly received the following...? *or* Did you correctly receive this message?
Contact	Establish radio contact with... (The obsolete code 'QSY', which meant the same thing, is often still used by pilots.)
Correct	That is correct.
Correction	An error has been made in this transmission (or message indicated). The correct version is...
Disregard	Consider that transmission as not sent.
How do you read	What is the readability of my transmission?
I say again	I repeat for clarity or emphasis.
Monitor	Listen out on (frequency).
Negative	No *or* permission not granted *or* that is not correct.
Over	My transmission is ended and I expect a response from you.
Out	My transmisison is ended and no response is expected.
Pass your message	Proceed with your message.
Read back	Repeat all, or the specified part, of this message back to me exactly as received.
Report	Pass required information.
Request	I should like to know... *or* I wish to obtain...

Roger	I have received all your last transmission. (Note: under no circumstances to be used in reply to a question requiring a direct answer in the affirmative (*affirm*) or negative (*negative*).)
Say again	Repeat all, or the following part of your last transmission.
Standby	Wait and I will call you. (Note: No onward clearance to be assumed.)
Verify	Check and confirm.
Wilco	I understand your message and will comply with it. (Abbreviation for 'will comply'.)

The words *over* and *out* are now rarely used in practice and the original form of *affirmative*, superseded in 1984 by *affirm*, is still to be heard. (Old habits die hard!) Also note that controllers who are recently ex-military, sometimes use standard RAF phrases such as *wait* (for *standby*) and *wrong* (for *correction*).

The clarity of radio transmissions is expressed by the following scale:

Readability 1 — Unreadable;
Readability 2 — Readable now and then;
Readability 3 — Readable but with difficulty;
Readability 4 — Readable;
Readability 5 — Perfectly readable.

Note that controllers in exasperation sometimes use non-standard phrases like 'Strength a half' for really awful radios! Another phrase in common usage is 'Carrier wave only', indicating that an unmodulated transmission is being received by the ground station, ie, it is just noise without the accompanying speech.

Communications

Aeronautical ground stations are identified by the name of the location, followed by a suffix which indicates the type of service being given.

Suffix	**Service**
Control	Area Control Service
Radar	Radar (in general)
Approach	Approach Control
Tower	Aerodrome Control
Ground	Ground Movement Control
Precision	Precision Approach Radar

Information   Flight Information Service
Radio   Aerodrome Air/Ground Communications Service

When satisfactory two-way communication has been established, and provided that it will not be confusing, the name of the location or the callsign suffix may be omitted. The basic rule is that the full callsigns of both stations must be used on the first transmission. For example:

Aircraft: Southend Tower GABCD.

ATC: GABCD Southend Tower pass your message.

Aircraft callsigns may take various forms but they must remain the same throughout the flight. However, if aircraft on the same frequency have similar callsigns ATC may instruct one of them to alter the format temporarily to avoid confusion. One other point is that aircraft in the heavy wake turbulence category must include the word 'heavy' immediately after the callsign in the initial call. This is to remind the controller that increased separation may be necessary for following aircraft.

The recommended methods of presenting callsign are summarised below.

	Example	
Type of callsign	**Full**	**Abbreviated**
(a) The five-character callsign corresponding to the registration marking of the aircraft, the first one or two letters being the national prefix	G–ABCD	GCD
(b) The five-character callsign referred to in (a) above, preceded by the R/T designator of the aircraft operator	British Midland G–BMAE	British Midland AE
(c) The five-character callsign referred to in (a) above, preceded by the type of aircraft (An American practice which is slowly spreading to Europe)	Cherokee G–AWTM	Cherokee TM
(d) The R/T designator of the aircraft operator, followed by the flight identification	Speedbird 835	No abbreviation permitted
(e) Alpha-numerical callsign corresponding with the aircraft registration marking	N786AQ	86AQ

In practice other variations are to be heard, some pilots using their company three-letter designator and flight number rather than the normal company name and flight number, eg GNT 401 for Granite 401. Either is correct and it is quite common for controllers, faced with an unfamiliar company designator on a flight progress strip, or simply forgetting what it stands for, to revert to the three-letter prefix.

The aim is to prevent incidents and potential accidents caused by callsign ambiguities but these still occur in sufficient numbers to cause concern. Regular bulletins of Mandatory Occurrence Reports (MORs) are circulated amongst pilots and controllers and these often contain reports of aircraft with similar callsigns taking instructions meant for each other by mistake.

Up to the mid-sixties airline operators generally used the aircraft registration letters for flight-planning purposes. As the ATC system became more sophisticated and traffic increased, the flight number became the prime means of identification. (On inter-continental flights this practice came into use much earlier.) There were several reasons for the change, one of the more mundane ones being the amount of extra work involved at the ATC Centres if the company had to change the aircraft on a route because of unserviceability or other reasons. In those days computer-printed flight progress strips were far in the future, the strips having to be hand-written by the 'A-Man', who acted as assistant to the Airways Controller, based on advance information from the flight plan.

Perhaps BEA might have decided that Vanguard G-APEP was to be replaced on, say, a London-Belfast trip, by G-APEN. Since each UK internal flight on airways might take up to eight flight strips, one for each en route reporting point, there was an awful lot of writing to be done at peak periods. The Airways Controller or 'D-Man', to use the jargon of the day, was not very happy to be given a collection of altered strips, so they all had to be written out again. Speaking from personal experience, the change to flight numbers saved a lot of writer's cramp. Unfortunately, the spotters under Amber 1 or Red 3 would gnash their teeth because they were no longer able to 'cop' (a spotter's jargon for seeing) the entire Vanguard fleet or whatever, without moving from the back garden!

In 1968 the flight plan system was amended to facilitate the introduction of the repetitive flight plan for scheduled services. The use of flight numbers became even more widespread because they were then the only form of identification known sufficiently far in advance of the departure. In the mid-seventies smaller charter operators in the United Kingdom who had formerly used the registration for their Piper Aztecs, Navajos and the like, began to use flight numbers instead. One of the main reasons for this was that many European controllers treated them as private aircraft and gave them low priority, even though they were *bona fide* commercial flights.

This greater use of flight numbers led to more callsign confusion and methods of improving the situation were investigated. One of the best was the alpha-numeric system which was employed by Dan-Air during two separate trials, the second being suspended in October 1987. A typical callsign was Dan-Air Bravo Six Foxtrot Echo. Unfortunately, international agreement could not be reached and the alpha-numeric method has been shelved for the time being. Further confusion has been caused by callsigns resembling flight levels or headings, so operators have agreed, as far as possible, not to allocate flight numbers which end in zero or five. In practice, this means figures below 500.

GLOSSARY OF AVIATION TERMS HEARD ON RADIO

See also Abbreviations and lists on pages 20, 21 and 49.

Abeam	Passing a specified point at 90 degrees to the left or right.
Active	The runway-in-use.
Actual	The current weather conditions.
Air Pilot	UK Aeronautical Information Publication.
Approved	
Departure Time	See pages 105 – 106.
ATIS	Automatic Terminal Information Service.
Avgas	Aviation gasoline.
Backtrack	Taxi back along the runway.
Bandboxed	Two or more frequencies monitored by one controller.
Base turn	The turn on to final from an instrument approach when it is not a reciprocal of the outbound track.
The Bell	Colloquial term for the Belfast VOR.
Blind transmission	A transmission from one station to another when two-way communication cannot be established but where it is believed that the called station is able to receive the transmission.

The Boundary	Boundary between Flight Information Regions or alternatively the edge of a Control Zone.
Box	Radio, Box One being the main set and Box Two the standby.
Breakthrough	Transmissions on one frequency breaking through on to another.
Build-ups	Cumulo-nimbus clouds.
CAVOK	See page 91.
CB	Also referred to as Charlie Bravo. Cumulo-nimbus clouds
Centrefix Approach	Self-positioning to final approach using the aircraft Flight Management System.
Charlie	That is correct (common HF usage).
Clearance limit	A specified point to which an ATC clearance remains effective.
Conflicting traffic	Other aircraft in the vicinity which may prove a hazard.
The Cross	Colloquial term for Dean Cross VOR.
The Data	Temperature, QNH, runway-in-use, etc.
Detail	Intentions during a particular training flight.
Direct	Flying from one beacon or geographical point straight to another.
Discrete	Separate frequency usually devoted to one aircraft for PAR talk-down, etc.
Div Arrival	Arrival message sent to destination and other agencies when an aircraft diverts en route.
Drift	The effect of wind on an aircraft (see page 15).
Established	Aligned or 'locked on' with the ILS.
Expected Approach Time	See page 51.
Fanstop	Practice engine failure.
Free call	A call to a ground station without prior co-ordination by landline between this and the previous ATC unit with which the aircraft was in contact.
Glidepath	The final descent path to the runway on an ILS approach.
Go around	Overshoot runway and rejoin circuit or carry out missed approach procedure.
The GOW	Colloquial term for Glasgow VOR.
GPU	Ground Power Unit.

Guard Frequency	International Distress Frequency which is continuously monitored by aircraft flying long-distance routes.
Heavy	See page 182.
Jet A – 1	Turbine fuel.
Land after	See page 61.
Localiser	See page 39.
Mach	Speed expressed as a ratio of the speed of sound, Mach 1.
MOR	Mandatory Occurrence Report.
Navex	Navigational Exercise.
Notam	Notice to Airmen.
Off blocks	The time the aircraft commenced taxying.
On Blocks	Time on parking stand.
Orbit	Circle, usually over a specified point.
The Park	Colloquial term for Brookmans Park VOR.
Pattern	American equivalent of circuit.
Pax	Passengers.
The Pole	Colloquial term for Pole Hill VOR.
Pop-up traffic	Traffic which suddenly appears on radar, perhaps because it has just climbed into coverage.
PPR	Prior permission by telephone required for landing.
Procedure turn	Similar to base turn except that the aircraft retraces its steps on an exact reciprocal of the outbound leg.
QAR	Quick Access Recorder.
QFE	Barometric pressure at aerodrome level.
QNH	Barometric pressure at sea level.
QSY	Change frequency to . . .
Radar overhead	Radar blind spot above aerial.
Radar vectoring	Specified headings given by radar (see page 52).
Regional	The QNH for a defined area (see page 33).
RVR	Runway Visual Range (see page 92)
Selcal	Selective Calling (see page 82).
SID	Standard Instrument Departure.
SIGMET	Significant met conditions (see page 92).
Slot time	See pages 105 – 106.
SNOCLO	Airfield closed during snow-clearing operations.

SNOWTAM	See page 93.
Special flight	A police, photographic survey or other flight for which special permission has been granted by the CAA.
Squawk	SSR code (see pages 66–67).
Stand	Numbered parking position on apron.
Standard Missed Approach	Procedure to be followed if an aircraft is unable to land from an instrument approach.
Stratus	Low-lying cloud layer.
Stud	Military pre-set frequency.
Tad	Tactical Air Deployment (frequency).
TAF	Terminal Aerodrome Forecast.
Teardrop	A 180 degree turn to land back on the runway from which one has just departed. Often used by circuit training aircraft when runway-in-use is changed.
Tech stop	En route diversion for technical reasons.
Three greens	Indication of wheels down and locked.
U/s	Unserviceable.
Volmet	See pages 93 – 94.
Vortex wake	See pages 63 and 101.
Wake turbulence	Alternative form of vortex wake.
Waypoint	A pre-selected geographical position used with a Flight Management System.
Wind shear	See pages 92 – 93.

Moving on from callsign presentation, there are certain other basic R/T rules with which pilots must comply. Aircraft flying in controlled airspace must obtain permission from the controlling authority before changing frequency to another station. This is one of the most common causes of acrimony between controllers and pilots; aircraft disappearing from the approach frequency just as a turn or other important instruction is required to be passed. After a brief delay the aircraft comes up on the tower frequency and has to be told to go back to approach. This sort of thing is irritating and can be dangerous. Of course, pilots sometimes take instructions intended for other aircraft, particularly if the callsigns are similar.

Another important point is that an ATC route clearance is not an instruction to take off or enter an active runway. The words *take-off* are used only when an aircraft is cleared for take-off. At all other times the word *departure* is used—the disaster at Teneriffe in 1977 was caused mainly by a flight crew interpreting a route clearance as also implying a take-off clearance. They must have known better but there were pressing distractions and so the fatal error was made.

There is a stringent requirement to read back route (or airways) clearances because of the possible seriousness of a misunderstanding in the transmission and receipt of these messages. If the controller does not receive a read-back, the pilot will be asked to give one. Similarly, the pilot is expected to request that instructions be repeated or clarified if any are not fully understood. The ATC instructions listed below are to be read back in full by the pilot.

Level instructions, heading instructions, speed instructions, airways or route clearances, clearance to enter, land on, take off on,

Control Tower at Sumburgh, Shetland Isles (CAA).

backtrack or cross an active runway, runway-in-use, Secondary Surveillance Radar operating instructions, altimeter settings, VDF information, and frequency changes.

Examples are:

ATC: GBFVM cleared to cross Bravo 1 at Ottringham Flight Level 180.
Aircraft: Cleared to cross Bravo 1 at Ottringham Flight Level 180, GVM.
ATC: GTE contact Castledon Approach 119.65.
Aircraft: 119.65 GTE.

Levels may be reported as altitude, height or Flight Level, according to the phase of flight and the altimeter setting, but a standard form of reporting is adhered to. An aircraft climbs, descends, maintains, passes, leaves or reaches a level, the following ATC instructions clarifying this:

Aer Lingus 920 climb FL 190.
Speedbird 231 report passing FL 160.
Swissair 842 report reaching FL 190.
British Midland 581 maintain 3,500 ft.
Aircraft: Manx 501 request descent.
ATC: Manx 501 descend FL 60.
Aircraft: Manx 501 leaving FL 90 for FL 60.

Sometimes a changing traffic situation may necessitate an intermediate halt to a descent or climb. 'Aer Lingus 920 stop descent FL 150.' Occasionally, for traffic reasons, a higher than normal rate of climb or descent may be requested to avoid eroding separation. 'Aer Lingus 920 climb to FL 190, expedite passing FL 150.'

Separations

The rules for separation of IFR traffic, particularly when radar is not available, are quite complicated and probably of little interest to the layman. Suffice it to say that the basic radar separations are five miles laterally (but three and up to ten in certain cases) and/or 1,000 ft vertically up to FL 290. Above this level 2,000 ft vertical separation is applied and above FL 450 for supersonic aircraft 4,000 ft is the norm.

For aircraft departing from an airport the minimum separation is one minute, provided the aircraft fly on tracks diverging by 45° or more immediately after take-off. Where aircraft are going the same way, and provided the first has filed a true airspeed (TAS) 40 kt or more faster than the second, the separation is two minutes. With a TAS of 20 kt or more faster than the second aircraft it becomes five minutes and in all other cases it is ten minutes. Radar may reduce some of these times and they are also affected by the demands of vortex wake separation and local procedures.

Chapter 3

Types of airspace

Flight Information Region (FIR)

The United Kingdom is divided into two FIRs, the London and the Scottish, the boundary between them being the 55°N line of latitude. Above 24,500 ft these areas are known as Upper Flight Information Regions, abbreviated to UIR. The London FIR comes under the London Air Traffic Control Centre at West Drayton, close to Heathrow, and the Scottish FIR under Scottish ATCC at Atlantic House near Prestwick. Southern Ireland comes under the jurisdiction of the ATCC at Shannon, the stretches of the Atlantic to north and south being controlled by Reykjavik and Shanwick Oceanic Controls, respectively. At Manchester Airport there is an ATC Sub-Centre which controls traffic below 15,000 ft over the North of England and the Irish Sea.

In November 1991 the UK adopted a new ICAO system which aims to classify airspace internationally so that it is perfectly clear to users from anywhere in the world which flight rules apply and what air traffic services they can expect within a particular airspace. Actual procedures remain unaffected, the main change being one of terminology. Special Rules Airspace, except for the Upper Heyford Mandatory Radio Area, no longer exists, and Special Rules Zones have been renamed Control Zones. The seven different categories of airspace are represented by the letters A, B, C, D, E, F and G, although Class C has yet to be adopted in the UK.

Class A

This consists mainly of airways which are normally ten miles wide and generally have a base between 3,000 ft and FL 55. With some exceptions they extend vertically to FL 245, the base of upper airspace in Britain. Aircraft flying in them are required to operate under IFR and are separated positively by ATC, using radar or procedural methods.

'Westbound' flights, which could in practice also be on north-west or south-west headings, fly at even thousands of feet and 'eastbound' flights at odd thousands. Some airways are activated for peak periods only, usually weekends and recognised holidays. Additionally the London and Manchester TMAs are nominated as Class A.

Class B

This consists of upper airspace extending from FL 245 up to FL 660 and is designated a Control Area. The Upper Air Routes lie within it, the majority of them following the line of the normal airways below, hence Bravo 1 and Upper Bravo 1. However, fuel saving requirements in the last decade or so have led to an increasing tendency for aircraft to fly direct routes between radio beacons sometimes several hundred miles apart. Some of these *ad hoc* routeings have resulted in the establishment of UARs to regulate their use and also 'DT' or Direct Track routes.

The whole of the upper airspace is covered by joint civil and military radar units to co-ordinate the large numbers of flights within it. The standard vertical separation above FL 245 is increased to 2,000 ft so that aircraft flying in opposite directions are 2,000 ft apart. Link Routes in the upper airspace connect the oceanic boundaries with UK and Continental domestic routes. Concordes have special supersonic Link Routes.

Class D

This is the airspace formerly classified as Special Rules airspace in the vicinity of principal airfields. It is known now as a Control Zone or Control Area.

Class E

Scottish TMA airspace below 6,000 ft (above 6,000 ft is Class D), Belfast TMA and the Scottish Control Zone outside Glasgow and Prestwick Control Zones.

Class F

Reserved for Advisory Routes, normally referred to as ADRs, which have been established where public transport aircraft use certain routes but not in sufficient quantity to justify the full protection of an airway. To distinguish them from airways, the suffix 'Delta' for 'discretionary', eg Whiskey Two Delta, is used. Most of the ADRs are to be found in Scotland and Northern England with a mere two (Red Eight Delta and

Overleaf: *Upper Airspace Control Area and ATS routes for Southern UK (CAA).*

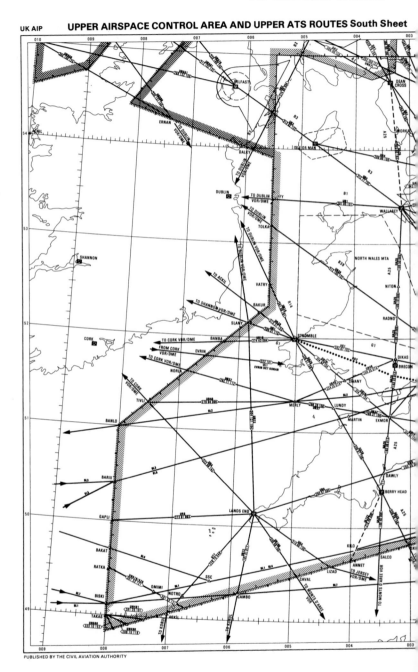

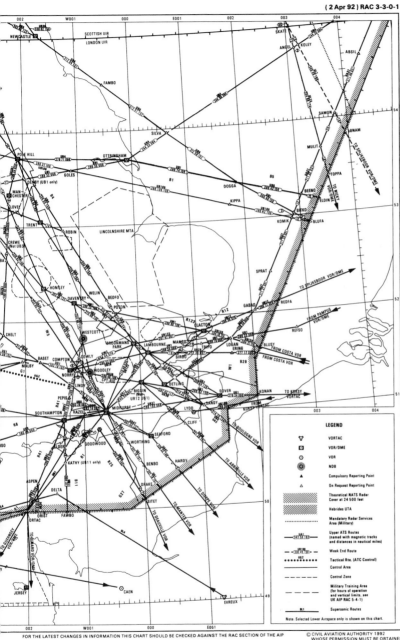

LEGEND

▽	VORTAC
◉	VOR/DME
⊙	VOR
◎	NDB
▲	Compulsory Reporting Point
△	On Request Reporting Point

Theoretical NATS Radar Cover at 24 500 feet

Hebrides UTA

Mandatory Radar Services Area (Military)

Upper ATS Routes (named with magnetic tracks and distances in nautical miles)

Week End Route

Tactical Rte. (ATC Control)

Control Area

Control Zone

Military Training Area (for hours of operation and vertical limits, see UK AIP RAC 5-4-1)

Supersonic Routes

Note: Selected Lower Airspace only is shown on this chart.

Green Four Delta) in the south. A few have achieved traffic density to
reach airway status, one of them being Bravo Two, formerly Delta Blue
22, between the Scottish TMA and Aberdeen. Unlike on airways, the
quadrantal rule is applied for level allocation (see page 17).

Class G

Unregulated airspace in the open FIR within which aircraft are allowed
to fly as they wish without hindrance or radio calls. In instrument
conditions pilots are expected to conform to a simple procedure called
the quadrantal rule which regulates altitude according to the aircraft's
heading.

Upper Heyford Mandatory Radio Area

Introduced by the USAF as a positive attempt to separate the large
numbers of light aircraft operating below 4,000 ft in the South Midlands
from high-speed jet traffic, mainly F-111s. Radio equipment and
compliance with instructions are compulsory.

Military Aerodrome Traffic Zones

The purpose of a MATZ is to provide a volume of airspace within
which increased protection may be given to aircraft in the critical
stages of circuit, approach and climb-out. It normally comprises the
airspace within five nautical miles radius of the airfield from the
surface up to 3,000 ft. In addition, a 'stub' out to five miles protects the
final approach path of the most used runway. Although it is not
mandatory for civil pilots to request permission to penetrate a MATZ,
it is obviously highly desirable for them to do so.

Military Training Areas

Military Training Areas are defined areas of upper airspace, within
which intense military flying takes place during weekdays and
occasionally, with prior notification, at weekends. Certain airways,
including Upper Alpha 25 and Upper Whiskey 39 are affected when
MTAs are active.

Aerodrome Traffic Zones

The dimensions relate to the midpoint of the longest runway and its
length. For example, if the longest runway is greater than 1850
metres, the boundary of the ATZ will be a circle of radius $2\frac{1}{2}$ NM
from the midpoint of that runway. Aerodromes with shorter
runways have smaller ATZs but the vertical limit remains 2,000
feet above aerodrome level. Both within or outside controlled
airspace pilots must either avoid the ATZ or obtain permission to
fly through it.

Danger Areas

The most common Danger Areas are weapons ranges but the term can also embrace parachuting and other potentially hazardous activities. Radar crossing services are available for some of them.

Prohibited and Restricted Areas

Most Restricted Areas are centred on nuclear power stations, over-flight being prohibited below 2,000 ft above ground level within a radius of two miles. A number of sensitive places in Northern Ireland are defined as Prohibited Areas, with varying dimensions.

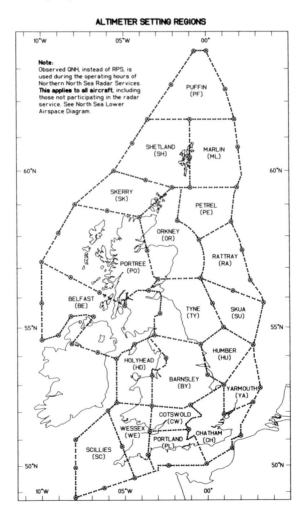

United Kingdom Flight Information and Altimeter Regions (CAA).

Chapter 4

Navigational aids

Radio navigational aids assist a pilot in threading his way through the airways, letting down at destination and then, if an Instrument Landing System is installed, following its beam down to the runway. The main types of navaid in the United Kingdom are described briefly below.

Non-Directional Beacon (NDB)

The commonest, and one of the simplest of aids is the Non-Directional Beacon. It is used to mark airways, when its useful range may be up to 100 miles, and as an approach and landing aid, sometimes referred to as a Locator Beacon, when its range will be about 15 miles. It consists merely of a radio transmitter in the medium frequency band which sends out a continuous steady note in all directions. A callsign of three letters in morse code is superimposed at regular intervals as a check that the desired beacon has been tuned in.

The Automatic Direction Finder (ADF), or radio compass, fitted in an aircraft will, when tuned to the appropriate frequency, indicate the relative position of the transmission source by means of a needle on a dial. The great disadvantage of the NDB is that it is very prone to interference. For example a thunderstorm cell in the area will often cause the cockpit needle to point to it in preference to the beacon, not a happy state of affairs!

VHF Omni-Directional Range (VOR)

VORs broadcast their signals in all directions but the signals vary around the compass in such a way that each direction has its own signal which cannot be confused with that of any other direction. If an aircraft receiver can pick-up and decode the signal from a VOR, it can tell the bearing (or radial as it is termed) from the station. As a

Right *ILS Approach Chart for East Midlands* (British Airways Aerad).

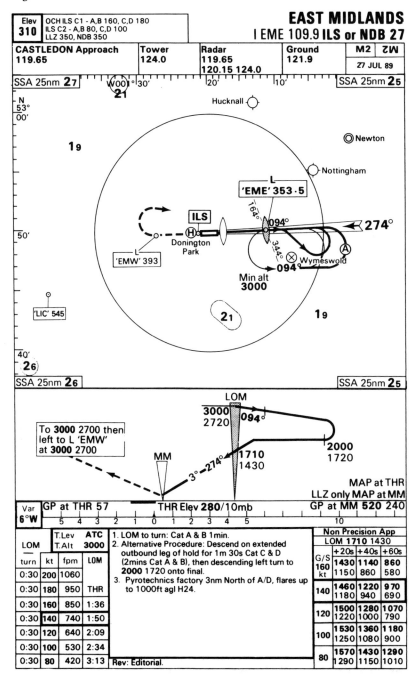

Elev 310	OCH ILS C1 - A,B 160, C,D 180 ILS C2 - A,B 80, C,D 100 LLZ 350, NDB 350				**EAST MIDLANDS** I EME 109.9 **ILS or NDB 27**	
CASTLEDON Approach **119.65**		**Tower** **124.0**	**Radar** **119.65** **120.15 124.0**	**Ground** **121.9**	**M2**	**ZW**
						27 JUL 89

SSA 25nm **27**   W00° 30'   20'   10'   SSA 25nm **25**

N 53° 00'

Hucknall

1 **9**

Newton

Nottingham

L
'EME' 353·5

ILS

164°   **094°**   **274°**

50'   H
Donington Park

L
'EMW' 393

344°   **094°**   Wymeswold   A

Min alt
3000

21   1 **9**

'LIC' 545

40'
26

SSA 25nm **26**   SSA 25nm **25**

LOM

3000
2720 **094°**

To **3000** 2700 then
left to L 'EMW'
at **3000** 2700

MM   **1710**
1430

3°-274°   **2000**
1720

MAP at THR
LLZ only MAP at MM

Var **6°W**	GP at THR 57	THR Elev **280**/10mb	GP at MM **520** 240

5 4 3 2 1 0 1 2 3 4 5   10

LOM — turn	T.Lev T.Alt	ATC **3000**		1. LOM to turn: Cat A & B 1min.		**Non Precision App**	

LOM
—
turn
	kt	fpm	LOM	1. LOM to turn: Cat A & B 1min.
				2. Alternative Procedure: Descend on extended
				  outbound leg of hold for 1m 30s Cat C & D
				  (2mins Cat A & B), then descending left turn to
				  2000 1720 onto final.
				3. Pyrotechnics factory 3nm North of A/D, flares up
				  to 1000ft agl H24.			

0:30	200	1060					
0:30	180	950	THR				
0:30	160	850	1:36				
0:30	140	740	1:50				
0:30	120	640	2:09				
0:30	100	530	2:34				
0:30	80	420	3:13	Rev: Editorial.			

Non Precision App
LOM 1710 1430

G/S	+20s	+40s	+60s
160 kt	1430 1150	1140 860	860 580
140	1460 1180	1220 940	970 690
120	1500 1220	1280 1000	1070 790
100	1530 1250	1360 1080	1180 900
80	1570 1290	1430 1150	1290 1010

convenience the receiver can add 180° to the 'From' determination and instruct the pilot which way to fly 'To' the station. A 'To/From' flag on the instrument face tells the pilot in which mode it is operating.

Distance Measuring Equipment (DME)

While VOR gives accurate, specific directional information, it cannot make explicit distance measurements. The pilot, however, may find his distance from the station by taking an intersection of radials from two VORs, or by doing a timed radial manoeuvre with a single VOR. A simpler answer is to use DME which is associated closely with VOR, the combination providing an accurate position fix. A special transmitter in the aircraft sends out pulses in all directions and these are received at the DME station on the ground. As each pulse is received an answering pulse is automatically transmitted and this is picked up in the aircraft. It is in fact the reverse of secondary radar (qv).

As the speed of radio waves is constant at 186,000 miles per second, a computer in the aircraft which measures the time interval between the transmission of a pulse and the receipt of the response can convert this time interval into a distance and display it to the pilot in nautical miles. The presentation is either by means of a mechanical meter or increasingly nowadays by LED (Light Emitting Diode) display. In both cases the distance is in miles and tenths. With some equipment, it is also possible for the 'time to go' to the beacon to be displayed.

It should be noted, incidentally, that the height of the aircraft affects the distance measurement; when directly above the station at 36,000 ft the instrument will show the aircraft as still being six miles from it. This is because the DME measures slant range rather than ground distance, but it is of little importance except when very close to the station.

DMEs are normally co-located with VORs and the frequencies of the two installations are 'paired'. For example, the VOR frequency of 112.7 MHz is always matched by a DME on Channel 74, a VOR on 114·9 by a DME on Channel 96 and so on. This means that aircraft equipment can be arranged so that the selection of a particular VOR frequency automatically means that the related DME channel is selected at the same time.

Instrument Landing System (ILS)

ILS is a pilot-interpreted aid which gives a continuous indication of whether the aircraft is left or right of the final approach track and also its position in relation to an ideal glide path to the runway. The latter is a standard 3°, giving an approximate rate of descent of 300 ft per minute. Certain airfields may have greater angles owing to high ground on the approach or other local considerations.

This information is augmented by marker beacons on the ground showing range; the outer marker at about four miles from touchdown, a middle marker at around 3,500 ft and sometimes an inner marker just short of the runway threshold. As the aircraft passes over them they give an audible signal. The outer marker transmits low-toned dashes, the middle marker alternates dots and dashes on a medium tone and the inner marker transmits dots (six per second) on a high tone. These markers cannot only be heard, they also light up lamps on a marker indicator on the instrument panel. The outer marker lights up a blue lamp, the middle an amber and the inner a clear lamp, each flashing in time with the codes. These signals, transmitted on a standard 75 MHz, can often be picked up by domestic radios when in the vicinity of an ILS system.

A transmitter with a large aerial array known as the Localiser is sited at the far end of the runway, transmitting its signals on either side of the centreline of the runway and approach. These signals, called blue on the right of the approach path and yellow on the left, overlap in a beam about 5° wide exactly along the approach centreline.

A second unit, the glide path transmitter, is sited at the nearer end and slightly to one side of the runway. Aboard the aircraft there is an instrument with two needles, one which pivots from the top of its case, moves like a windscreen wiper and is actuated by the signals from the Localiser and the other which pivots on the left side of the case, moves up and down and is operated by the transmissions from the glidepath aerial. When the two needles are crossed at right angles, the aircraft is lined up perfectly for a landing. Any deviation can rapidly be corrected by an experienced pilot.

Initial approach on to the ILS is normally achieved by Approach Radar, the aim being to place the aircraft on a closing heading of about 30° to the final approach at a range of between seven and nine miles. The aircraft should be at an appropriate altitude so that the glide path can be intercepted from below rather than attempting to 'chase' it from above. The final turn-on can be done by radar direction, but these days it is usually done automatically by coupling the ILS with the autopilot. Where no radar is available a procedural ILS is flown, similar to an NDB approach with the exception that the procedure turn will intercept the ILS and enable the pilot to establish himself on it.

ILSs are divided into three categories as follows:

Cat 1 – Operation down to 60 m decision height with Runway Visual Range in excess of 800 m.

Cat 2 – Operation down to 60 m decision height with RVR in excess of 400 m.

Cat 3 – Operation with no height limitation to and along the surface of the runway with external visual reference during the final phase of landing with RVR of 200 m.

Sub-divisions are Cat 3b with RVR of 45 m and a planned Cat 3c with RVR of zero. They both require guidance along the runway and the latter also to the parking bay. Special lighting is required for Cat 2 and 3 ILSs, together with safeguarded areas around the sensitive aerial systems to avoid fluctuations caused by vehicles or taxying aircraft.

Microwave Landing System (MLS)

The MLS is so-called because it works in the much higher frequency microwave band, as opposed to the VHF band used by ILS. This creates a number of advantages, not the least of which is a high accuracy. This means that all MLS installations will be built to ICAO Cat 3 standards. Instead of the marker beacons associated with ILS, MLS will normally have continuous distance information provided by Precision DME (P-DME).

In addition, non-standard offset or curving approaches can be made to avoid obstacles or noise-sensitive areas and the glide path is adaptable to high angle approaches by STOL aircraft or helicopters. The CAA is currently evaluating MLS equipment at Heathrow (Runway 27R) to gain the technical and operational experience necessary for the approval of future installations in the United Kingdom. A private system has also been evaluated at Yeovil. Even so, ILS is expected to remain in use until at least 1998.

Decca

The Decca Navigator provides position fixing ability over an area up to about 300 miles around its transmitter by use of a group (or chain) of special long wave transmitters about 70 to 100 miles apart which radiate in unison. The information thus received enables a pen on a moving map display to trace the path of the aircraft over the ground.

Doppler

The Doppler navigation system is self-contained and produces the desired information on position through a measurement of aircraft velocity by means of Doppler radar and measurement of direction by means of a sensor such as a gyro or magnetic compass. The two sets of information are then processed in a computer.

Inertial Navigation System (INS)

This operates independently of ground stations, being based on a computer aboard the aircraft which derives its input from gyroscopic accelerometers. A pre-determined journey can be programmed in, the output of which will direct the autopilot to fly the required tracks. This enables aircraft to fly direct routeings without reference to radio beacons if first requested from, and approved by, ATC.

Satellite Navigation

Currently there are two systems: GLONASS, the GLobal Orbiting NAvigation Satellite System developed by the former USSR; and the American GPS, Global Positioning System. A joint system combining the GLONASS and GPS satellites is planned so that worldwide coverage will be increased significantly and a greater measure of redundancy introduced to guard against satellite failure. Global positioning is the most accurate form of navigation technology under development and it could play a major role in increasing airspace capacity as well as improving safety.

Omega

A long-range area navigation system which uses VLF (Very Low Frequency) signals from eight ground stations located to provide near world-wide coverage.

Transponder

The transponder is not a navigation aid in the true sense, but its use certainly improves the service which ATC is able to give. Like so many other developments, it was born in World War 2 when it became apparent that it would be useful to be able to distinguish between our own aircraft and those of the enemy, as depicted on a radar screen. IFF (Identification Friend or Foe) was invented to meet this need but the basic device, now called a transponder, has become indispensable in civil, as well as military, aviation.

The transponder is a small airborne transmitter which waits until a radar pulse strikes its antenna and then instantly broadcasts, at a different frequency, a radar reply of its own—a strong synthetic echo. Since ordinary 'skin return' (the reflection of the ground radar pulse from the aircraft structure) is sometimes quite weak, especially at great distances or with small aircraft, the transponder helps the radar operator to track targets that might return an echo too weak to display.

The transponder is simple in concept but in practice is a complex, sophisticated device. It is triggered into either of two modes of reply by the nature of the ground radar pulse. Without delving too deeply into the technicalities, Mode A is employed for identification and Mode C for altitude information. (Modes B and D, by the way, are reserved for research and future development.) At the UK Control Centres, radar replies are channelled into a computer which decodes the pulses, converts them into a letter and number display, and places a label alongside the appropriate target on the radar screen. The information includes the callsign and altitude of the aircraft.

This Secondary Surveillance Radar (SSR) has many advantages. One of the most important is that aircraft identification is easy to achieve and eliminates the necessity of requesting a turn of at least 30° from the original heading to confirm which blip is which on the screen. R/T loading is reduced considerably because altitude information is presented continuously to the controller and the pilot no longer needs to make constant checks.

When Traffic Alert and Collision Avoidance System (TCAS) is fitted to aircraft, the equipment reacts to the transponders of other aircraft in the vicinity to determine whether or not there is the potential for a collision. TCAS is currently under worldwide evaluation, so there may be references to it on R/T. Warnings are given in two steps: typically 40 seconds before the assumed collision, a Traffic Advisory (TA) warning indicates where the pilot must look for the traffic; then between 20 and 30 seconds before the assumed collision a Resolution Advisory (RA) gives the pilot advice to climb, descend or remain level. The two warnings, TA followed by RA, can only be received if the conflicting aircraft is transponding on Mode C or Mode S. Where both aircraft in an encounter are fitted with TCAS Mode S, the transponders will communicate with each other to agree which aircraft is to pass below, and which above, the other. Mode S is a datalink system which has a number of potential applications in ATC, one being the eventual replacement of many routine radio messages. Warnings appear on a small cockpit display indicating the relative positions of the conflicting aircraft in plan view and elevation, together with an aural warning spoken by a synthetic voice.

Secondary radar differs from primary radar in that the 'echo' returned to the ground station is augmented by an authentic signal triggered from the aircraft's transponder equipment. Interference from weather and other causes is virtually eliminated. This is not the case with primary radar which is not quite the magic eye some of us would believe; it suffers from all sorts of interference. Depending on the wavelength of a particular radar, weather clutter can swamp the screen with returns from rain or snow. There are ways of removing, or at least reducing, this clutter, but the aircraft echo can be lost too, especially if it is a small one. It is not uncommon therefore to hear a controller say that he is unable to give a radar approach due to rain clutter and offer an alternative, such as an ILS approach.

Ground Proximity Warning System (GPWS)
The Ground Proximity Warning System is not a navigational aid but it provides an audible warning to the pilot if an aircraft experiences any of the following conditions:

(a) An excessive sink rate;
(b) An excessive terrain closure rate;
(c) An altitude loss after take-off or overshoot;
(d) Proximity to terrain when not in the landing configuration;
(e) A deviation below the glide slope.

In the first four conditions, the warning consists of an audible tone and a spoken warning over a cockpit loudspeaker, 'Whoop, whoop. Pull up'. For the last condition the warning 'Glide slope, glide slope' is used. The warning is repeated as long as the conditions exist.

Aircraft Flight Manuals instruct pilots to climb immediately to a level where the warning is no longer being received. If a pilot gets a 'pull up' warning, his recovery action is to establish the power setting and attitude which will produce the maximum climb gradient consistent with the aircraft configuration. If a 'glide slope' warning is received, recovery action is to apply power to regain the ILS glide slope.

Unfortunately, the GPWS is an extremely sensitive piece of equipment and spurious warnings can be caused by several factors. One of these is a sudden variation in terrain, even though it is well below the aircraft. GPWS incidents can occasionally be heard being discussed on air band frequencies.

Flight Checks
Some of the navaids, particularly ILS, require regular check flights to ensure that their performance remains consistent. These checks, normally flown by the CAAFU's HS 748 or Fieldair's Navajo aircraft, are not as intensive as those made when the equipment was originally brought into service but they are still quite time-consuming.

Chapter 5

Area or Airways Control

Since messages between the Air Traffic Control Centres (ATCCs) and aircraft on the UK airways system are those which are most easily monitored from all parts of the country, this seems a logical point at which to begin. There are two ATCCs, London and Scottish, supported by a Sub-Centre at Manchester. The dividing line between them is latitude 55°N (roughly the Scottish border) and the Sub-Centre handles traffic below FL 130 on the airways around Manchester and over the Irish Sea.

Transmitter/receiver stations are sited at various strategic positions around Britain and linked to the ATCCs by land line. The aim is to achieve a balanced coverage over the whole area with no 'dead' spots. Similarly, the radar stations are 'remoted' on high ground, where possible, to improve range. London ATCC (LATCC) is served by radar heads at Heathrow, Ash near Canterbury, Ventnor on the Isle of Wight, Clee Hill in Shropshire, Burrington, Devon and St Annes near Blackpool. Additional service is provided on a Eurocontrol agency basis from Mount Gabriel in Eire, a station which extends SSR cover out to 15°W in the south-west approaches.

More information on SSR will be found in a separate section of this book but, briefly, the main function of primary radar is to provide aircraft position. Secondary Radar, or SSR, depends for its operation on a transponder carried in the aircraft which, on receipt of pulses from a ground interrogator, will transmit coded reply pulses back to the ground. When these are decoded by the display equipment, they give the Flight Level of the aircraft together with a four-figure identifying number known as a *squawk*. The primary and secondary information received by the radar stations is processed in a common 'plot extractor', converting the basic radar data into digital form and automatically sending the information to the ATCCs over land lines.

At the ATCC display processing equipment employing modern

computer technology is used to decode the combined radar information from several antenna and displays either a manually selected radar station or a composite area mosaic picture. The SSR squawk is paired with the aircraft callsign in the computer and this callsign label is displayed on the screen instead of the code. This enables the controller to match the radar picture with the strips on his flight progress board.

When the mosaic picture is selected at LATCC, the computer divides the London FIR into 16 mile squares, each of which has radar cover from a 'preferred' radar and a 'supplementary' radar. This avoids the blind spots possible if only one radar were in operation. Should the preferred radar fail, the supplementary will take over automatically, information from a third radar head being upgraded in turn to supplement it.

All incoming primary and secondary digital data is continuously recorded and the tapes are kept for 30 days before being erased and reused. The same applies to all ATC radio messages, whether they be Area, Tower or Approach. The purpose of these recordings is to help an investigating authority to build up a picture of the events surrounding an accident or incident.

To facilitate traffic handling, LATCCs airspace is broken up into sectors, each with its own radio frequencies. Aircraft are passed from one sector to the next with co-ordination between the controllers concerned. From mid-evening as traffic decreases, sectors are 'closed down', the frequencies being 'band-boxed', to use the jargon. Hence nothing may be heard on what is in daytime a busy airways frequency. By the early hours the whole FIR may be controlled by only two frequencies. When the morning shift comes on duty the sectors are activated again to meet the new traffic flow.

Before computers came on the scene in British ATC in the 1970s, flight progress strips at the ATCCs were hand-written in vast quantities. Today the system is automated, apart from a shut-off period for computer maintenance in the small hours of the morning, and it would be advantageous to describe briefly what happens when a particular flight leaves, for example, Liverpool for Heathrow.

If the flight is a scheduled one, it will be on a 'stored plan' in the LATCC computer's bulk store file, if not it will be input on a teleprinter at Manchester Sub-Centre. At the appropriate time as programmed into the computer, usually about 40 minutes before Estimated Time of Departure (ETD), warning strips will be printed by flight strip printers at Manchester and at any location at LATCC

The Sectors of the London Air Traffic Control Centre

Remote Radio and Radar Sites

London Air Traffic Control Centre Remote Transmitter Sites and their frequencies

Chedburgh, Suffolk: 127.95, 128.7, 129.6, 133.45, 134.25
Clee Hill, Shropshire: 124.75, 128.7, 131.2, 133.6, 133.9
Daventry, Northamptonshire: 121.025, 129.2, 133.7
Davidstow Moor, Cornwall: 124.75, 131.2, 132.6, 132.95, 133.3, 133.6, 134.175, 135.15
Grantham, Lincolnshire: 123.95, 124.6, 127.65, 128.125, 131.05, 133.8, 135.525
Greenford, Middlesex: 121.075, 123.9, 125.8, 125.95, 126.3, 126.45, 128.25, 128.4, 128.9, 129.2, 132.05, 132.8, 133.7
Kelsall, Cheshire: 128.05, 129.1, 134.425
Mount Gabriel, Eire: 132.95
Preston, Lancashire: 128.125, 127.45, 129.1
Rothwell, Humberside: 131.225, 133.325, 134.25, 135.075, 135.275, 135.625
Snaefell, Isle of Man: 128.05, 134.7
Swingfield, Kent: 127.1, 127.95, 128.25, 129.6, 132.45, 133.45, 134.9
Trimmingham, Lincolnshire: 124.6, 128.125, 131.05, 133.525, 134.25, 134.7
Ventnor, Isle of Wight: 124.275, 124.75, 127.7, 132.3, 133.3, 134.45
Warlingham, Surrey: 123.9, 124.6, 125.8, 125.95, 126.3, 126.45, 127.1, 127.7, 128.4, 128.625, 128.9, 130.925, 132.05, 132.45,
  134.45, 134.9, 135.05, 135.575
Winstone, Gloucestershire: 132.6, 132.8, 133.9, 135.25

Note that some frequencies may be offset up or down by 2.5, 5 or 7.5 kHz (see page 133).

where advance information of the flight is required.

When Manchester receives the actual time of departure from Liverpool, via a direct telephone link, an activation message will be input to the computer via a keyboard. This will generate an update message for the sectors at the Sub-Centre and those sectors at London which have warning strips. Additionally 'live' strips will be printed at any sector or location concerned with the flight that did not have a warning strip. In all cases the computer will have calculated and printed times for en route reporting points based upon the airborne time input at Manchester. The forecast winds at various levels will have been programmed in and thus automatically taken into account.

The flight of an aircraft from Heathrow to Manchester serves as a good example of how traffic is fed through the airways system. When the departing aircraft comes onto the LATCC Departure Radar Controller's frequency and has complied with the minimum noise routeing element of its Standard Instrument Departure, it is started on its climb to cruising level, using radar separation where necessary between it and other arriving, departing or transitting traffic. To ease the task of the Departure Controller in regard to co-ordination with other sectors concerned with the airspace, there is an internal procedure which permits him to climb the aircraft to an arbitrary level of FL 120 without reference to other sectors.

However, before it reaches this Flight Level or, alternatively, when the aircraft is approaching the sector for which the Daventry Sector Controller is responsible, prior co-ordination is carried out. When this has been done, the aircraft is instructed to contact the Daventry Sector (still with the same London Control callsign.)

Daventry Sector continues the aircraft's climb to its cruising level, once again using radar to resolve any conflictions with other traffic. By this time it is also possible to check the computer on the elapsed time between reporting points and, if these deviate by three minutes

Left *Plessey AR5 airways radar site at Burrington, Devon* (CAA).

or more, the estimates for the rest of the flight are revised and a new
ETA is passed to Manchester.

As the flight nears the Manchester TMA boundary co-ordination
takes place by direct telephone line between Daventry Sector and the
TMA Controller. Descent instructions dependent upon the Manchester traffic situation are then issued and the aircraft transferred to
the Manchester Control frequency. The Manchester TMA Controller
has a radar display similar to that used by the Daventry Sector and, as
the aircraft descends into his airspace, its callsign and level will be
visible on his screen. He will also have displayed in front of him the
flight progress strips generated by the computer which have been
updated by any revised estimates. The descent will be continued until
the aircraft comes under the jurisdiction of the Manchester Approach
Controller and positioned on the ILS as described in the next chapter.

Ideally, traffic is given an uninterrupted climb to cruising level and,
from a convenient point, a continuous descent to final approach. In
practice, however, the presence of other traffic rarely makes this
possible. Traffic climbing to, say, FL 180 may be given an initial limit of
FL 120 against conflicting traffic at FL 130. By the time it is approaching
FL 120, the other aircraft may be well out of the way and the controller
will be able to instruct the pilot to continue his climb to the required
level. Before the days of SSR height read-outs, the Area Controller in
this example would ask the pilot to report passing FL 110 and then
would assess the situation with regard to further climb.

Part of the London Air Traffic Control Centre at West Drayton, Middlesex (CAA).

The phraseology used in Area Control is mainly self-evident and some, concerning level changes has already been covered in an earlier chapter. Common phrases to be heard are as follows:

Aircraft: Speedbird 345 request descent.

ATC: Speedbird 345 maintain FL 110 expect descent after Lichfield.

ATC: Air France 045 descend to cross Honiley FL 170 or above. After Honiley descend to FL 130.

The standard airways position report is a little gem of brevity dating back decades to when procedural airways control was first developed. A typical one goes like this:

Aircraft: Logan 231 Dean Cross 45 FL 90 Pole Hill 10.

This means that the aircraft was over the Dean Cross VOR at time 45, maintaining FL 90 and estimating over the Pole Hill VOR at ten minutes past the next hour.

Nowadays, with comprehensive radar coverage of the airways system, a pilot may be instructed to omit position reports when flying in certain areas, his progress being monitored by the SSR read-out. This reduces the need for R/T considerably.

Certain phrases concerning the operation of transponders are listed below. Since SSR in the United Kingdom is confined mainly to the ATCCs, they will most commonly be heard on airways frequencies. Few Approach Control units have SSR capability as yet, but the number is slowly increasing. The use of the word *squawk*, by the way, seems to have been inspired by the wartime instruction to operate the IFF, (Identification, Friend or Foe), 'Make your cockerel crow' and the pilot's confirmation that the IFF was switched off after landing 'Cockerel strangled.'

Phrase	**Meaning**
Squawk (code)	Set the code as instructed.
Confirm squawk	Confirm the code set on the transponder.
Recycle	Reselect assigned code.
Squawk ident	Operate the special position identification feature.
Squawk low	Select 'low sensitivity' feature.
Squawk normal	Select normal feature.
Squawk standby	Select the standby feature.
Squawk Charlie	Select altitude reporting feature.
Stop Squawk Charlie	Deselect altitude feature.
Verify level	Check and confirm your level. (Used to verify the accuracy of the Mode C derived level information displayed to the controller.)

Chapter 6

Approach Control

An arriving aircraft is transferred from Area to Approach Control at a specified release point. This is not obvious from R/T transmissions because it is passed by land line between controllers shortly before the aircraft comes on to the approach frequency. It may be a position, time or level. The transfer of control is made deliberately flexible to react to differences in the flow of traffic. For example, if the release is 'out of FL 50' the Approach Controller may not alter the heading of the aircraft until he has received a 'passing FL 50' report. The reason for this is that Area Control may have been separating the inbound aircraft from other traffic above FL 50.

Ideally, the arriving aircraft should be released in plenty of time to enable it to carry out a straight-in approach and at the same time to lose height. However, should a busy traffic situation exist, it might be necessary to put it into a holding pattern based upon a radio beacon. The release would then be at a specified level in the holding stack. The holding patterns are a standard oval 'racetrack', the direction of turn and headings being published in navigational charts or approach plates.

At airfields without radar, traffic is separated by procedural methods, the first aircraft making an instrument approach from, say, 3,000 ft, aircraft continuing to hold above at 1,000 ft vertical intervals. As soon as the first aircraft reports visual with the ground or approach lights, and there is a reasonable likelihood of a successful landing, the second aircraft is cleared for the approach and so on. If the aircraft carries out a missed approach prior to becoming visual, it must climb to the safe terrain clearance altitude, in this instance 3,000 ft. Hence it is not hard to see why this altitude is left vacant at the beacon until the first aircraft breaks cloud.

The decision height is the level at which the pilot on a precision approach must carry out a missed approach if he fails to achieve the required visual reference to continue the approach to a landing. A precision approach is defined as being provided by an ILS, MLS or PAR facility. All other procedures, including SRAs, are non-precision and the term Minimum Descent Height is used instead. The major revision of obstacle clearance criteria described in the previous editions of this book has now been virtually completed by the CAA.

The previous obstacle clearance limit—the minimum safe height to which an aircraft may descend either on an instrument approach or in the event of a missed approach—has been replaced by an obstacle clearance height. This is published on the approach charts for each airfield, aircraft being divided into five speed-related categories, resulting in a reduction of the obstacle clearance heights for the more manoeuvrable types.

The obstacle clearance criteria are, of course, tied in with company minima for visibility and cloud base, below which a public transport flight is not allowed even to attempt an approach. So far, there are no such statutory provisions for non-public transport flights. However, recommended minima are published for the approach aids at each airfield for the guidance of pilots and these will be passed on R/T when conditions demand.

The term Expected Approach Time is often heard at non-radar equipped airports. This indicates to a pilot that if he has a radio failure he must not commence an instrument approach until this specific time to allow preceding aircraft to descend and land. 'No delay expected' means that a pilot can begin his approach as soon as he reaches the beacon. If his estimate for the beacon is 12, the next aircraft's EAT will be 19, the third's 26 and so on.

A standard seven minutes is assumed to complete the let-down procedure and three minutes will be added to this if an aircraft arrives from certain points of the compass and has to realign itself in the correct direction for the descent. The controller will calculate the figures and update them as necessary. Note that EATs are not issued in busy TMAs when the delay is likely to be less than 20 minutes.

Pilots' interpretations of instrument let-downs vary enormously, the seven minute standard ranging from five to ten or more, depending upon wind strength, aircraft performance and other factors. One other phrase used in connection with EATs is the rarely heard 'delay not determined.' This is used to meet certain eventualities, such as a blocked runway, when it is not known how long an aircraft may have to hold.

Where Approach Radar is in use, as well as giving a release, the

ATCC also transfers radar identity in what is called a handover (a 'handoff' to the Americans). The Approach Controller is thus certain that the aircraft he is directing is the correct blip. The object is to pass headings (vectors) to the pilot to enable him to lock onto the ILS beam by the shortest practicable route commensurate with losing height. If there is no ILS, a Surveillance Radar Approach (SRA) will be given or, when the weather is suitable, radar positioning to a visual final.

In effect a radar directed circuit is flown, the terms downwind, base leg and final (see page 71) all being used where necessary, although the area of sky covered is far bigger than in the normal visual traffic pattern. A closing heading of about 30° is recommended so that when the aircraft intercepts the ILS only a gentle turn is necessary to lock on. The aim is to intercept the standard 3° glide path at approximately 7 to 8 miles out on the extended centreline of the runway. As a 3° glide path is roughly equal to 300 ft of descent per mile, the aircraft should be between 2,000 ft and 2,500 ft at this point.

Subsequent landing aircraft are vectored not less than five miles behind, or further depending upon the vortex wake category of the preceding traffic (See Chapter 13). Bigger gaps may also be built in to give space for departing aircraft at single-runway airports. At certain locations, Heathrow for example, reduction of the separation to 3 miles is authorised to ensure maximum utilisation of the arrival runway. The vortex rules still apply of course. It is quite an art to arrange traffic in line astern with the correct spacing, particularly at Heathrow where four holding stacks serve the airport. Speed control is also used extensively to even out the flow, a minimum of 170 kt being permissible for jets and 160 kt for large propellor-driven aircraft. It is not uncommon to see a slow turbo-prop aircraft only lowering its wheels on short final at Heathrow so as to keep the speed up as long as possible. (According to the book, any speed restriction must be lifted at 4 miles on final approach, but pilots often press on to help the traffic flow.) Within the TMAs during the intermediate stages of the approach, a speed limit of 250 kt is imposed on all traffic to make the Radar Controller's task a little easier.

The Approach Controller passes an 8 mile check on intercom to his colleague in the Tower who will already have details of the arriving aircraft. If there are no pending departures at the runway holding point, a landing clearance may be given at this point but it is more usual to give this at the 4 mile range, approximately equal to the outer marker on the ILS. Alternatively, once the pilot reports established on the ILS, Approach may tell him to 'Contact the Tower and report passing the outer marker.'

Pilots expect to receive a landing clearance at around 4 miles on final approach, but this is not always possible owing to departing traffic or a previous landing aircraft being slow to clear the runway. Two miles is the absolute minimum for large transport aircraft because an overshoot is a fairly major operation. The phrase 'expect late landing clearance' is sometimes heard because light aircraft in a busy circuit may, of necessity, receive a very late landing clearance. They may even be told to go around if they get too close to the one in front.

For a runway not equipped with ILS the Radar Controller is normally able to offer a Surveillance Radar Approach. If the weather is poor this can be down to ½ mile from touchdown, assuming that the radar is approved for this purpose. With certain types of radar,

Standard Terminal Arrival Charts for London Heathrow (CAA).

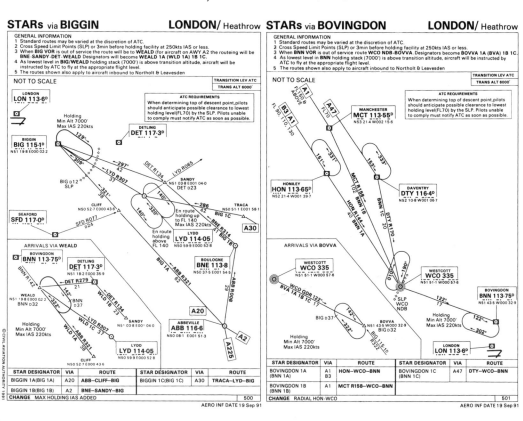

approaches to 2 miles only may be allowed. This ensures a reasonable chance of seeing the approach lights and making a successful landing in all but the worst weather.

Where only one Approach Controller is on duty and the ILS fails, he may be unable to offer a ½ mile SRA because of the necessity for continuous transmissions during the last 4 miles of the approach. This of course means that any other traffic cannot communicate with him until the talk-down is complete. If a second controller is available, the first can do a ½ mile SRA on a discrete frequency while his colleague continues to sequence traffic onto long final for handover as soon as the preceding aircraft has completed its approach.

SRAs to 2 miles, however, do not require continuous transmissions and the controller can talk to other traffic as necessary, although he must time his calls so that range checks and the associated advisory heights are passed at the correct intervals. The differences between ½ mile and 2 mile SRAs are apparent when one compares the respective phraseology.

The advisory heights are based upon a glide path of 3°, therefore, at 6½ miles the aircraft should be a height of 2,000 ft. Some airfields have non-standard glide path angles because of local obstructions, the advisory heights being adjusted accordingly. It is assumed that the aircraft is flying on QFE, but if the pilot advises that he is using QNH the runway threshold elevation is added to the advisory heights and rounded up to the next 25 ft, the term 'altitude' being used in place of 'height' where necessary.

Phraseology for SRA terminating at ½ mile from touchdown

During the Intermediate Procedure	*This will be a Surveillance Radar Approach, terminated at ¹/₂ mile from touchdown. Check your minima, step down fixes and missed approach point.*
If a change of frequency is required for final approach	*Contact . . . on* (frequency) *for final approach. After landing contact Tower on . . .* (frequency.)
Before commencing final descent	*Check wheels.*
To alter course of aircraft	*Turn left/right (. . . degrees) heading . . .*
Azimuth information	*Closing* (final approach) *track from the left/right. Your heading (of . . .) is good. Slightly left/right of track.*

Approaching 6½ miles from touchdown	*Approaching 6 ¹/₂ miles from touchdown —commence descent now to maintain a 3° glide path.*
At 6 miles from touchdown	*6 miles from touchdown—height should be 1,850 ft.*
At 5½ miles from touchdown	*5 ¹/₂ miles from touchdown—height should be 1,700 ft.*
No landing clearance received by 2 miles from touchdown	*Go around—I say again, go around—climb on heading . . . to . . . ft.* (Further instructions.) *Acknowledge.* (The reason for overshooting is to be given as soon as convenient.)
If during the latter stages of the approach, an aircraft reaches a position from which it appears to the controller that a successful instrument approach cannot be completed	According to circumstances, EITHER: *Continue visually, or go around.* (Further instructions.) *Over.* OR: *Go around—I say again, go around—climb on heading . . . to . . . ft.* (Further instructions.) *Acknowledge.* OR: *Climb immediately, I say again, climb immediately on heading . . . to . . . ft.* (Further instructions.) *Acknowledge.*
At 5 miles from touchdown	*5 miles from touchdown— height should be 1,550 ft.*
At 4½ miles from touchdown	*4 ¹/₂ miles from touchdown—height should be 1,400 ft.*
At 4 miles from touchdown	*4 miles from touchdown—height should be 1,250 ft—do not reply to further instructions.*
Landing Clearance (Normally passed between 4 and 2 miles from touchdown)	*Cleared to land runway . . .* (Surface wind also given if necessary.)
At 3½ miles from touchdown	*3 ¹/₂ miles from touchdown—height should be 1,100 ft.*
At 3 miles from touchdown	*3 miles from touchdown—height should be 950 ft.*
At 2½ miles from touchdown	*2 ¹/₂ miles from touchdown—height should be 800 ft.*
At 2 miles from touchdown	*2 miles from touchdown—height should be 650 ft. Check minimum descent height.*

At 1½ miles from touchdown	*1 ½ miles from touchdown—height should be 500 ft.*
At 1 mile from touchdown	*1 mile from touchdown—height should be 350 ft.*
At ½ mile from touchdown	*¹/₂ mile from touchdown—approach completed. Out.*
Avoiding action or breaking off approach on instructions from Approach/Aerodrome Control	*Turn left/right ... degrees heading ... climb to ... ft—acknowledge.*

Phraseology for SRA Terminating at 2 miles from touchdown

	This will be a Surveillance Radar Approach, terminated at 2 miles from touchdown. Check your minima, step down fixes and missed approach point.
If a change of frequency is required for final approach	*Contact ... on (frequency) for final approach.*
Before commencing final descent	*Check wheels.*
To alter course of aircraft	*Turn left/right (... degrees) heading ...*
Azimuth information	*Closing (final approach) track from the left/right. Your heading (of ...) is good. On track. Slightly left/right of track.*
Approaching 6½ miles from touchdown	*Approaching 6½ miles from touchdown— begin your descent to maintain a 3° glide path.*
At 6 miles from touchdown	*6 miles from touchdown—height should be 1,850 ft.*
At 5 miles from touchdown	*5 miles from touchdown—height should be 1,550 ft.*
At 4 miles from touchdown	*4 miles from touchdown—height should be 1,250 ft.*
Landing Clearance (Normally passed between 4 and 2 miles from touchdown)	*Cleared to land Runway ... (Surface wind also given if necessary.)*
At 3 miles from touchdown	*3 miles from touchdown—height should be 950 ft.*
At 3 miles, or any convenient point during the approach	*Advise when runway/approach lights in sight. Check minimum descent height. After landing contact ... on ... (frequency).*
At 2 miles from touchdown	*2 miles from touchdown—height should be*

If the pilot has not reported lights in sight	650 ft. I cannot assist you further. *Continue the approach, or go around at your discretion.*
Avoiding action or breaking off approach on instructions from Approach/Aerodrome Control	*Turn left/right ... degrees, heading ... climb to ... ft.* (Further instructions.)—*Acknowledge.*
No landing clearance received by 2 miles from touchdown	*Go around—I say again, go around.* (Further instructions.) *Acknowledge.*

Approach Control Phraseology

Since all major airports now use radar to direct their traffic, I shall deal with this aspect first. An aircraft must be identified before it can receive a radar control or advisory service, in other words, the controller must be sure that one particular blip on his screen is the aircraft that he is directing. This is simple with a radar handover from another ATC unit or by means of SSR, but at airfields outside controlled airspace, where aircraft may approach from random directions with no prior notification, a standard procedure is observed.

ATC: GVM report heading and level.

Aircraft: GVM heading 140 at 2,500 ft.

ATC: GVM for identification turn left heading 110.

The identification turn must be at least 30° different from the original heading. When the pilot reports steady on the new heading, and the controller is sure that he has related the correct blip on his screen with the aircraft, he transmits: 'GVM identified 12 miles south of (airfield)'.

The service to be given is then added.

ATC: This will be radar vectoring to a visual approach runway 23, nominal glide path angle 3°, obstacle clearance limit 320 ft. Check your minima.

(The weather and pressure settings are then passed as a separate transmission.)

If in the initial call the aircraft makes the turn requested and is still not observed on the radar, perhaps because it is out of range, in weather clutter, or below cover, the controller will say 'GVM not identified. Resume own navigation.' D/F will then be used to home the aircraft towards the airfield for eventual radar pick-up.

When identified, the aircraft will be vectored, that is given headings to steer to fit it into the approach sequence or, if traffic is light, direct to final approach. Outside controlled airspace the aircraft may be vectored around unidentified traffic. Information will be given by use of the twelve hour clock, twelve o'clock being straight ahead, three o'clock over the pilot's right shoulder and so on. The distance and relative direction of movement is also given, together with any information on speed, type of aircraft if known, etc. Typical traffic information is passed in this form, 'ABC123 unknown traffic ten o'clock, five miles crossing left to right, fast moving.'

If the pilot does not have the traffic in sight he may request avoiding action. This may, in any case, be initiated by the controller if he considers it necessary. Sometimes rapid action is required to avert the risk of collision: 'ABC123 avoiding action turn left immediately heading 110'. A few incidents have occurred where, by using a too relaxed tone of voice, the controller failed to convey to the pilot the urgency of the required action and the pilot's more leisurely response led to an awkward situation which might have been averted. The CAA eventually instructed all controllers to ensure that their tone of voice does not lull a pilot into a false sense of security!

At locations with no radar, procedural methods are used. The same applies when radar is normally available but unserviceable or seriously affected by weather clutter, or if the pilot wishes to carry out a procedural approach for training purposes. On transfer from the ATCC, the first call will go something like this:

Aircraft: Inverness Approach Loganair 916 descending to FL 60, estimating INS at 42.

ATC: Loganair 916 cleared for beacon approach descend 4,500 ft. Report beacon outbound.

Subsequent reports will be made when 'base turn complete' and, if the beacon is several miles out on final approach, rather than on the airfield, a 'beacon inbound' call will be made as well. These standard calls help the Tower Controller to plan his traffic, bearing in mind that there may be no radar to give him ranges from touchdown.

Where the airport is equipped with ILS, permission to make a procedural approach is given thus: 'GMB cleared ILS approach runway 27, report outer marker outbound QFE 1008'. Subsequent exchanges would be:

Aircraft: GMB outer marker outbound.

ATC: GMB report established ILS inbound. (The phrase 'report procedure turn complete' may be substituted.)

Aircraft: GMB established ILS inbound.

ATC: GMB report outer marker.

Aircraft: GMB outer marker.

ATC: GMB contact Tower 118.1

In good weather, by day or night, even though nominally flying IFR, a pilot may request permission to make a visual approach. This may be granted subject to certain provisos, the most important of which is that the pilot must have the airfield in sight and a reasonable assurance exists that he will be able to complete the landing visually. Standard separation continues to be applied between this aircraft and other arriving and departing traffic. During daylight hours only, IFR flights may be cleared to approach maintaining VMC and their own separation, if reports indicate that this is possible.

It remains for me to mention the QGH, a military procedure which is only available at a handful of civil airfields, usually where a University Air Squadron is based. The QGH dates back to World War 2 but is, nevertheless, highly effective in bringing aircraft safely down to a position from which an approach can be continued visually. This particular Q-Code meant 'Controlled descent through cloud' and uses a cathode ray tube VDF to home the aircraft to the overhead at a safe altitude. Subsequent bearings bring it down a safety lane onto final approach. During the procedure, the pilot's replies are used to obtain D/F bearings and additional transmission may be requested using the words 'Transmit for D/F.' Immediately the aircraft has passed overhead the VDF aerial, turn instructions are given to get it onto the outbound track:

ATC: V91 D/F indicates that you have passed overhead. Turn left heading 120. Report steady.

On completion of the overhead turn and when bearings indicate that the aircraft is outbound, heading corrections derived from a series of bearings are given by the controller as required to make good the outbound track. Descent instructions and the appropriate pressure settings are also given at this point. 'V91 descend to 1,000 ft QFE 1006, report level'. The controller times the outbound leg with a stop watch (usually three minutes) and then gives the aircraft a turn onto a heading to intercept the final approach track. Further D/F checks ensure that it remains within the safety lane and the pilot is told to descend to decision height and report airfield in sight.

The civilian counterpart of the QGH is the VDF Approach which is virtually the direct opposite, in that the pilot interprets the QDM information, rather than the controller. VDF approaches are uncommon these days, reflecting the greater availability of radar and ILS. Apart from this they require a lot of practice by the pilot to perfect them and were never very popular!

Chapter 7

Aerodrome Control

The Aerodrome Controller's function is defined as the issuing of information and instructions to aircraft to achieve a safe, orderly and expeditious flow of traffic and to assist pilots in preventing collisions between:

(a) Aircraft in flight in the vicinity of the aerodrome traffic zone

(b) Aircraft taking off or landing

(c) Aircraft moving on the apron

(d) Aircraft and vehicles, obstructions and other aircraft on the manoeuvring area (ie, the runways and taxyways)

The apron may also come under the jurisdiction of the marshaller, who makes sure that aircraft are parked in the required places. This is particularly important at airports where all or part of the apron is out of sight of the tower. At larger airports, self-manoeuvring markings are painted on the concrete to guide pilots to the stand which he has been allocated on R/T, thus obviating the need for 'the man with the bats'. It would be impossible to control all the service vehicles moving about the apron so these are confined, as far as possible, to lanes outlined in white paint. Airfield fire and maintenance vehicles which need to go on runways and taxyways are controlled on a UHF domestic frequency. At some airfields the Tower frequency may be used for this.

To smooth the running of the larger airports, it may be necessary to split the duties of Aerodrome Control into Air Control and Ground Movement Control (referred to as GMC). The latter's responsibility covers aircraft moving on the apron and aircraft and vehicles on the manoeuvring area, except on runways and their access points. R/T loading at Heathrow necessitates a further sub-division of GMC named Delivery, on which clearances and other information is passed.

Apart from the 'Mark 1 eyeball' and a pair of binoculars, the Tower Controller has few aids. The most useful, but installed at very few places, is the Distance From Touchdown Indicator, colloquially known from its initials as a 'Dufftyscope'. It is a small daylight-viewing cathode ray tube, its picture being derived from the main approach radar, showing the final approach line out to about ten miles.

At airports with only one runway and a high movement rate, Manchester and Gatwick for example, it is invaluable in judging whether or not there is sufficient room to clear a departing aircraft to take off or to allow an aircraft in the circuit to turn in ahead. The Radar Controller is required to give 8 mile and 4 mile checks for traffic on final approach to his colleague in the Tower. The aim is to confirm landing clearance at about 4 miles but certainly at not less than 2 miles.

Runway occupancy is governed by the following rules:

(*a*) An aircraft shall not be permitted to begin take-off until the preceding departing aircraft is seen to be airborne or has reported 'airborne' by R/T and all preceding landing aircraft are clear of the runway in use.

(*b*) A landing aircraft will not be permitted to cross the beginning of the runway on its final approach until a preceding departing aircraft is airborne.

There is, however, a phrase 'land after' which seems to puzzle some pilots who probably think it is a place in Wales! Its purpose is to increase runway utilisation by permitting a landing aircraft to touch down before a preceding aircraft which has landed is clear of the runway. The onus for ensuring adequate separation is transferred from controller to pilot. The provisos for this are:

(*a*) The runway is long enough to allow safe separation between the two aircraft and there is no evidence to indicate that braking may be adversely affected.

(*b*) It is during daylight hours.

(*c*) The controller is satisfied that the landing aircraft will be able to see the preceding aircraft which has landed, clearly and continuously until it is clear of the runway.

(*d*) The pilot of the following aircraft is warned.

There is one other runway procedure which is authorized only at Heathrow and Gatwick where arriving aircraft are 'cleared to land after' (the phrase also being unique). Certain conditions must be met and the procedure is also allowed behind departing traffic.

At some airfields the Tower and Approach function may be combined on one frequency. This is perfectly satisfactory with light to medium traffic flows, but on busy weekends the R/T congestion can be serious, pilots having difficulty in getting a word in edgeways.

Airfields outside controlled airspace possess an Aerodrome Traffic Zone, through which flight is prohibited without a clearance. The circuit direction is a standard left hand, although this may vary for different runways to avoid overflying built-up areas, hospitals and the like. The reason for the left hand pattern is said to date back to the First World War when aircraft like the Sopwith Camel turned much more easily to the left than the right, owing to the torque effect of the rotary engine. When larger aircraft with side-by-side seating were introduced, the pilot sat on the left and this has become traditional. In helicopters, however, this is reversed!

Circuit height is normally 1,000 ft, but at airfields such as Manchester-Barton it is 800 ft, which sometimes leads to confusion when trainee pilots land elsewhere. These days, some pilots tend to fly enormous 'bomber circuits', much to the annoyance of ATC and other aircraft in the circuit.

The circuit is divided into four legs; crosswind, downwind, base, and final approach. The first aircraft to report downwind will be told to 'report final'. ('Number one' may be added to this.) The second will be told 'Number two, follow the Cherokee on base', and so on. If the circuit is very busy the Tower may instruct a pilot to 'report before turning base, four aircraft ahead.' When he does this he will be given an update on his position in traffic, there perhaps being only two ahead by this time.

The standard circuit-joining procedure is to arrive overhead the field at 2,000 ft, descend on the dead side, ie the one opposite the live downwind leg and let down to 1,000 ft. Whilst watching for departing traffic, the pilot then joins the crosswind leg over the upwind end of the active runway. (Wags should note that there is a cemetery under the dead side at Cambridge Airport.)

This should ensure that a joining aircraft does not conflict with one just airborne, as there have been numerous cases in the past of collisions because of careless rejoins a mile or so off the end of the runway. Of course a fast climber like a Rockwell 680 can easily be at 1,000 ft by the time it reaches the end of a longish runway, so it is up to the Tower to make sure that a joining aircraft does not cross its path.

Scheduled and other large aircraft are usually fed straight into the final approach, which can sometimes be tricky. One way to achieve this safely if there is circuit traffic, is to instruct the trainer to continue downwind until he has the arriving aircraft in sight and then follow it. The other solution is an orbit—a 360° turn—always away from the final approach, to be continued until the traffic is sighted. The first method has the disadvantage that a strong tailwind may carry the aircraft into the next county, with perhaps an inexperienced pilot losing sight of the aerodrome. An orbit may be impracticable because of following traffic in the circuit. There is a limit to the number of aeroplanes you can orbit safely in a circuit!

If things are particularly congested and large aircraft are expected, trainers can always be told to land and taxi back to the holding point to await further take-off clearance. Another complication is vortex wake, a phenomenon once referred to as slipstream or propwash, but now known to be a rapidly revolving cylinder of air from each wingtip. This can be so violent that it can overcome the control forces of a following aircraft and invert it. Aircraft in the United Kingdom are placed in four categories depending upon maximum total weight at take-off. These are heavy, medium, small and light. More details are to be found below.

Helicopter operations are less of a problem than might be imagined; the main one being crossing the active runway. However they can clear it quickly and can thus be slotted between arriving and departing aircraft, remaining below 500 ft until clear of the traffic zone. The same applies to their arrival, although at places like Liverpool with an adjacent wide river, pilots are understandably reluctant to approach or depart at low level. In this case, the normal procedure is to change the direction of the circuit traffic away from the helicopter.

Overflying helicopters are treated like any other crossing traffic, either cleared overhead above 2,000 ft if the circuit is busy, or asked to report a few miles away and given traffic information so that they can fly through the pattern without conflict.

The Aerodrome Controller is, of course, pre-warned of arriving traffic by Approach or at some places he handles both functions on the same frequency. Similarly, for departing IFR aircraft he will have the flight progress strips on his pending board, made up when the flight plan was filed with ATC.

At certain busy airports pilots on VFR flights, local, landing away or circuits, are required to 'book out' over the telephone with ATC, giving brief details. This is particularly important with circuit training as the Tower Controller may refuse to accept more than a certain number, dependent upon weather conditions, scheduled traffic, existing congestion and other factors. At smaller airfields, pilots merely call for taxi clearance from the parking area stating their requirements. Training flights are often referred to by the word 'detail' as in 'Coventry Tower GAXVW request taxy clearance, two on board circuit detail.' This is a throwback to military jargon, as is the term 'fanstop' for a practice engine failure after take-off.

Aircraft on IFR flight plans should first request permission to start engines so that ATC can warn of any likely delays and thus minimise fuel wastage. If there is no delay, 'Start up approved' is passed, together with the outside air temperature in degrees Celsius. The QNH, QFE and runway in use may also be given in the same transmission, although this is optional. The alternative is to pass them when taxy clearance is given. In practice, pilots often call in advance for this 'airfield data', acknowledge it and say 'call you again for start'.

Traffic on the congested holiday routes to the Mediterranean and other parts of Europe is subject to complex rules known as departure flow regulation. They require the aircraft to take off at a specified time, ATC being allowed a small margin before and after this to cover any

Landing Chart for Manchester (CAA).

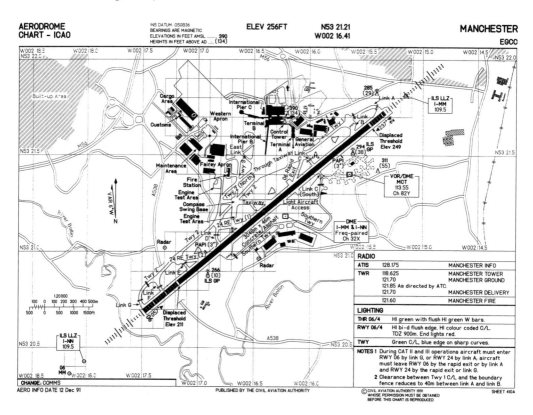

taxying delays or short waits for landing traffic. These Approved Departure Times (ADTs) were formerly known as slot times and this terminology is still heard occasionally on R/T. Further details will be found on page 105.

For example, a system known as Passive Slot Allocation is used for scheduled airline flights into London's airports from various British cities. Since the flight details are already stored in LATCC's computer it is a simple matter to allocate the ADTs well in advance by means of a FAX to the operator and local ATC.

Other domestic traffic within the UK is also regulated at peak periods. For example, the Channel Islands airports become very busy during the summer and flow control is employed to reduce congestion. Routes over the Irish Sea and, on occasion, into Scotland are also subject to flow regulation. A time band normally of 10 minutes, within which an

Landing Chart for Heathrow (CAA).

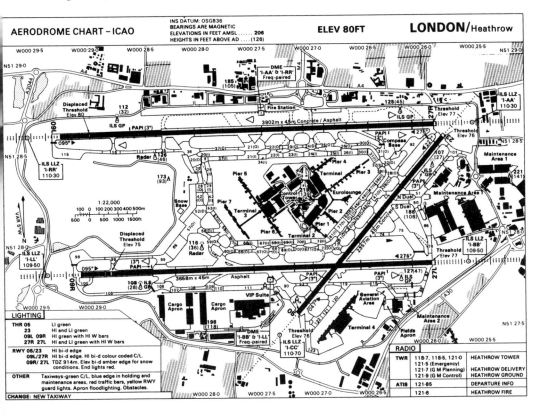

aircraft must cross a specified point, is used as an alternative to an ADT.

If there are no problems, taxy instructions will be given to the appropriate runway. In the meantime, ATC will have obtained an airways clearance from the parent ATCC by land line and this is passed to the aircraft at a convenient moment. (Preferably not while the crew are picking their way gingerly out of a crowded apron!) Local procedures vary from one airport to another and it may be necessary to contact the ATCC again as the subject nears the runway for permission to let it take off. Sometimes a restriction may be applied to separate it from overflying traffic, such as: 'Not above 2,500 ft until further cleared by Manchester Control.'

On occasion, the ATCC may allow the aircraft to take off with the condition that Approach Radar will separate it from inbound conflicting traffic. It will then be given a suitable radar heading to fly after departure and/or a level restriction. As soon as it is airborne the aircraft will be transferred to the Approach frequency and it will only be handed over to the ATCC when the confliction has been resolved ('Clean' in ATC slang).

Where no local restrictions are applied the Tower will put the aircraft over to the ATCC immediately after take-off. The departure time is also passed to the ATCC by telephone to be fed into the computer. At the busiest UK airports, including Heathrow, Gatwick and Manchester, the flow of arrivals and departures is designed so that the two do not conflict. The ideal is a 'conveyor belt' system but, although in practice this is virtually impossible to achieve, it comes quite near to being so. Of necessity the other lesser airfields in a TMA, for example Liverpool in the case of Manchester, are somewhat subservient. Their traffic flows are very much subject to those of their busier neighbours, although on the credit side, sometimes more flexible.

Often, if the weather is good, pilots on IFR Flight plans may elect to go VFR. This saves en route navigational charges and it is also a way to avoid delays at busy periods when an airways clearance is not immediately forthcoming from the ATCC. However, pilots who try to beat the system and rejoin controlled airspace further down the airway will not get much sympathy! Public transport flights are not permitted to do this but cargo and mail pilots often make the request. A typical ATC acknowledgement of a request to go VFR is: 'Atlantic 991 roger, IFR flight plan cancelled at time 36.'

The SSR code or *squawk* as it is known, is allocated according to a predetermined system. The United Kingdom participates in the internationally agreed Originating Region Code Assignment Method (ORCAM). This was developed by Eurocontrol and endorsed by ICAO. Since there are insufficient code blocks to develop a world-wide system it has been necessary to group certain countries into Participating Areas. The ICAO EUR region is divided into five of these areas, the United Kingdom falling into PA West.

ORCAM is designed to reduce R/T and cockpit workload by allocating an SSR code which will be retained by the aircraft from take-off to touchdown. This helps controllers in forward planning, particularly in areas of radar data processing. Each ATCC is allocated two blocks of codes, one for internal flights (Domestic) and the other (ORCAM) for international flights. The ATCC with jurisdiction over the airspace first entered by an aircraft will assign a discrete code from one of its blocks. The code will depend on the destination and will be retained throughout the flight within the Participating Area, being transferred from centre to centre along the route. See Appendix 7.

Approach Control units with SSR capability have their own small block of codes which they can allocate to traffic crossing their area, provided of course that the aircraft is transponder-equipped. Fortunately nowadays most private aircraft can comply with this. Mention of the special *squawk* 7000 is often made on R/T. Pilots flying outside controlled airspace and Aerodrome Traffic Zones and who are not receiving a radar service are advised to set 7000, the conspicuity code, on the transponder. As the name implies, this makes the aircraft show up better on radar and the more sophisticated transponders will also indicate the altitude being maintained.

Aerodrome Control Phraseology

Aircraft: Luton Tower Britannia 835A request start-up.

ATC: Britannia 835A start-up approved, temperature plus 8.

These start-up requests should always be made by aircraft which intend to fly airways, as there may be unexpected delays. Far better to postpone starting for a few minutes than waste fuel at the holding point. The phrase 'Start-up at your discretion', together with an expected departure time, may be used so that the onus is on the crew to start engines at a convenient time. Note that the words 'at your discretion' are used by controllers to imply that any traffic delays, getting stuck in soft ground and similar misfortunes will henceforth be the pilot's fault! Controllers have very definite responsibilites and they are understandably reluctant to take on any extra ones.

Aircraft: London Ground Alitalia 235 Stand E3 request pushback.

Liverpool Tower (Author).

ATC: Alitalia 235 pushback approved.

Many airports have nose-in parking at the terminal to save apron space and to facilitate passenger handling. Aircraft thus have to be pushed backwards by a tractor before they can taxy for departure.

Aircraft: Liverpool Tower GBDNR on the Western Apron request taxy for local.

ATC: GNR taxy to holding point runway 09 via Western Taxyway, QNH 1008.

Taxy instructions must always specify a clearance limit, which is the point at which an aircraft must halt and ask for further permission to proceed. The limit is normally the holding point of the runway in use but it may be an intermediate position, perhaps another runway which is also in intermittent use. To maintain a smooth operation, controllers try to anticipate calls from taxying aircraft so that they do not actually have to stop at intermediate points.

The ideal is to establish a circular flow of taxying aircraft so that the ones just landed do not get in the way of those moving towards the holding point. Alas, many airports have inadequate taxyway systems with two-way flows and bottlenecks, perhaps in the worst cases, as at Coventry, having runway access at only one end. A refusal to give crossing clearance of an active runway is given in the form: 'GVW hold short runway 23.' Permission to proceed is: 'GVW cross runway 23, report vacated.'

When ready for take-off, permission is sought from the Tower. If the runway is occupied by traffic which has just landed the aircraft will be told to 'line up and wait'. The American phrase 'taxy into position' is sometimes tried when a foreign pilot seems to have difficulty in understanding what is meant. (Controllers always have something up their sleeves to break the language barrier and we have all had to resort to plain speech to convey our meaning to some uncomprehending student pilot!)

If there is traffic on final, the aircraft at the holding point may be told: 'After the Cherokee on short final, line up.' Care must be taken that there is no possibility of confusion with another aircraft which may have just landed. Where a preceding aircraft is beginning its take-off roll, the second aircraft may be told: 'After the departing F27, line up and wait.' The use of the words 'cleared immediate take-off' means that the aircraft must go without delay to leave a runway free for landing traffic. It is only to be used where there is actual urgency so that its specific meaning is not debased.

I have already covered the circuit joining procedure, so a few examples of phraseology will suffice.

Aircraft: Coventry Tower GAYMN at Ansty for landing.

ATC: GMN join right hand downwind runway 05, QFE 1004; *or* GMN cleared straight-in approach runway 23, QFE 1004.

Aircraft: GMN downwind.

ATC: GMN Number 2, follow the Cessna 150 on base.

Aircraft: GMN Number 2, traffic in sight.

OR

ATC: GMN extend downwind, number 2 to a Cessna 150 4 miles final on radar approach.

Aircraft: GMN wilco.

Note that the obsolete standard phrase 'Cleared to final Number 2' etc may still be heard for some time as controllers under pressure occasionally revert to what they have been saying for the past decade or so. The word 'clear' or 'cleared' was swept away in the changes to R/T jargon in mid-1984 and is now reserved solely for landing, take-off and route clearances in order to reduce dangerous misunderstandings.

Having already explained the criteria for issuing landing and take-off clearances, it only remains for me to mention a few extra points. Aircraft on what used to be known as 'circuits and bumps' may wish to do a 'touch and go' landing; in other words, the aircraft lands, continues rolling and takes off again without a pause. The wording 'cleared touch and go' is the only one approved officially but pilots may ask for a 'roller', the military equivalent.

Instructions to carry out a missed approach may be given to avert an unsafe situation, such as when one aircraft is too close behind another on final. 'GTE go around, I say again, go around. Acknowledge.'

Depending on local procedures, a departing aircraft will be retained on the Tower frequency until it is clear of the area or changed to Approach immediately. Airways flights will of course be transferred to the ATCC just after take-off or as soon as they have been separated from any conflicting traffic. When the landing roll is complete, the arriving aircraft will be told to clear the runway in the following manner:

Typical Left-hand Circuit

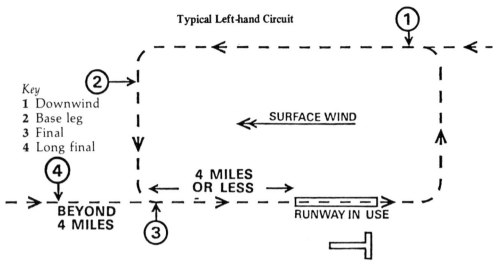

Key
1 Downwind
2 Base leg
3 Final
4 Long final

Above *Critical positions in the Traffic Circuit*

Left *Night scene in the Tower at Manchester* (CAA)

Below *Aerodrome Chart for Stansted* (CAA).

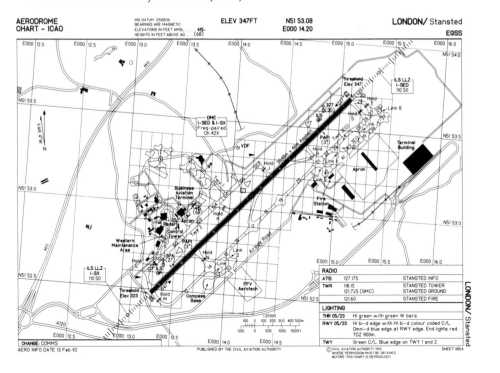

ATC: GMN vacate left; *or* GMN taxi to the end, report runway vacated; *or* GMN take next right. When vacated contact Ground 118.35.

The appropriate taxying instructions are then passed. Airborne and landing times may be passed by the Tower, although there is no official requirement for this.

Interestingly enough, controllers are not responsible for reminding pilots to put their wheels down on final, except when a radar approach is being provided. However, if an aircraft landed wheels-up in broad daylight, the controller would no doubt come in for some criticism, apart from the dent to his professional pride! Fortunately it is a rare occurrence these days but I once earned a pint from a Cessna 337 pilot whom I reminded just in time. (Cheap at the price—the saving in repairs would have paid my year's salary!)

One last point is defined as 'Essential Aerodrome Information' and refers to any obstruction or unserviceability which is likely to affect operations. It is always prefixed 'caution' and some examples follow:

Caution work in progress ahead north side of the taxyway.

Caution VASIs runway 27 unserviceable.

Caution large flock of birds north of runway 27 near the fast turn off.

Chapter 8

ATC at London's airports

Because of its intensity, Heathrow traffic is handled rather differently from that of other British airports. Inbound aircraft are directed by LATCC to one of four VORs located at Bovingdon, Lambourne, Biggin and Ockham. If traffic is light they may not actually route overhead these beacons but are vectored by radar directly to intercept the ILS for the runway in use. As the traffic flow increases, aircraft may arrive at the beacons faster than the airport is able to receive them, allowing for the requisite separation on approach. Hence the term 'stacking' (in ATC more usually referred to as 'holding'). The aircraft fly an oval racetrack pattern aligned in a specific direction. The outbound leg from the beacon is flown for one minute, then a rate one turn (a change of direction of 3° per second) onto a one minute inbound leg, finally a further rate one turn to the beacon, and so on.

During Heathrow's busy periods six controllers work as a team. They consist of two Approach Controllers, two Number One Radar Controllers, a Number Two Radar Controller and a Special VFR Controller. Each Approach Controller with his Number One radar man controls the traffic from either Bovingdon and Lambourne in the north or from Ockham and Biggin in the south. As the aircraft nears the reporting point LATCC releases it to Heathrow Approach on intercom as pre-warning that it is about to call. On contact the pilot is told to enter the hold or, if there is no delay, vectored directly into the landing sequence. The frequencies in use are London Approach (North) on 119.2, London Approach (South) on 119.5 (119.2 only at quieter times), and No 2 Radar Controller on 120.4. The S/VFR controller operates on 119.9.

The Approach Controllers and the Number One Radar Controllers work closely together, instructing pilots to adjust their height, speed and heading so that two orderly streams of aircraft, one from the north, the other from the south are brought onto the approach path.

Aircraft in these two streams are handed over to the Number Two Radar Controller so that he can integrate them into a single stream of aircraft approaching the runway.

Radio display for the London TMA of a busy time. Callsign and height information is shown together with codes for destinations eg KK for Gatwick and LL for Heathrow (CAA).

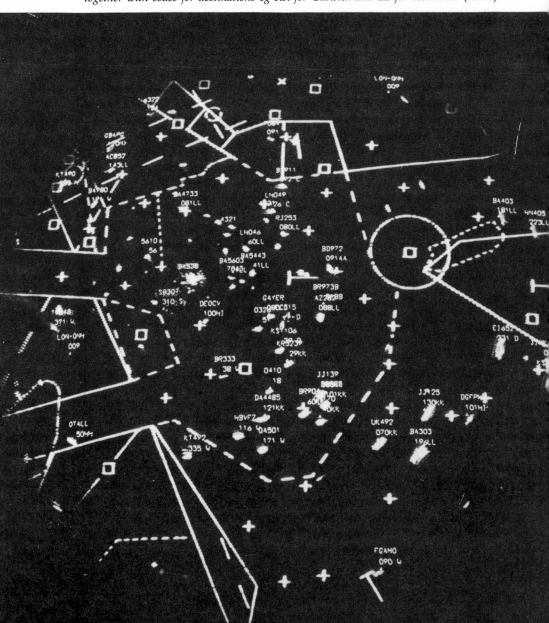

At this stage a correct landing interval must be established and the Number Two Radar Controller ensures that all aircraft are correctly separated, depending on the prevailing weather conditions and type of aircraft involved. The vortex wake separations are explained in Chapter 13 but there are other considerations. For example, a DC-9 following a Shorts 360 will obviously have no problem with vortex wake but will catch up rapidly if this is not allowed for. Similarly, if visibility is on limits an aircraft may be slow to clear the runway and the 'land after' procedure cannot be applied, resulting in an overshoot if the next aircraft is too close behind.

The Special VFR Controller is responsible for helicopters and light aircraft which want to land or merely transit the London Control Zone within the levels for which Heathrow Approach is responsible. Inbound aircraft are fitted into the approach pattern to cause as little inconvenience as possible to the main commercial traffic. Helicopters are required to follow special routes in the London area, designed where possible to keep them over the River Thames and the most thinly populated areas.

The usual destination is the Westland Heliport at Battersea. All inbound helicopters have to route via the River Thames, initially positioning to Kew Bridge, Barnes or London Bridge, depending upon the direction from which they are approaching. There are numerous compulsory and on request reporting points and helicopters may be held at a number of positions to await onward clearance. They are all located at easily recognizable places such as Hampton Court, Sunbury Lock, and Hanworth.

When the two streams of approaching aircraft are satisfactorily merged into one, and as each aircraft is established on the ILS at a distance of six to eight miles from touchdown, control is transferred to Air Arrivals Control in the Tower. Like any other Tower Controller he issues landing clearances, and passes wind checks and details of surface conditions where appropriate. The frequency is 118.7.

After the aircraft has landed and left the runway it will be transferred to the Ground Movements Controller on 121.9 who directs it to the parking stand. He continues to monitor its progress and co-ordinates its movements with those of other aircraft and vehicles. Any airport has its quota of service vehicles but Heathrow inevitably has more than most. There is, for example, a full time mobile bird control unit; its radio callsign is *Seagull*. *Checker* is the airport surface and lighting inspection vehicle.

The maintenance of runways and taxyways and their associated

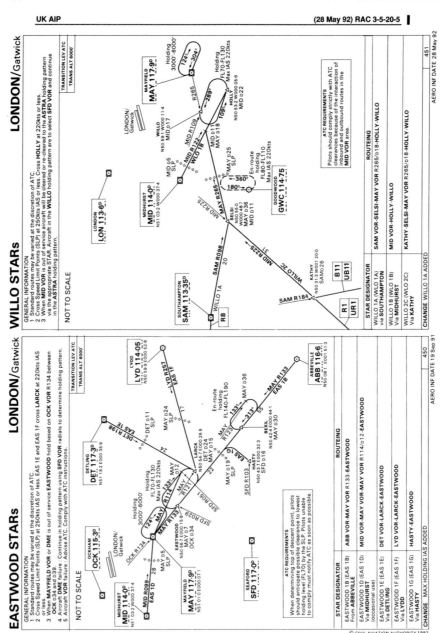

Standard Terminal Arrival Chart for Gatwick (CAA).

lighting is one of the biggest problems for Ground Movement Control. One controller told me that there is almost always some part of the airport being dug up or resurfaced. Each controller has an airport plan on which he notes the current unserviceable areas before taking over watch in the Tower. For easy reference Heathrow is divided up into numbered blocks.

To help things run smoothly at night or in poor visibility a radar called the Aerodrome Surface Movement Indicator (ASMI) is used to monitor aircraft and vehicle movements. Its aerial is mounted on top of the Tower and scans the airport at very high speed so that the radar picture is continuously renewed. Runways and taxyways show up clearly on the display, as do the aircraft and vehicles which need to be tracked. Like television, it is bright enough for daylight viewing.

At night the aircraft are assisted by green centreline and red stop bar lights set flush with the taxyway. These can be illuminated in sections to allow a discrete route to be signalled to ensure that no two aircraft are in or crossing the same section at any one time. This complex lighting system is operated by an ATC assistant on instructions from the Ground Movements Controller. The lighting control panel is a mimic diagram, ie it is designed in the form of an airport plan with switches which directly operate the lighting in the corresponding section on the airport.

When an aircraft is ready for departure, the pilot, having noted the data on the continuous broadcast on the ATIS, calls the Ground Movement Planner on 121.7 (call sign *Delivery*) for permission to start engines. This may be granted at once or a start time given to minimise ground delays and thus save fuel. Also taken into consideration are the number of other aircraft which have started up, air route congestion and ADTs issued by LATCC.

Once start-up clearance is given the pilot is told to contact GMC when ready to taxy. The latter is responsible for issuing push-back clearance from the stand by a tractor. Guidance is then given to the runway in use, and as this is approached, the aircraft is handed over to the Air Departures Controller on 118.5 who arranges the aircraft in a departure sequence to achieve the maximum use of the runway concerned.

For example, when two aircraft of a similar type are departing in succession, one for a north bound destination followed by one to the south, they may be allowed to leave one minute apart. However, due to the variety of aircraft types using Heathrow, this time interval may be increased depending on aircraft type and specific departure route.

Immediately it is airborne the aircraft is transferred to London Control and fitted into the airways system.

The pair of westerly (27) runways tends to be used most frequently because of prevailing winds. One is normally used for landings and the other for departures, but a local agreement ensures a change from one to the other at around 1500 hours local time each day in order to spread the noise more evenly. When the tail wind component is no greater than 5 knots on Runway 27 Right and Left, they will be used in preference to Runway 09 Right and Left, provided the runway surface is dry. When the cross-wind component on these main runways exceeds 20 knots Runway 05/23 will normally be made available if there is a lesser cross-wind component affecting it.

ATC at Gatwick is somewhat less complex because of the single runway operation and the two, rather than four, holding stacks known as WILLO and Eastwood. Traffic from and to London City Airport is handled by a facility known as Thames Radar which is co-located with Heathrow Approach. Because of its proximity to London City, Biggin Hill's IFR traffic is also co-ordinated by Thames Radar. Traffic at Stansted, currently with just one holding stack, continues to grow. Its airspace is expected to be incorporated in the CCF (see page 6) in 1995 when a second stack will be established.

Chapter 9

Oceanic Control

Although traffic over the North Atlantic communicates with ATC by means of the HF radio band, VHF being too restricted in range, aircraft requesting clearance to enter the Shanwick Oceanic Control Area from overhead the United Kingdom can be heard on certain VHF frequencies. ATC in the Shanwick OCA is provided by the Oceanic ATCC at Prestwick, supported by the communications station at Ballygireen near Shannon in Eire, hence the composite callsign Shanwick Oceanic. Jet aircraft are required to request oceanic clearance while east of 2°W (roughly Manchester–Bournemouth) or as early as possible if departing from a point west of 2°W, so it is easy to intercept their transmissions in much of the United Kingdom.

For sub-sonic aircraft over the Atlantic there is a procedure known as the organised track system. As a result of passenger demands, time zone differences and airport noise restrictions, much of the North Atlantic air traffic is contained in two flows—westbound in the morning and eastbound in the evening. Because of the concentration of the flows and the limited vertical height band which is economical for jet operations, the airspace is comparatively congested. The track system is thus designed to accommodate as many aircraft as possible on the most suitable flight paths, taking advantage of any pressure systems to provide a tail wind where possible.

Prestwick OACC is responsible for the day track system and Gander for that at night. In each case, planners on both sides of the Atlantic consult with one another and co-ordinate as necessary with adjacent OACCs, as well as with domestic ATC agencies, to ensure that the system provides sufficient tracks and Flight Levels to satisfy anticipated traffic demands.

On completion of negotiations the organised tracks system is sent out by the OACC concerned by signal to all interested parties in Europe and North America. The daytime system is usually published by Prestwick between midnight and 01:00 hours. Gander usually publishes its night system between noon and 13:00 hours. In addition, the track co-ordinates are broadcast on frequency 133.8 and this can be heard in many parts of the United Kingdom on a normal air band radio. The tracks are known as Alfa, Bravo, Charlie and so on, the most northerly being Alfa.

Each oceanic flight plan received from the departure airport includes the track, Flight Level and cruise Mach number requested. (Mach number being a proportion of Mach 1, the speed of sound.) When the pilot requests an oceanic clearance, the Planning Controller attempts to fit the flight into the planned slot according to the aircraft's requested level, Mach number and boundary estimate.

Once the clearance is accepted by the pilot, the information is relayed to the relevant ATCC and, where necessary, to adjacent OACCs. Then the clearance is fed into Prestwick's computer which prints the appropriate en route flight strips and passes the information to Gander's computer. This flight strip gives all relevant flight details and computed times of arrival at specific reporting points along the track, normally at intervals of 10° of longitude. This flight strip is used by the controller to monitor the progress of the flight through the OCA.

Compared with the brief content of domestic airways clearances, these oceanic clearances are fairly long-winded because of the need to specify a large number of latitude and longitude positions, although in certain circumstances they can be abbreviated. It is useful to record these messages on tape for subsequent analysis, the same going for other ATC transmissions when you are using an air band radio for the first time.

Most flights across the North Atlantic are handled in this way, but some aircraft may wish to operate outside the organised track system, for example on flights between Europe and the Caribbean, or between Europe and the West Coast of the USA. These too are handled by Shanwick, as are transatlantic flights by Concorde. The latter operate along fixed tracks, normally between 50,000 ft and 60,000 ft. Because of the extremely small number of aircraft flying within this height band it is usually possible for the OACC to issue a clearance before take-off. This allows Concorde to operate on a supersonic 'cruise climb profile', which is the best in terms of fuel economy.

Unique to oceanic control is the method by which aircraft request clearances. Irrespective of geographical location, an aircraft will always use one of two frequencies, either 123.95 or 127.65 MHz. Aircraft registered west of 30°W use the first one, those registered east of 30°W the second. In practice this generally means that British airlines use 127.65 and American, Australian and Canadian airlines use 123.95. 135.525 is used as a stand-by.

Concorde flying over the Atlantic is a special case because an idealised flight profile would commence with an uninterrupted climb to supersonic cruise, followed by an uninterrupted descent to destination. Sonic boom considerations and the presence of other traffic obviously render this impossible so, in order to avoid supersonic flight over the UK land mass, a typical flight to the USA via the Woodley and Lyneham beacons climbs initially to around FL 260 and maintains Mach .95 until the 'nominal acceleration point' after crossing the coastline south of Brecon. The final tactical consideration for clearance for transonic acceleration along the Bristol Channel is made by the Radar Controller at LATCC. Likewise, on the return trip the transonic deceleration is completed over the sea prior to crossing the coast.

Concorde has special, unvarying oceanic tracks, known as 'Sierra Mike' when westbound and 'Sierra November' when eastbound. 'Sierra Oscar' is a reserve track in both directions. Air France Concorde flights to North America depart from Paris Charles de Gaulle and enter the London UIR south-west of Lands End. They then route to the same oceanic entry point at 50°N 08°W. Supersonic Link Routes numbered SL1 to SL7 connect the oceanic tracks with domestic airspace.

Outside VHF range, aircraft crossing the Atlantic communicate with ATC by means of HF radio. The same applies to any ocean or underdeveloped land mass where the short range of VHF radio waves would prove an embarrassment. More than 200,000 commercial, military and general aviation flights overflew the North Atlantic during 1991 alone and the ownership of an HF receiver opens up a whole new area of interest for the enthusiast.

In Britain there are a wide variety of listening possibilities, principally the civil stations (nets) controlling traffic over the Atlantic from Polar regions to the Equator, the US Air Force's extensive network and those of the RAF and airline operators. There are nearly 140 ATC centres operating on HF around the world and, depending on the performance of one's receiver and other factors, many of them can be monitored. During the transatlantic slack periods (ie between the late morning/early afternoon westbound flights and the eastbound flights in the early hours of the morning) one can listen in to other parts of the world. For example, aircraft in the Far East in the late afternoon, Africa in the evening, and then, for an hour or so either side of midnight, the Caribbean and the eastern seaboard of the USA are very busy.

HF stations use a block of radio frequencies to circumvent the effects of atmospheric conditions. HF transmissions 'bounce off' the ionising layers which lie above the earth but, since the layers are affected by day and night conditions, a suitable range of daytime frequencies might suffer severe interference at night and vice versa. Although having very long range, HF lacks the clarity of the VHF channels and the atmospheric noises and constant chatter make it very tiring for crews to maintain a continuous listening watch.

The answer is SelCal, short for Selective Calling. By this method, crews need not monitor the frequency, but when the ground station wishes to communicate with them a tone is sent and decoded by the cockpit equipment. A 'bing-bong' sound can be heard on the radio and on the flight deck a chime or light signal alerts the pilots to respond by R/T. Each aircraft with SelCal capability is allocated a four-letter code by ARINC (Aeronautical Radio Inc), an American company which acts as agent to ICAO to perform this function.

On the first contact with the controller, the SelCal will normally be checked and here is where the interest lies for the aircraft registration collector. The SelCal code remains with the aircraft as long as the 'box' does, despite changes of ownership. ARINC does not make public the registration/SelCal tie-ups but painstaking detective work by enthusiasts has tracked most of them down. The Aviation Society in Manchester publishes an extensive list in *High in the Sky* which is available from them or specialist bookshops. The Society's magazine and also that of LAAS International (see pages 144 – 145) list new allocations.

Over the Atlantic, position reports are passed in a similar fashion to those on VHF, ie the present position and a forward estimate for the next one. The positions are given in terms of latitude and longitude, 56 North 10 West being an example, or as a reporting point or beacon when nearing a land mass. Approximately one aircraft per hour is requested by the Oceanic Control Centre to 'Send Met', and will include weather information with each position report. This consists of outside air temperature, wind speed and direction derived from INS equipment, plus any other relevant observations. A typical position report is: 'Position Swissair 100 56 N 20 W 1235 Flight Level 330 estimate 56 N 30 W 1310, next 56 N 40 W.'

The airspace between 27,500 ft and 40,000 ft over most of the North Atlantic is known as MNPS (Minimum Navigation Performance Specification) airspace. Aircraft flying within it are required to carry a certain scale of navigation equipment so that they can be flown accurately within the parameters of the ATC clearance. In this congested area, mostly unmonitored by radar, any deviation could be dangerous.

This is reflected in the fairly large lateral separation between flights, vertical separation being the same as that described on page 17. Aircraft which do not meet the MNPS requirements are separated laterally by 120 nautical miles, which is reduced to 90 miles in certain designated airspace. A spacing of 60 miles is allowed for aircraft which meet the MNPS. The same applies to supersonic aircraft operating at or above FL275. The rules for longitudinal spacing, ie one aircraft following another on the same track, are too complicated to list here but vary from 15 down to 10 minutes and sometimes less. It all depends upon speed, which is expressed as a Mach number.

The Oceanic Controllers at Prestwick do not talk to the aircraft directly but teletype their instructions to specialised, usually ex-marine, radio operators at Ballygireen just north of Shannon Airport. The latter talk to the aircraft and teletype the responses back to Prestwick. This is not as inefficient as it sounds because HF communications can be so distorted that experienced radio operators do better than the controllers themselves and the short delay in reply is insignificant with such long distances between aircraft.

The majority of short wave aircraft communications use Single Side Band (SSB) signals. Without going into too many technicalities, the AM (Audio Modulation) method employed by VHF transmissions is built up of three components; a lower side band, a carrier, and an upper side band. By removing the carrier and one of the side bands, the power of the signal is compressed into a smaller band width which boosts reception at long range and reduces interference. However, an ordinary short wave receiver which may have the necessary frequency bands (2 – 28 MHz) will pick up SSB as something which has been described as 'sounding like Donald Duck'. To make the signal intelligible, the carrier has to be reintroduced and this is done by a Beat Frequency Oscillator (BFO). Modern short wave receivers usually have this incorporated but older sets will have to be modified. BFOs can be bought separately or built at home with the aid of a circuit diagram.

Unfortunately, a basic HF set with SSB costs considerably more than the equivalent simple VHF radio. However, for about £110 the Sangean ATS803A will do the job admirably. It is a revamped version of a set previously marketed under different names by Comet (Sangean ATS803), Curry's (Matsui MR4099), Dixon's (Saisho SW5000) and Tandy (Realistic DX–44). It has digital tuning which is highly desirable with

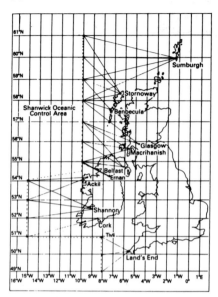

Map showing entry points into the Shanwick Oceanic Control Area (produced from information supplied by the CAA).

HF as there are so many operational frequencies and it obviously helps to identify them precisely for future reference. The built-in aerial is only useful for strong local signals like Shanwick, and for wider coverage one needs a long wire aerial. The longer (10 to 30 yards) and higher the better, orientated as near horizontal as you can and if possible at right angles to the direction of the station you most want to listen to, eg N/S for Atlantic traffic. Beware of short circuits in the rain from whatever tree or pole you have attached it to, not to mention lightning strikes!

If you are rich enough to move up-market for higher performance, the Lowe HF 150 and HF225 at around £330 and £430 respectively are said to have the performance of much more expensive receivers. The Kenwood range includes the R-2000 and R-5000 retailing at around £550 and £875 respectively. Ideally, the enthusiast needs a scanner which can monitor VHF and UHF air band as well as HF air communications, but it is only now that modern electronics have made this possible in a convenient package. The receivers concerned are the AR3000A, which covers 100 kHz to 2036 MHz and costs around £765, and the AR1500, the first *hand-held* scanner to feature HF SSB as well as VHF and UHF air band. It retails at £279.

Of course, for these sort of prices you are getting far more than the air bands. The radios mentioned above and others, including the Icom and Yaesu ranges, are communications receivers in the fullest sense of the word. The AR3000A spans virtually the entire radio spectrum from long wave broadcasts up to the limits of current usage. For a full appreciation of the capabilities of short wave radios the reader is recommended to consult Arthur Miller's *Short Wave Radio Listener's Handbook,* also published by Patrick Stephens Limited.

We now move on to an outline of what can be heard relatively easily on HF in Britain. Don't expect to get the quality of VHF air band—HF listening can be hard work as signals fluctuate! The North Atlantic HF network is divided into 'families' of frequencies to obtain a balanced loading of communications on the oceanic track system. Each family uses a primary frequency with a secondary one for use when reception is poor. The frequencies are shared by several Oceanic Control Centres, including Shanwick (Shannon/Prestwick) which serves aircraft between roughly 45 North and 61 North and between 10 West and 30 West. The Iceland OCC at Reykjavik is responsible for traffic north of 61 North and Gander works aircraft to the west of 30 West.

Santa Maria in the Azores looks after traffic south of Shanwick's area and from 15 West to 40 West. New York OCC controls flights over a large proportion of the south-west of the North Atlantic, and with favourable reception conditions those from the Caribbean and South America can be heard as well. San Juan in Puerto Rico is responsible for aircraft south of New York's area, using the same frequencies.

Long Distance Operational Control Facilities (LDOCF) are operated by or on behalf of many airlines throughout the world for company messages similar to those heard on VHF air band. Some of these stations are equipped to provide direct voice communications between flight crews and their company operations using phone patch techniques. Alternatively, the ground radio operator will accept messages for relay over the normal telephone or telex circuits. British Airways handles its own aircraft by HF from Heathrow, along with those of many other companies subscribing to the service. Portishead Radio is operated by British Telecom for phone patches into the international public system. A similar service is provided by Berne Radio in Switzerland and Stockholm Radio in Sweden. Of course, many of the messages may not be in English!

Military aircraft use HF frequencies within broadly the same range as do civil aircraft, so you can listen to both with the same radio, unlike VHF/UHF. Military radio traffic is, however, a lot more varied and much less predictable than civil. It is also difficult to find out enough background information to understand some of the things to be heard, which is perhaps just as well! Further information can be found in Chapter 16.

A fairly simple way of expanding the capabilities of an HF receiver is to use it to monitor Radio Teletype, known as 'Ritty' from its initials RTTY. A personal computer is required or alternatively a RTTY module. The radio's speaker extension is connected by lead into the PC or module and the read-out is displayed on screen and printed out if desired. The Aeradio stations around the world churn out masses of information, much of it weather reports and forecasts, but the interesting items for enthusiasts are the flight plans which are also sent by this method.

RTTY is a very specialised branch of airband 'listening' and these notes are included merely to alert readers to the possibilities. There are several frequency and reference guides available, a good source being *Short Wave Magazine*'s Book Service. Suppliers of RTTY reception equipment advertise regularly in this magazine and a regular column 'Decode' covers the subject in detail. Aeronautical information is of course only a small fraction of the data sent worldwide in RTTY mode.

A selection of HF frequencies

Do not expect to hear the distant ones routinely. *Civil Air Route Regions (ICAO)*, frequencies and major ground stations involved: AFI = African; CAR = Caribbean; CEP = Central East Pacific; CWP = Central West Pacific; EUR = European; MID = Middle East; NP = North Pacific; SAM = South America; SAT = South Atlantic; SEA = South East Asia; SP = South Pacific. Virtually all frequencies listed are USB.

NAT-A (southern tracks)	3016 5598 8825 13306	New York, Gander, Shanwick, Santa Maria
NAT-B (N/SAm-regd a/c)	2899 5616 8864 13291	Gander, Shanwick, New York
NAT-C (Eur/Asia-regd a/c)	2872 5649 8879 11336 13306	Gander, Shanwick, New York
NAT-D (polar routes)	2971 4675 8891 11279 13291 17946	Cambridge Bay, Gander, Shanwick, Iceland
NAT-E (Mid-Atlantic)	3476 6628 8906 11309	New York, Santa Maria tracks
EUR-A	3479 5661 6598 10084 13288 17961	Berlin, Malta
CAR-A	2887 5550 6577 8846 8918 11387 11396 13297 17907	New York, Paramaribo, San Juan, Panama
MID-1	2992 5667 8918 13312	Ankara, Baghdad, Beirut, Damascus, Kuwait, Bahrain, Cairo, Jeddah
MID-2	3467 5601 5658 10018 13288	Bahrain, Karachi, Bombay, Lahore, Delhi, Calcutta
SEA-1	3470 6556 10066 13318 17907	Calcutta, Dhaka, Madras, Colombo, Male, Cocos, Kuala Lumpur
SEA-2	3485 5655 8942 11396 13309	Hong Kong, Manila, Kuala Lumpur
SEA-3	3470 6556 11396 13318 13297	Manila, Singapore, Jakarta, Darwin, Sydney, Perth

AFI-1	3452 6535 6673 8861 13357 17955	Casablanca, Canaries, Dakar, Abidjan, Roberts
AFI-2	3419 5652 8894 13273 13294 17961	Algiers, Tripoli, Niamey, Kano
AFI-3	3467 5658 11300 13288 17961	Cairo, Jeddah, Khartoum, Addis Ababa, Bombay, Mogadishu, Nairobi
AFI-4	2878 5493 6586 8903 13294 17961	Lagos, Brazzaville, Luanda, Windhoek, Johannesberg, Lusaka
AFI-5/INO-1	3476 5634 8879 13306 17961	Seychelles, Johannesberg, Lusaka, Mauritius, Colombo, Perth
SEA-1	3470 6556 10066 13318 17907	Colombo, Madras, Calcutta, Kuala Lumpur, Cocos, Dhaka
SEA-2	3485 5655 8942 11396 13309	Hong Kong, Manila, Kuala Lumpur, Singapore, Beijing
SEA-3	3470 6556 11396 13297 13318	Singapore, Cocos, Perth, Sydney, Darwin, Manila, Jakarta
CEP-5	2869 3413 5547 5574 8843 11282 13261 13354 17904	Honolulu, San Francisco
CWP-1/2	2998 4666 6532 6562 8903 11384 13300 17904	Hong Kong, Manila, Guam, Tokyo, Honolulu, Port Moresby
NP-3/4	2932 5628 6655 10048 11330 13273 13294 17904	Tokyo, Cold Bay, Anchorage, Honolulu
SP-6/7	3467 5643 8867 13273 13300 17904 21964(?)	Sydney, Auckland, Nandi, Tahiti Honolulu, Pascua
SW/SAM-8	2944 4669 6649 10024 11360 17907	Pascua (Easter Island)
SAM-1	2944 4669 6649 10024 11360 17907	Pascua, Panama, Lima, Santiago, Cordoba, Punta Arenas
SAM-2	3479 5526 8855 10096 13297 17907	Manaus, Belem, Recife, Brasilia, Rio, Montevideo, La Paz, Leticia
SAT-1	3452 6535 8861 13357 17955	Recife, Salvador, Brasilia
SAT-2	2854 5565 11291 13315 17955	Paramaribo, Cayenne, Dakar, Canaries

Base Stations: Portishead *5610* 6634 8170 8185 8960 *11306* 12133 17405 18210 19510 20065; Berne 4654 6643 8936 *10069* 13205 15046 18023; Stockholm 5541 8930 11345 13342 17916 23210; ARINC 6640 11342 17925 21964

Company frequencies (may be used by other carriers as well): British Airways 5535 8921 10072 13333 17922; KLM 5532 5645 8924; South African 8893 8933; Iberia 5529 8936 13327; Gulfair 5538; Saudia 5545 21994; Jordanian 9003 13225; Pakistan 8930; Lufthansa 4687 5645 6637 10078; Varig 5553 8924 11366; Air France 6526 6637 10093; El Al 8837; Balkan 11384; Air India 10072; MEA 13330; LTU 8921; BWIA 8924; Interflug 4745 17975; Singapore 5526; Eastern 5535; Qantas 6526 10093 13342; Kenya 6640 8927; LOT 8924; Zimbabwe 8950; Nigeria 8963; Aeroflot 11312 13220. NB Some US carriers use European base stations.

VOLMET: RAF 4722 11200; New York 3485 6604 10051; Shannon 3413 5640 8957 13264

Rescue: 3023 3488 3939 5420 5670 *5680* 5695 6760 8893 9025 18271 8364 (International Distress)

RAF STICS (Architect): 4742 5729 6190 6690 6738 8190 9032 11204 *11234* 11244 13257 15031 18018 23220

UK Air Defence Region Sector Operations Control (call-sign Buchan/ Boulmer/ Neatishead/ Portreath/ Benbecula): 3120 3939 4707 4710 *4739* 5747 6686 6693 6715 *6733* 6740 6748 6765

US GCCS (call-sign *Croughton*): 3067 5302 5370 5703 *6750* 6757 9011 9921 10537 *11176* 11180 11207 *11243* 13214 13244 16454

USAFE: 3046 3109 4477 6753 9025 11257

Royal Canadian Air Force: Lahr Military: 3092 4704 5690 6705 9006 11233 13231 13257 15031 18012

NASA: 5190 5246 5810 9043 10780 13600 20186 20192 20198

Frequencies in *italics* are those most commonly used. They are quoted in kilohertz but by inserting a decimal point in the appropriate place they can be converted to megahertz, eg 5616 kHz = 5.616 MHz, 10096 kHz = 10.096 MHz.

Chapter 10

Flight Information Services

An ATC service can be provided only by licensed controllers but at certain small airfields an Aerodrome Flight Information Service (AFIS) is in operation. The AFIS Officers, AFISOs for short, are also required to be licensed and many of them are flying instructors doing this ground job on a part-time basis. Air band listeners will notice certain differences in the R/T phraseology used by AFISOs, reflecting the fact that their instructions are of an advisory nature only. For example, where a licensed controller would say 'cleared take-off', an AFISO would say 'take off at your discretion.'

The aerodrome air/ground service (A/G) is a rudimentary one, for which no qualifications are required, although persons providing it must possess an 'Authority to Operate.' It is usually encountered at private aerodromes used by perhaps one or two company aircraft, Wrexham in North Wales and Shipdam in Norfolk being examples. Basic information is passed to the pilots, covering such essentials as the wind direction and whether the runway is clear. The callsigns for AFIS and A/G are 'INFORMATION' and 'RADIO', respectively.

The Flight Information Service provided by licensed controllers at ATCCs on a 24-hour basis is somewhat different and requires further explanation. The London FIR outside controlled airspace is divided into three, west and east of Alpha 1 and north of Bravo 1, with separate radio frequencies. For the Scottish FIR, one is considered sufficient because of the lighter traffic.

The FIR controller is able to offer the following services; weather information, changes of serviceability of radio navigation aids, aerodrome conditions, proximity warnings and any other information pertinent to safety. Because of the multiplicity of possible reporting points in the FIR, ranging from disused airfields to towns and coastal features, it is difficult to assess the possibility of collision and therefore no positive control or separation can be provided. The other problem is that of civil and military aircraft on random tracks and for whom there is no requirement to contact the FIR.

Outside controlled airspace, a Radar Advisory Service is provided by certain ATC units, subject to the coverage of the radar equipment and the unit's workload. Where such a service is given by an airfield approach unit, it is usually limited to a range of 40 km from the aerodrome traffic zone. Pilots are informed of the bearing, distance, and, if available, the level of the conflicting traffic with advice on the action to be taken to maintain separation if the pilot does not have the traffic in sight. If the pilot decides to ignore the advice given, whether he has visual contact or not, he is responsible for any avoiding action that may subsequently prove necessary.

An alternative is the Radar Information Service, in which the participating pilot is warned of conflicting traffic. No avoiding action is offered and the pilot is wholly responsible for maintaining separation from other aircraft, whether or not the controller has passed traffic information. A pilot wishing to take advantage of an RAS or RIS must first establish verbal agreement with the controller, no radar service being provided until this agreement has been reached. A request for an RAS to be upgraded to an RIS will be accepted subject to the controller's existing workload.

Since mid-1983, military ATC radar units have been providing a Lower Airspace Radar Advisory Service (LARS) to any aircraft outside controlled airspace which requests it. The upper limit is, with certain exceptions, FL 95, and the service is given within about 30 miles of each participating unit. Overlapping coverage ensures that Eastern England and the Midlands and South are well-served, but over Wales and the North-West there are only Brawdy, Valley and Shawbury. Whenever possible aircraft will be handed over from one controller to the next and pilots told to contact the next unit.

A typical small airfield with air/ground service—Caernarfon, North Wales. (Andy Rackham, Air Supply)

Chapter 11

Weather and Air Traffic Control

Met observations at the larger airports are made every 30 minutes at 20 minutes past and 10 minutes to each hour. At the less busy airports they are made once in each hour. Special observations, known as SPECIs (pronounced 'Spessys') must be made within these times if certain changes are observed, eg at the onset or cessation of hail or thunderstorms. If there is a Met Office available, the observations will be done by met staff who are all employees of the Ministry of Defence. Otherwise they are made by ATC personnel who are required to hold a Met Observer's Certificate, gained after a short course at the Met College.

There is a standard format which is passed to the aircraft, consisting of the wind direction in degrees True and its average speed in knots with a note of any significant gusts. This is, however, normally read by the controller in degrees Magnetic direct from the dial in front of him so that it can be related by the pilot to the magnetic heading of the runway. The visibility is passed in metres and kilometres in increments of 100 m when 5,000 m or less and in whole kilometres when greater than 5,000 m. The distance is determined from the known ranges of conspicuous landmarks visible in the locality. The next item is the weather, eg drizzle, fog, rain and so on.

Cloud base is measured by means of a cloud base recorder which scans the sky overhead with a laser beam. Unfortunately, it may give inaccurate low readings when haze, mist or smoke is present. At less well-equipped airfields, cloud base is found by estimation, with experience a surprisingly accurate method. Pilot reports can be requested to confirm the base. At night estimation is difficult so a vertical searchlight is often used. The angle of the 'spot' on the cloud can then be found by sighting with a simple instrument known as an alidade. Simple pre-calculated trigonometry enables the cloud height to be read off a table.

A third method, a small hydrogen or helium-filled balloon of about 2 ft diameter, can be used to measure a lowish base in daylight. The balloon rises at a known rate and can thus be timed with a stop-watch until it disappears into the cloud. It is, however, time-consuming and necessitates heavy, and in the case of hydrogen, highly inflammable, gas cylinders being stored adjacent to the Tower, so few airfields still use it today.

Cloud amount is given in oktas, ie eighths, and height in feet up to and including 5,000 ft. Cloud above this level is of academic interest only to aircrew so is not reported. Not more than three layers are reported, the exception being when cumulo-nimbus cloud, known as Cb or Charlie Bravo, is present. If necessary this can be reported as a fourth group with some emphasis as its turbulence and lightning discharges are an obvious hazard to aircraft.

Air temperature is passed in degrees Celsius, together with the dew point if the two figures are significantly close, indicating that fog may be about to form. The QNH and QFE (Threshold QFE at certain airfields) is given in millibars. These units may one day become hectopascals in the United Kingdom and are already referred to as such in certain European ATC systems. American aircraft occasionally ask for the pressure settings in inches of mercury so a table is kept handy in the Tower for a quick conversion.

Where the weather conditions meet particular criteria—visibility of 10 km or more, no precipitation, no thunderstorm or shallow fog, no cloud below a level of 5,000 ft above aerodrome elevation and no Cb at any level—the visibility and cloud groups are omitted and the word 'CAVOK' (pronounced 'cav OK') is passed. This is derived from the phrase Ceiling and Visibility OK but it seems to confuse a lot of private pilots!

At the busiest UK airports the current met observation is transmitted continuously on the appropriate Terminal VOR or Information frequency by means of a pre-recorded tape. A transcript of a typical broadcast for Newcastle on the Newcastle VOR is as follows: 'This is Newcastle Arrival Information Juliet. 13:20 weather, 300 at 15 knots, 8 kilometres recent rain, 7 okta 1,500 ft, temperature plus 8, dew point plus 7, QNH 1001 millibars. Landing runway 33. Report Information Juliet received on first contact with Newcastle Approach.'

The significance of Juliet is that each observation is given a code letter, beginning with **Alpha** and working through the alphabet, starting once more when Zulu is reached. The controller is thus sure that the pilot has copied the latest observation. These automatic transmissions are very useful in reducing R/T loading as crews can monitor them at their leisure and the controller does not have to pass repeated weather information. It will be noted that the QFE is not included in the ATIS broadcast (Automatic Terminal Information Service). Because of its vital importance this is left to Approach Control to pass.

Runway Visual Range, or RVR as it normally referred to, makes available a more localised assessment of how far the pilot is likely to be able to see along the runway. Measurement only begins when the official met report gives a general visibility of 1,500 m or less and it is essential to enable the pilot to decide whether or not it is within the limits of what are known as 'company minima' for landing or take-off.

RVR is calculated by either the human observer method or by means of electronic equipment. The former requires a person, usually an airport fireman, to stand on a vehicle adjacent to the runway threshold at a specified height to simulate pilot eye-level. He then counts the number of lights or, at some locations, marker boards, that he can see down one side of the runway. The total is passed by radio to the Tower and the RVR read off a pre-computed table.

The Instrumented RVR system, called IRVR, measures the opacity of the atmosphere and gives a constant read-out in the Tower of the RVR at three fixed points on the runway, referred to as touchdown, mid-point and stop end, and can easily be switched manually to the opposite end if required.

The term *sigmet* is sometimes heard on R/T, this being a warning of such hazardous phenomena as thunderstorms, severe turbulence and severe airframe icing. Another jargon word is *nosig*, short for no significant change, and sometimes appended to aerodrome forecasts when passed on the radio. The term *trend* is employed to indicate the way the weather is likely to go, codes like *tempo* for a temporary change being added as appropriate.

A hazard which has always been with us but has only recently become recognised is that of wind shear. In the last seven years there have been at least a dozen serious accidents to large airliners directly attributable to wind shear and pilots can often be heard reporting its presence on final approach to the Tower so that following aircraft can be warned.

Briefly, wind shear is a change of windspeed and/or direction between two points in the atmosphere. By such a definition it is almost always present and normally does not cause undue difficulty to the pilot. However, on take-off or landing what amounts to an instantaneous change in headwind can be dangerous. An instantaneous decrease in headwind on the approach will tend to increase the rate of descent and an instantaneous increase in headwind will tend to decrease it. In both cases the pilot is faced with a rapid change in airspeed, coupled with a departure from the glide path and either a 'hot and long' or a short landing become likely.

Horizontal wind shears are generally outflows from the bases of Cb clouds or are caused by the passage of active weather fronts. Local topographical features, both natural and artificial, can also cause shear. Buildings and other large structures close to runways can spark off turbulence and rotor effects, with marked differences in wind direction. Since wind shear is obviously invisible, much experimental work is being carried out with acoustic Dopplers, Doppler radar and optical lasers to try to detect and measure it. Heathrow is unique in the United Kingdom in having a wind shear alerting service. Certain weather criteria are used to assess its possible presence and this is backed up by pilot reports. The alert message is inserted in the arrival and departure ATIS broadcasts.

Another major hazard to aircraft is fortunately easier to measure. This is braking action when the runway is icy, or if snow or slush is present. There are two methods of determining it; the simple Tapley Meter decelerometer and the sophisticated (and expensive) device which has largely superseded it, the Mu Meter. The latter consists of a runway friction measuring trailer towed by a vehicle travelling at 40 mph. It provides an automatic print-out of the mean co-efficient of friction at three equi-distant points along the runway. When manual mode is selected, further readings can be obtained as required. The lower the figure the worse the braking action, eg something like 0.25 would indicate a very icy surface, 0.85 would be a dry runway.

The word *snowtam* refers to an ingenious system of describing and tabulating runway conditions under snow, slush or ice and the degree to which they are cleared or about to be cleared. Braking action as determined above is also included. A series of letters and figures, each referring to a specific detail, can easily be decoded on receipt by telex.

Finally, in many parts of the country it is possible to pick up the broadcasts of the London and Scottish Volmet Services, the Vol part of the title being derived from the French word for flight. Weather conditions in a standardised form are transmitted continuously for the main UK and selected European airports. Pilots can thus monitor Volmet whilst en route and note the current conditions at their destination and suitable alternatives without having to make specific calls for the information. If their destination is a smaller airfield not on the Volmet they can either call it direct or request the information via London or Scottish Flight Information who will obtain it by telephone.

There are three separate broadcasts on different VHF frequencies:
London Volmet North—126.6 MHz;
London Volmet South—128.6;
London Volmet Main—135.375;
Scottish Volmet—125.725.

Volmet North is sent out from Great Dun Fell in Cumbria, South and Main are both transmitted simultaneously from Davidstow Moor in Cornwall, Ventnor, Isle of Wight and Warlingham, south of London. The rather mechanical speech is due to the fact that the message is made up from a store of individual words and short phrases on tape, which are selected by a computer and then joined to form the required sentences.

The presentation of the information is as described above but where significant changes are expected, one of the following will be heard:

Gradu The change is expected at a constant rate.

Rapid The change is expected in a short period of less than 30 minutes.

Tempo The change is expected to last for less than one hour.

Inter Frequent changes are expected, fluctuating almost constantly.

Trend A change is anticipated but it is expected to occur slowly throughout the period.

London Volmet Main broadcasts the half-hourly reports for Heathrow, Gatwick, Stansted, Manchester, Glasgow, Amsterdam, Dublin, Brussels and Paris/Charles de Gaulle. London Volmet South is responsible for Birmingham, Bristol, Luton, Bournemouth, Southampton, Norwich, Southend, Cardiff and Jersey. London Volmet North transmits those for Gatwick, Manchester, Isle of Man, East Midlands, Tees-side, Liverpool, Blackpool, Newcastle and Leeds. Scottish Volmet broadcasts for Aberdeen, Aldergrove, Edinburgh, Glasgow, Inverness, Heathrow, Prestwick, Stornoway and Sumburgh.

Chapter 12

Airfield visual aids

Airfield lighting ranges from the rudimentary edge lights found at many smaller locations to the complex and impressive systems to be seen at major airports. The paraffin flares from an earlier era, known as 'goosenecks', are still in use at a few places as emergency lighting, but are gradually being replaced by portable battery lamps which are easier to handle but no more effective.

On certain instrument runways the caution zone, ie the last 600 m, may have yellow rather than white lights. In addition the centreline is usually delineated by flush-fitting lights for the whole length. These are colour-coded to give an indication of the distance remaining in poor visibility. The lights are coloured red over the final 300 m and alternately red and white between 900 m and 300 m from the runway end.

As well as centreline lighting, all runways which comply with Precision Approach Category 2 and 3 lighting standard are provided with Touchdown Zone lights (TDZs). These consist of many flush-fitting white lights set into each side of the centreline in the first 900 m of the runway. A row of green threshold lights marks the beginning of the paved surface and a similar line of red ones marks the stop end.

Approach lighting is usually non-existent at small aerodromes and at others varies in standard, depending upon the approach aids and type of traffic handled. The approach lights at major airports begin at an average distance of 300 m out from the threshold and extend for a further 900 m out on the approach. They consist of a centreline and up to five cross-bars in white lights. Where Category 2 and 3 lighting standard is required, red supplementary approach lighting is provided within the basic system for the inner 300 m as an extra aid for landing in marginal weather conditions. All lighting is controlled in intensity from the Tower, the criteria being laid down clearly for differing met conditions.

The lights are displayed all the time at busy airports but the normal requirement for them to be on in daylight hours is whenever the visibility is less than six kilometres and/or the cloud base less than 700 ft. At night when traffic is light at some places, the lights are turned on 15 minutes before an ETA and left on until 15 minutes after an aircraft has departed.

Taxyway lights are standardised as green for the centreline and blue for the edges. The latter are used only to delineate apron edges and as an extra guide for bends in taxyways. The lights are 15 m apart which is reduced to 7½ m for Category 3 systems. Red stop bars mark holding points, especially those at runway entrances. There may also be traffic lights for airfield vehicles. Both can be operated from the Tower and the stop bars normally have a short time delay so that they revert to red after an aircraft has passed. London Heathrow has a particularly elaborate system of lighting for the control of taxyways.

Fast turn-offs, or rapid exit taxyways as they are coming to be known, only have their centreline lights lit from the runway direction. The lights in the opposite direction are now required to be blanked off to prevent inadvertent infringement of an active runway. This was yet another result of the enquiry into the Teneriffe collision.

Runway guard lights, consisting of a pair of alternately flashing lights and known colloquially as 'wig-wags', may be located at either side of holding positions. The purpose of these yellow lights is to improve the conspicuity of holding points and to warn pilots of the proximity of an active runway.

Once a pilot on approach is within sight of the runway, visual guidance is provided by the Precision Approach Path Indicator—PAPI for short—or, at some smaller aerodromes, Visual Approach Slope Indicators (VASI). Four PAPI lights are placed in line to the left of the runway threshold. They are arranged so that when the pilot is on the approach path two appear white and the other two are red. When a third light shows red, the pilot knows he is getting slightly low, when all four are red he is significantly below the glide path. Conversely, four white indicators tell him he is too high.

From the pilot's point of view, PAPI gives crisper indications and is usable right down to touchdown—VASI cannot be used below 200 ft. PAPI is effective out to a range of about 20 km, compared with about 5 km for VASI. It also performs better when the pilot is looking into bright sunlight.

VASI shows lights of two colours and is arranged to form two pairs of white/red wingbars extending each side of the runway; they are generally located at 300 m and 1,500 m up the runway from the threshold. The indications given are:

All bars white—high approach

Near bars white, far bars red—normal approach

All bars red—low approach

The normal VASI system may not provide sufficient wheel clearance over the threshold for very large aircraft due to the difference in height between the pilot's eye level and the landing gear. To meet this problem the three-bar VASI is installed at airports regularly used by such aircraft. A third pair of wing bars is sited further along the runway to form another approach channel above the normal one.

A number of the smaller airfields have an installation called LITAS (Low Intensity Two Colour Slope System). It is basically similar to VASI but has lights of lower intensity placed generally on the left hand side of the runway only. Interpretation of the information is identical to that for VASI and, although designed for use at night, the system has been found to give assistance by day in anything other than bright sunlight.

The other major visual aids on airports are the painted markings on the manoeuvring area. All runways in regular use will have centreline and threshold markings, the latter varying from the designator number alone to separate 'piano keys' and designator, depending upon the importance of the runway and its associated instrument aids. Whilst threshold markings are usually at the end of the runway, they sometimes need to be displaced upwind if, for example, there are obstacles like a public road on the approach. Arrows then indicate that the first portion of the runway is sterile for landing.

All runways more than 1,600 m long without VASI or PAPI, and all precision instrument runways, will have an additional symbol 300 m from the landing threshold known as the 'fixed distance marker'. The apparent distance between this and the threshold marking, seen from the approach, should aid pilots in judging their angle of descent and the two markings also bracket the optimum Touchdown Zone on the runway.

Touchdown Zone markings, extending for a distance of at least 600 m from the threshold, will be provided on precision approach runways with such aids as ILS. These are intended to give added texture by day and, except in fog, added texture by night in the light of landing lamps. Yellow lines delineate the centres of taxiways and at certain airports self-manoeuvring stand markings enable aircraft to be

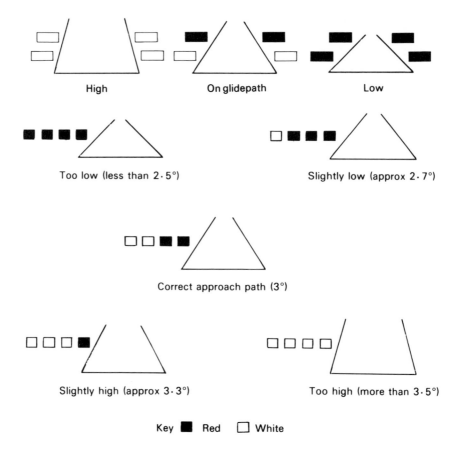

High   On glidepath   Low

Too low (less than 2·5°)   Slightly low (approx 2·7°)

Correct approach path (3°)

Slightly high (approx 3·3°)   Too high (more than 3·5°)

Key ■ Red   □ White

Standard VASIs (above) and PAPIs (below) and how they are interpreted. (CAA).

taxyed to the correct parking position without the aid of a marshaller.

At airfields which accept non-radio equipped aircraft ground signals will be displayed for guidance. These are normally to be found in front of the Control Tower, but not always, which gives rise to a funny story. One day a pilot who had suffered a radio failure landed at Blackpool. On reporting to the Tower, he complained that he could not make any sense from the ground signals. Further conversation revealed that he was trying to interpret the strange shapes on the crazy Golf Course adjacent to the airport's public enclosure!

Obviously not all the following ground signals can be seen at any one airfield but they cover all those to be seen at UK civil locations.

This list does not include signs peculiar to military airfields.

(*a*) Direction for landing or take-off: A large white 'T' signifies that aircraft will land or take-off in a direction parallel to the 'T' and towards the cross-arm. A white disc above the cross-arm of the 'T' indicates that the direction of landing and take-off do not necessarily coincide.

(*b*) A white 'dumb-bell' means that aircraft movement on the airfield is confined to paved surfaces only. A black strip across each disc of the dumb-bell at right angles to the shaft signifies that aircraft taking off and landing shall do so on a runway, but that ground movement is not confined to paved surfaces. A red letter 'L' superimposed on the dumb-bell signifies that light aircraft are permitted to take off and land either on a runway or on the area designated by a further 'L' (painted white) elsewhere on the aerodrome.

(*c*) A red and yellow striped arrow indicates that a right hand circuit is in force. This can also be shown by a rectangular green flag flown from a mast.

(*d*) A red square with one yellow diagonal bar warns that the state of the manoeuvring area is poor and pilots must exercise special care.

Standard runway markings (CAA).

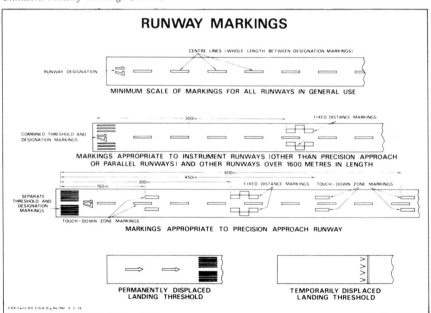

MINIMUM WEATHER CONDITIONS

SURFACE VISIBILITY		COLOUR	BASE OF LOWEST CLOUD LAYER
RN/RAF Km (nm)	USAFE★ Km (Stm)		**RN/RAF - of ⅜ or more** USAFE★ - of ⅝ or more
8(4·3)	8(5)	Blue	2500ft AGL
5(2·7)	5(3)	White	1500ft AGL
3·7(2)	3·7(2·3)	Green	700ft AGL
1·8(1)	1·6(1)	Yellow	300ft AGL
0·9(0·5)	0·8(0·5)	Amber	200ft AGL
Less than **0·9(0·5)**	0·8(0·5)	Red	Below 200ft AGL
Black A/D not usable for reasons other than cloud or visibility minima. Black will precede actual colour code.			

★ Includes USAFE bases in UK and Canadian, Netherlands & West German bases in 2ATAF.

RAF colour codes for aerodrome availability/weather state.

(e) A red square with a yellow cross superimposed along the diagonals declares that the airfield is unsafe for the movement of aircraft and that landing is prohibited. (Usually found at grass airfields which are water-logged in the winter months!)

(f) A white letter 'H' marks the helicopter landing area.

(g) A double white cross signifies that glider flying is in progress. (A yellow cross indicates the tow-rope dropping area on the runway.)

(h) 'Aerodrome Control in operation' is shown by a red and yellow checkered flag or board. (Aircraft may only move on the manoeuvring area with ATC permission.) A black letter 'C' on a yellow board indicates the position at which a pilot can report to the ATC unit or to the person in charge of the aerodrome.

(i) On grass aerodromes areas of 'bad ground' are marked by triangular orange and white markers, alternating with orange and white flags. Similar coloured markers outline the aerodrome boundary.

Chapter 13

Airport operations and procedures

Vortex wake

Behind each wingtip of an aircraft in flight and, in the case of a helicopter, the tip of each rotor blade, a trailing cylinder of rapidly rotating air is created, known as a vortex. The heavier the aircraft, the more intense the effect, which is quite capable of rolling a following aircraft onto its back if it gets too close. These hazardous wake vortices begin to be generated when the nosewheel lifts off the runway on take-off and continues until it touches down on landing. To minimise the danger controllers apply a system of spacing which is outlined below.

In the United Kingdom aircraft are divided into four vortex wake categories according to their maximum total weight at take-off:

Heavy—136,000 kg or greater;
Medium—less than 136,000 kg and more than 40,000 kg;
Small—40,000 kg or less and more than 17,000 kg;
Light—17,000 kg or less.

There are, however, a few exceptions to this. Helicopters generate more intense vortices from their rotors than fixed wing aircraft of the same weight, therefore Sikorsky S61Ns and larger types are included in the small category. Several aircraft types have been grouped into vortex categories which do not conform to those listed above. For example, the Boeing 707, DC-8, VC-10 and IL-62 series have been classified as medium, as experience has shown that the characteristics of these types conform more to that group. Similarly, it has been decided to place the BAe 146 in the small category.

The medium category embraces aircraft in the BAC 111/Boeing 737/DC-9 class, together with propellor aircraft like the Hercules and Electra. Small includes the Viscount, Friendship and Herald, and light anything from executive jets downwards.

DAVENTRY SIDs   **BIRMINGHAM**

GENERAL INFORMATION
1 SIDs reflect Noise Preferential Routeings.
2 Initial climb straight ahead to 825' QNH (500' QFE).
3 Climb gradients in excess of 3·3% are necessary for ATC seperation purposes.

TRANSITION ALT
4000'

NOT TO SCALE

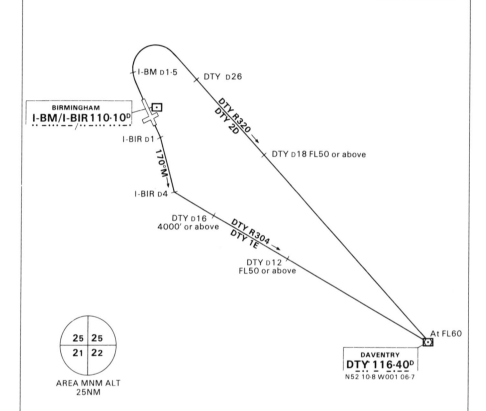

I-BM D1·5   DTY D26

BIRMINGHAM
I-BM/I-BIR 110·10^D

DTY R320
DTY 2D

I-BIR D1

170°M

DTY D18 FL50 or above

I-BIR D4

DTY D16
4000' or above

DTY R304
DTY 1E

DTY D12
FL50 or above

At FL60

DAVENTRY
DTY 116·40^D
N52 10·8 W001 06·7

25	25
21	22

AREA MNM ALT
25NM

SID	RWY	ROUTEING (incl. Noise Preferential Routeing)	ALTITUDES	AIRWAY ROUTE
DTY 2D	33	Climb straight ahead to **I-BM** D1·5 or 500' QFE whichever is later, then turn right to intercept **DTY VOR** R320 by **DTY** D26 then continue to **DTY VOR**.	Cross **DTY** D18 FL50 or above **DTY VOR** at FL60	B3 W1 South-Bound
DTY 1E	15	Climb straight ahead to **I-BIR** D1 or 500' QFE whichever is later, then turn right to track 170°M. At **I-BIR** D4 turn left to establish on **DTY VOR** R304 to **DTY VOR**.	Cross **DTY** D16 4000' or above **DTY** D12 FL50 or above **DTY VOR** at FL60	
CHANGE		REVISED PROCEDURE - DTY 2D		051

Arriving Flights

Where flights are operating visually (IFR flights operating under the reduced minima in the vicinity of aerodromes, VFR flights, or a mixture of the two), pilots are to be informed of the recommended spacing.

For other flights the spacing listed below is to be applied between successive aircraft on final approach.

Leading aircraft	Following aircraft	Minimum distance
Heavy	Heavy	4 miles
	Medium	5 miles
	Small	6 miles
	Light	8 miles
Medium	Medium	3 miles
	Small	4 miles
	Light	6 miles
Small	Medium or small	3 miles
	Light	4 miles

Aerodrome Operations

The minimum spacing listed below is to be applied between successive aircraft, both IFR and VFR flights.

(a) Aircraft departing from the same runway or from parallel runways less than 760 m apart (including grass strips).

Leading aircraft	Following aircraft		Minimum spacing at time aircraft are airborne
Heavy	Medium Small Light	Departing from the same take-off position	2 minutes
Medium or small	Light	Departing from the same take-off position	2 minutes
Heavy (Full length take-off)	Medium Small Light	Departing from an intermediate take-off point	3 minutes

Opposite *Daventry Standard Instrument Departure (SID) Chart for Birmingham (CAA).*

| Medium or small | Light | Departing from an intermediate take-off point | 3 minutes |

(*b*) Operations on a runway with a displaced landing threshold if the projected flight paths are expected to cross.

Leading aircraft	**Following aircraft**		**Minimum spacing at time aircraft are airborne or have touched down**
Heavy arrival	Medium Small Light	departure	2 minutes
Heavy departure	Medium Small Light	arrival	2 minutes

(*c*) Operations on crossing and diverging runways or on parallel runways greater than 760 m apart.

The spacings below are to be applied whenever the projected flight paths of the aircraft cross.

Leading aircraft	**Aircraft crossing behind**	**Minimum distance**	**Time equivalent**
Heavy	Heavy	4 miles	2 minutes
	Medium	5 miles	3 minutes
	Small	6 miles	3 minutes
	Light	8 miles	4 minutes
Medium	Medium	3 miles	2 minutes
	Small	4 miles	2 minutes
	Light	6 miles	3 minutes
Small	Medium or small	3 miles	2 minutes
	Light	4 miles	2 minutes

(*d*) Opposite direction runway operations. A minimum of two minutes spacing is to be provided from the time a heavy aircraft making a low or missed approach crosses over the take-off position of a medium, small or light aircraft departing from the opposite direction runway.

En-route and Intermediate Approach

No special longitudinal spacings based on time are required. When a medium, small or light aircraft is positioned by radar to cross behind or follow the same track as a heavy aircraft, the minimum spacing shall be 5 miles.

Departure flow regulation

At airports handling international traffic one will hear frequent references on the Tower or Ground Movement frequencies to Approved Departure Times. These were known previously as 'slot times' and this term is sometimes heard as well. During the peak summer months some countries are unable, for a number of reasons, to cope with the extra traffic. For instance, over 50 European and 27 UK airports are currently sending aircraft to the Mediterranean. Spain has about nine airports to receive the majority of them, with Palma the most popular destination. When the number of aircraft wishing to fly outstrips the capacity of the foreign ATC systems, the flow of traffic has to be regulated to ensure safe separation both nationally and internationally. This means that aircraft have to be held on the ground at the departure airports until such time as they can be accepted.

In the early 1970s a Departure Flow Regulation (DFR) section was set up at LATCC. Recently moved to Heathrow, its Flow Managers provide departure times about two hours ahead for up to 800 aircraft per day and liaise directly with the other ten Flow Management Units in Europe. This ensures an organised system of queuing for all flights as well as enabling airlines to plan aircraft and crew utilisation. When the ATC system in any part of Europe is in danger of being overloaded, a queue starts to form as a result of delaying departure times and so a list of airways with DFR restrictions is published in a NOTAM well in advance of the summer season. This is the theory but, as we all know, there are so many variable factors that the aims are often impossible to achieve.

For the uninitiated, the term Notam is an abbreviation of Notice to Airmen and is defined as 'a notice containing information concerning the establishment, condition or change of any facility, service, procedure or hazard, the timely knowledge of which is essential for the safe and efficient operation of aircraft.' Urgent NOTAMS are sent out by telex, those of lesser importance as Supplements to the UK Air

Information Publication.

Complications arise as different airways have different restrictions depending on destination, Flight Level or routeing, and countries overflown. If the system becomes overloaded, the flow of traffic has to be reduced. The DFR controller thus has the responsibility of allocating the correct number of aircraft at the intervals prescribed for a particular airway, route, Flight Level or destination.

The ADT stipulates that an aircraft must not be airborne before a specified time, but an allowance is added to this to cover taxying delays or holding for landing traffic. This can cause the GMC or Tower Controller something of a headache as extra-careful planning is often necessary to make sure that the aircraft gets away on time. The situation is not helped by pilots who taxy excruciatingly slowly or arrive at the runway threshold five minutes before the ADT!

Noise abatement

In an effort to minimise noise nuisance to local residents most airports have their own noise abatement procedures. These are devised by the aerodrome operating authority in conjunction with airlines and local airport consultative committees. Over built-up areas minimum noise routes have been defined which carefully route aircraft away from the more densely populated areas. Engine climb power is also reduced for the period when the aircraft must fly over certain conurbations.

At Heathrow different parallel runways are used for take-off and landing and these are alternated regularly so that noise is spread more equitably over the areas beneath the flight paths. Runways 27 Left and 27 Right are the preferred ones, provided the tail wind component does not exceed a certain figure and, in addition, flights are severely restricted at night. At Manchester the direction of approach is changed at regular intervals and at both locations noise levels are monitored. Operators whose aircraft exceed the permitted values are penalised.

Minimum Noise Routes (MNRs) are integrated with the lower end of Standard Instrument Departures, which are themselves designed to cause the least disturbance to those living below. Similarly, **Continuous Descent Approaches have been brought into operation**, particularly at Heathrow, to reduce noise and, as a bonus, to speed up the arrival rate. Headings and Flight Levels at which aircraft are to leave the holding pattern are passed by ATC. On receipt of descent clearance the pilot descends at the rate he judges to be best suited to achieve continuous descent. The object is to join the glide path at the appropriate height for the distance without recourse to level flight.

BRECON/DUBLIN/IOM SIDs LIVERPOOL

GENERAL INFORMATION
1 SIDs reflect Noise Preferential Routeings.
2 Initial climb straight ahead to 585' QNH (500' QFE).
  Rwy 27. Aircraft of more than 5 730kgs (12 500lbs) climb straight ahead at max rate
  to 1 085'QNH (1 000'QFE).
3 After completion of the initial turn onto outbound heading, all jet aircraft shall reduce power so as to
  maintain a rate of climb of at least 500' per minute.
4 Cruising levels at FL150 and below will be allocated en-route by 'Manchester Control',
  cruising levels above FL150 will be allocated en-route by 'London Control'.
5 Max IAS 250kts below FL100 unless otherwise authorised.

TRANSITION ALT
4000'

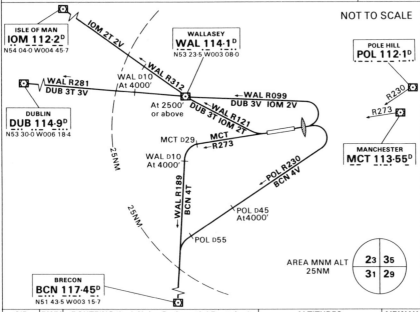

SID	RWY	ROUTEING (incl. Noise Preferential Routeing)	ALTITUDES	AIRWAY ROUTE
BCN 4T	27	Straight ahead on **MCT VOR** R273. At **MCT** D29 turn left to intercept **WAL VOR** R189 to **BCN VOR**.	Cross **WAL VOR** R189 D10 at 4000'	A25 South-bound
BCN 4V	09	At Rwy 27 MM or 500' (QFE) if sooner turn right to intercept **POL VOR** R230. At **POL** D55 turn left onto **WAL VOR** R189 to **BCN VOR**.	Cross **POL** D45 at 4000'	
DUB 3T	27	Straight ahead to intercept **WAL VOR** R121 to **WAL VOR**. At **WAL VOR** turn left onto **WAL VOR** R281 to **DUB VOR**.	Cross **WAL VOR** at 2500' or above **WAL VOR** R281 D10 at 4000'	B1 West-bound
DUB 3V	09	At Rwy 27 MM or 500' (QFE) if sooner turn left to intercept **WAL VOR** R099 to **WAL VOR** . At **WAL VOR** turn right onto **WAL VOR** R281 to **DUB VOR**.		
IOM 2T	27	Straight ahead to intercept **WAL VOR** R121 to **WAL VOR**. At **WAL VOR** turn right onto **WAL VOR** R312 to **IOM VOR**.	Cross **WAL VOR** at 2500' or above **WAL VOR** R312 D10 at 4000'	B3 West-bound
IOM 2V	09	At Rwy 27 MM or 500' (QFE) if sooner turn left to intercept **WAL VOR** R099 to **WAL VOR**. At **WAL VOR** turn right onto **WAL VOR** R312 to **IOM VOR**.		
CHANGE ALTITUDES				305

AERO INF DATE 3 May 90

SIDS for Liverpool (CAA).

The procedure requires that aircraft fly at 210 kt during the intermediate approach phase. ATC may request speed reductions to within the band 160 kt to 180 kt on, or shortly before, the closing heading to the ILS and 160 kt when established on the ILS. Aircraft unable to conform to these speeds are expected to inform ATC and state which speeds they are able to use. Since wheels and flaps remain retracted until the final stages, less engine power is needed which results in a much quieter approach.

Standard Instrument Departures (SIDs)

SIDs have been developed for the main runways of major airports, the routes terminating at an airway, Advisory Route or at a radio navigational fix. Minimum Noise Routes are also built in. All aircraft departing from an airport under IFR are required to follow the appropriate SID, unless and until authorised to do otherwise by the relevant ATC unit.

Each SID for a particular runway has a designator which incorporates the name of the radio beacon on which it is based. An example is the Honiley Three Tango from Runway 27 at Liverpool:

Straight ahead to Wallasey DME 9, turn left to intercept Wallasey VOR Radial 134. At Wallasey DME 24 turn right onto Honiley Radial 331 to Honiley VOR.

The heights to be observed are:

Cross Wallasey DME 17 3,000 ft or above. Cross Wallasey DME 28 at 4,000 ft.

VOR/DME holding procedures

These procedures are already in extensive use in the USA and the United Kingdom is following suit. An example is DAYNE, south of Manchester Airport, an 'offset' holding pattern for traffic inbound to Manchester and Woodford. Its axis is aligned on Trent VOR Radial 315, its position between Trent DME 13 and 17 miles.

The pilot flies towards the VOR/DME on this designated inbound radial and on reaching the holding fix position carries out a procedure turn onto the reciprocal outbound track. This outbound track is flown until the limiting DME distance is attained and the pilot then turns the aircraft to intercept the inbound VOR radial back to the holding fix position.

In the event of a ground equipment failure at the VOR/DME installation, a standby procedure is published, based on an alternative VOR/DME or other radio beacon. In the case of DAYNE, the holding pattern is defined additionally by a radial and distance from the Manchester VOR/DME.

Aircraft type and airfield designators

For flight planning and flight progress strip presentation aircraft types have been allocated a designator of not more than four characters, by ICAO. Where possible this conforms to the manufacturer's designation, or at least to part of it. For example Boeing 707, 737, 747 are represented by B707, B737 and B747, an HS74 is an HS 748, an SH36 a Shorts 360, and an S210 a Caravelle.

The codes are often used on R/T, most being fairly obvious, but some are obscure. Controllers occasionally ask a pilot for his aircraft type and get an answer which is not very enlightening. Space does not permit a comprehensive listing which would run into many hundreds of entries, but commonly heard designators are listed in Appendix 4.

One other point is the use of four-letter designators for airfields. These are rarely heard on R/T but are allocated by ICAO on a world-wide basis for flight planning and telex purposes. British airfields are prefixed 'EG', hence EGLL—Heathrow, EGKK—Gatwick and EGCC—Manchester. A few European examples are EDDH—Hamburg, LFPO—Paris Orly, EBOS—Ostend, LSZH—Zurich and LEMD—Madrid. American airports are prefixed 'K', as in KJFK—Kennedy, KLAX—Los Angeles.

Airbus A320 cockpit with fully integrated displays, setting the standard for future aircraft (Airbus Industrie).

Chapter 14

Air displays

From an ATC point of view, displays are fairly straightforward to control provided that the organisers have scheduled the items in a sensible order. Proper pre-planning in liaison with ATC is essential to avoid non-radio light aircraft clashing with jet aerobatic teams and similar embarrassments. I have known pilots without radio over-running their time slot and either ignoring or failing to see frantic lamp signals from the Tower while a Buccaneer or some such fast jet orbits in the distance with fuel dwindling rapidly. On another occasion we were horrified to see a formation of Turbulents take-off without permission while the Red Arrows were still performing. Fortunately they were on their final manoeuvre and to the crowd it probably looked like brilliant timing!

Timing is of course paramount to the continuity of a display. How many times do we hear the complaint that there were long gaps, causing the crowd to lose interest? The usual reason is that almost inevitably one or more of the items on the programme fails to turn up. Vintage aircraft are particularly temperamental, although their modern brethren can be just as bad. It thus becomes a major operation to close up the vacant slots and there are a number of ways this can be done. Since many shows now average 3–4 hours in duration and always seem to run late after the first hour or so, some of the time can be absorbed with ease. Pilots can usually be coaxed into extending their individual demonstrations slightly and it is not unknown for airline passengers to find themselves taking part if they happen to be arriving aboard a schedule during the show! ATC is normally in radio contact with a display co-ordinator who can communicate directly with the pilots on the flight line who are waiting their turn to perform. Rapid reshuffling is therefore possible but it often leads to some heated exchanges on the air!

Ideally, the next aircraft on the programme should be taking off as the previous one turns final, leaving no break in the proceedings. (The Farnborough shows have always been noted for this smooth flow.) Aircraft approaching from other airfields are held either on radar or at a distinctive and usually pre-arranged geographical position until they can be fitted in. I have witnessed high performance aircraft like the F-15 hold in the overhead at 10,000 ft or so and arrive almost vertically.

R/T is kept to a minimum during airshows; the last thing a pilot wants is unnecessary chatter during a complex sequence. He is usually advised the number of minutes to go as his slot nears its end and is expected to abide by this. The aircraft type is quite often used as a call-sign but military aircraft, apart from the Battle of Britain Memorial Flight as one example, normally employ their RAF or USAF callsigns. Since many military aircraft, particularly fighters, are only UHF-equipped, you will obviously not hear them talking to ATC on VHF. Portable UHF equipment will have been installed in the Tower at civil airfields for the occasion.

Aerobatic teams generally have their own discrete frequency although the leader will be monitoring the Tower channel in case there are any panic calls about a lost Cessna 150 blundering through the area! (It happens...) Orders from the Red Arrows' leader are a miracle of brevity on the R/T—'Smoke on go' being an oft-quoted example.

Far more entertaining is airband listening during the morning before an air display when some of the participants arrive and mingle with visiting aircraft, pleasure flights and the inevitable club pilot who wants to get in a few circuits before being grounded for the rest of the day. The results approach chaos and one feels for the Tower Controllers who are trying to sort it all out. I once had to scatter everybody to different points of the compass to allow four Jet Provosts low on fuel to make a priority landing. Another time a Bonanza's nose wheel collapsed and a non-radio Tiger Moth was dissuaded from landing on top of him by a quick-draw red flare!

Nowadays, air races are often sandwiched into air displays and are quite popular with ATC because we can sit back and watch, leaving the starting to the race marshallers. The drama comes at the end of the race when, if the handicappers have done a good job, 15 to 20 aircraft are all downwind for landing at the same time. Since it is impossible to apply normal rules for runway occupancy to this congestion, controllers tend to opt out of the situation by giving wind checks and muttering 'Land at your discretion' and similar platitudes to pilots who call on final. Half the aircraft may be non-radio anyway and, as race pilots' airmanship is usually pretty good, they can safely be left to themselves to sort things out.

With the numbers of air displays in Britain increasing every year, the CAA have issued a booklet for the guidance of organisers. This is CAP 403 *Safety Arrangements at Flying Displays, Air Races and Rallies.* The reader is also recommended to sample David Ogilvy's book *Flying Displays* (Airlife Publications) for an excellent guide to the pitfalls of their organisation and running.

Enthusiasts tend to deplore the extensive market areas seen at most displays but they do have one advantage—the presence of numerous aviation suppliers. Their wares range from books and magazines to air band radios and navigation charts. The major outlets which make regular appearances include *Aviation News*, *FlyPast* magazine, Air Supply, Flightdeck (The Airband Shop), Midland Counties Publications, Air-Britain, and The Aviation Hobby Shop.

Chapter 15

Emergencies

Emergency situations with aircraft are fairly common and although the word conjures up images of catastrophic failure or fire in the air, few are very dramatic, even if they do give the pilot some worrying moments. The most numerous are cockpit indications of undercarriage malfunctions which may necessitate a low run past the Tower for a visual check that the wheels are down. There is no guarantee that they are locked, though, but it gives the pilot some encouragement! Almost invariably the green lights come on when the jolt of the landing activates a stuck micro-switch.

Other frequent problems are doors coming open in flight, failed generators and lost fuel filler caps. On most light aircraft an open door is a noisy and draughty inconvenience rather than an actual hazard but there are some types on which the adverse effect on the airflow can reduce control. Hence, unlike in the USA where a pilot has formally to declare an emergency before the safety services are alerted, a British controller uses his own judgment and almost always puts them on a Local Standby, working on the saying 'Better safe than sorry'. There is also the possibility that a minor problem with the aircraft may distract a pilot enough to make him misjudge the landing.

There are six standard categories of emergency beginning with the self-explanatory 'Aircraft Accident'. A 'Full Emergency' is arranged when it is known that an aircraft is, or is suspected to be, in such trouble that there is a danger of an accident. The problems include the thankfully rare fire in the air and the not uncommon engine failure on multi-engined aircraft. In the latter case an experienced and properly trained commercial pilot should have no difficulty in making a safe landing as he is required to practice asymmetric flying at regular intervals and pass a check. The safety services are alerted, however, and at larger airports this usually means the outside services will be summoned automatically as a back-up.

Next comes the 'Local Standby' which I have mentioned already and the 'Aircraft Ground Incident' which covers occurrences other than accidents. These include fuel spillages and bomb scares on parked aircraft. A 'Weather Standby' is instituted 'when weather conditions are such as to render a landing difficult or difficult to observe.' Bad visibility is one obvious instance, a cross-wind component of 25 kt or more is another. The final category is 'Domestic Fire' which, as its title implies, covers such things as grass fires on and adjacent to the airfield and fires in its buildings. At major airports the Rescue and Fire-fighting Services have the use of a common frequency of 121.6 to talk directly with the aircraft crew when necessary. UHF frequencies for the control of ground vehicles, including fire appliances, are not published, but can be found around 453-458 MHz.

A pilot requiring immediate assistance is expected to transmit a distress message with the prefix 'Mayday, Mayday, Mayday'. If the situation is less urgent the prefix 'Pan, Pan, Pan' is used. Unfortunately, pilots, particularly phlegmatic British ones, are loath to make too much of a fuss so if you hear a 'Mayday' call, things have really reached the critical stage! The announcement of the loss of one engine, provided there are more than one, is usually delivered in a matter-of-fact manner, together with a request for a diversion. This calm approach is sometimes self-defeating—a controller who would be sparked into instant action to clear a path for an aircraft which has abruptly turned into a glider in the circuit, may think he has misheard if the magic word 'Mayday' is not used and waste time asking for a repeat.

Aircraft in distress or lost, if they are not already in two-way contact with an ATC unit, may call on the International Distress Frequency of 121.5 MHz. If they have a transponder the code 7700 can be selected to indicate an emergency. (This activates an alarm at every radar station able to receive the signal and also makes the radar blip pulsate to attract the controller's attention.) The Distress Frequency is monitored continuously by the RAF Distress and Diversion Cell at West Drayton in Middlesex and at Prestwick in Scotland, which serve the areas south and north of 55°N, respectively. They can provide a service to civil aircraft in emergency in addition to that for military aircraft on 243 MHz UHF.

South of a line from Preston to the Humber there is a reasonable chance of fixing the position of aircraft at quite low levels transmitting on 121.5, except over the hilly areas of Wales and South-West England. This 'Fixer Service', as it is known, takes bearings automatically from several receivers and projects them as lines on a large wall map. Where they intersect is the aircraft's position and remarkable accuracy can be achieved. Most of the larger airports keep the distress frequency selected and are thus able to hear any calls and relay bearing information to the D & D Cell if requested.

Pilots are encouraged to make practice Pan calls on 121.5, having first of all asked permission in case there is a real emergency in progress. It is extremely impressive to hear how quickly D & D can fix the aircraft's position. Aircraft on transatlantic flights are required to monitor 121.5 continuously and there have been many occasions when a high-flying airliner has relayed distress messages from some wave-hopping light aircraft on a delivery flight and alerted the rescue services.

Transmissions from aircraft in distress have priority over all other messages. When a pilot is already in contact with an ATC unit, assistance should be sought on the frequency in use, otherwise a call should be made on 121.5. On hearing a distress call, all stations must maintain radio silence on that frequency unless they themselves are required to render assistance and should continue to listen on the frequency concerned until it is evident that assistance is being provided.

The recommended form of the distress message to be transmitted is somewhat long-winded and it would have to be a very cool pilot who remembered to include everything (and in the right order!) even assuming he had time to make the full call. I have heard three; they were all in the circuit area and all there was time to say was Mayday three times, callsign and 'Engine failure'. Two of them got down safely but the helicopter crashed, although not too badly I'm glad to say.

The information to be passed goes like this:
(*a*) Name of the station addressed (when appropriate)
(*b*) Callsign and type of aircraft
(*c*) Nature of the emergency
(*d*) Intention of the person in command
(*e*) Present position, Flight Level/altitude and heading
(*f*) Pilot's qualifications as appropriate: (1) Student pilot; (2) No instrument qualification; (3) IMC rated; (4) Full Instrument Rating.

Pilots are invited to use the callsign prefix 'TYRO' when calling a military ATC unit or the D & D Section, to indicate lack of experience. This code word will ensure that controllers do not issue instructions which the pilot may have difficulty in following.

The standard acknowledgment is 'GABCD (station) Roger Mayday.' Further instructions follow without delay. It may be necessary to impose radio silence on all stations in the area or any particular station which, usually unintentionally having just come onto the frequency, interferes with emergency transmissions. In either case the messages should take this form: 'All stations Hurn Approach stop transmitting, Mayday' or 'GAMPT stop transmitting, Mayday'.

It may be a good idea to transfer aircraft from the frequency to avoid interfering with calls from or to the aircraft in distress. 'Mayday. All stations contact Hurn Tower on 125.6. Out.' When an emergency situation has been resolved, the station which has been controlling the traffic will broadcast a message that normal working will be resumed. 'Mayday all stations Hurn Approach time 04 distress traffic GABCD ended. Out.'

When an aircraft is operating on a flight plan and fails to turn up within 30 minutes of its ETA, the controller at the destination is required to confirm the ATD (actual time of departure) from the departure airfield. Other set procedures known as Preliminary Overdue Action are put into effect. After one hour, or sooner in certain cases, Full Overdue Action is taken by the parent ATCC and a search launched for the missing aircraft.

Aircraft on a flight for which a plan has not been filed have no such protection, although they are required to 'Book out' with the ATC unit at the departure aerodrome, assuming one exists. The departure, together with time en route, fuel endurance and number of souls on board, are recorded but no further action need be taken and if an aircraft goes missing, it is often some time before people start asking questions, usually sparked off by anxious relatives.

Flight plans must be filed at least 30 minutes before requesting taxy clearance or start-up approval. A pilot may file one for any flight but for certain categories they are mandatory. These include all IFR flights within controlled airspace, those which cross an international boundary, and for any flight where the destination is more than 40 km from the aerodrome of departure and the aircraft's maximum total weight exceeds 5,700 kg. In addition, a pilot is advised to file a plan if he intends to fly over the sea more than ten miles from the coast or over sparsely populated areas where search and rescue operations would be difficult.

For scheduled airline routes and other regularly recurring IFR flights with identical basic features, a repetitive flight plan saves operators and crews the chore of filing a separate plan each time. Often referred to as a 'stored plan', it is submitted by an operator for storage and repetitive use by ATC units for each individual flight.

Airmisses

Now, a word about airmisses, which the press prefers to call 'nearmisses'. A pilot is entitled to file an Airmiss Report when he considers that his aircraft may have been endangered by the proximity of another aircraft in flight, to the extent that a definite risk of collision existed. A sense of proportion is required for this, however, as light aircraft in traffic circuits occasionally get horrendously close to one another, usually through inexperience and/or not keeping a good look-out.

Pilots flying under IFR in controlled airspace may well file if they see another aircraft which they believe is closer to them than required by the separation rules. In a radar-controlled environment this may be four instead of five miles, which a pilot flying under VFR would consider ludicrous.

All Airmiss Reports are investigated, not so much as to allot blame but to try to prevent a recurrence by examining the circumstances. The degree of actual risk of collision is assessed and regular summaries of the most serious ones are published for restricted circulation in the aviation world. Inevitably, some are leaked to the press and suitably exaggerated! One they never heard about unfortunately was the large pink pig which an Army helicopter pilot nearly rammed one hazy day over the River Thames. It was an advertising balloon which had broken its moorings and drifted away!

Radio failures

If an aircraft suffers a radio failure there are published procedures to which the pilot is expected to adhere. A squawk of 7600 set on the transponder will alert an ATC unit to his problem, provided that it has SSR capability. If essential navigation equipment has failed also, pilots are advised as a last resort to carry out a special procedure to alert the Radar Controller to the fact that they need assistance. The aircraft is to fly at least two triangular patterns, before resuming course, as follows:

Aircraft speed	Length of leg	Transmitter failure only	Complete failure
300 kt or less	2 minutes	Right hand turns	Left hand turns
More than 300 kt	1 minute		

If the controller should notice such a manoeuvre (and RAF experiments show that they often do not!) he is to advise the Distress & Diversion Cell of the position and track and continue to plot the aircraft whilst it is in radar cover. A shepherd aircraft will then be sent out to lead it, hopefully, to a safe landing.

Quite often the failure is of the transmitter only and the controller can instruct the aircraft to make one or more turns and check if the pilot is complying. If it becomes obvious that the receiver is working, normal radar service is resumed. There are some subtle ways by which the aircraft's altitude and other information can be ascertained, such as 'After passing FL 50 turn left heading 270.'

There are occasions when an aircraft receiver is working correctly but the reply transmitted is unintelligible at the ground station because the speech is badly distorted or non-existent, perhaps because the microphone is unserviceable. Military pilots are briefed to use a special code which makes use of the carrier wave only. The pilot presses his transmitter button a certain number of times according to the following code:

One short transmission—Yes (or an acknowledgement);

Two short transmissions—No;

Three short transmissions—Say again:

Four short transmissions—Request homing;

One long transmission (two seconds)—Manoeuvre complete (eg, steady on heading);

One long, two short, one long—The aircraft has developed another emergency.

A controller will be alerted to the presence of an aircraft with this kind of failure if he hears, or sees on the VDF, four short carrier wave transmissions. The controller should then interrogate the pilot, using the callsign 'Speechless Aircraft' if the identity of the aircraft cannot be discovered, to find out what assistance is required. He must be careful to ask questions which can be answered with a direct yes or no. The code is now recommended for use by civilian pilots as it can easily be explained by the controller during the first few transmissions.

Chapter 16

Military Air Band

Military ATC employs a block of frequencies between 225 and 400 MHz, audio modulated (AM) as in the civil VHF air band. They are referred to as Ultra High Frequencies (UHF) and are normally spaced 25 kHz apart. Theoretically this produces 7,000 separate channels, and although many are in use for airfield and area ATC, it leaves a very large number available for a variety of uses. These include in-flight refuelling, bombing and gunnery range operations, air-to-air frequencies for formation flying and, in the case of the USAF in Britain, numerous ops and Command Post channels.

Blocks of frequencies, known as TADs from the acronym for Tactical Air Deployment, are allocated for air defence interception purposes by RAF radar units. Each channel has a code number such as TAD 122. An anomaly is the use by the USAF of a few frequencies around 142 MHz. To save time-consuming manual tuning many military aircraft have pre-set radio frequencies, referred to as Studs and used in the same way as the push buttons on a car radio. For example, the current allocation for a Hawk based at RAF Valley is as follows:

Stud 1: Ground Movements Control; Stud 2: Tower; Stud 3: Departures; Stud 4: Mona; Stud 5: Quiet frequency; Stud 6: Approach; Stud 7: Radar; Stud 8: Radar; Stud 9: NATO common; Stud 10: Low level; Stud 11: Air-to-air; Stud 12: Air-to-air; Stud 13: Air-to-air; Stud 14: London Mil; Stud 15: London Mil; Stud 16: Scottish Mil; Stud 17: Llanbedr Approach; Stud 18: Llanbedr Tower; Stud 19: Duty Instructor/Ops; Stud 20: not allocated.

Military aviation in Britain is organised much the same as its civil counterpart. Most airfields have a Ground Movements Controller as well as a Tower Controller who is known also as the 'local' controller. The controller who sequences traffic onto final approach is the Director, the next stage being the Talkdown Controller who uses Precision Approach Radar (PAR) to bring the aircraft down to visual contact with the runway. PAR, discontinued in civil ATC about 20 years ago in favour of ILS, uses two radar displays. One shows the aircraft and final approach in plan view, the other the picture from the side which monitors deviations above and below the glidepath. The pilot can thus be given height information as well as heading corrections.

The RAF makes considerable use of ILS installations, but few are rated more accurate than the minimum civil Category 1 (minimum of 200 ft cloud base and 600 metres RVR). Efforts are being made to improve this situation to counter the planned demise of PAR, MLS being seen as the eventual replacement for both systems. QFE has now been dropped in favour of QNH for altimeter settings prior to landing.

RAF rules governing runway occupancy, separation and other procedures are similar to those in civil ATC. R/T phraseology is, however, somewhat different, although it is planned to bring it into line with civilian practice as an ongoing process. R/T exchanges are often clipped and difficult for the layman to understand, and the use of oxygen mask microphones tends to depersonalise voices. It does, however, make many RAF transmissions instantly identifiable as such!

Military aviation thrives on initials and code words. Among the many to be heard on UHF are PD (practice diversion), RTB (return to base), and Homeplate (base). The Americans have their own jargon such as Code One (a fully serviceable aircraft), RON (remain overnight), TOT (time on target), Lima Charlie (loud and clear), Victor freek (VHF frequency), and Uniform (UHF frequency.)

London Air Traffic Control Centre (Military) is co-located with the civil ATCC at West Drayton near Heathrow Airport to form the London Joint Area Organisation (LJAO). To meet the requirements of all airspace users, the civil controllers provide air traffic services to en route GAT (General Air Traffic) flights usually within the airways system and within fixed geographical sectors, and the military controllers give a service in a more flexible fashion to OAT (Operational Air Traffic) flights. OAT flights are generally those that cannot conform to the requirements of flights within airways and other regulated airspace.

Within the airways system GAT, including military traffic operating as GAT, is normally given priority over OAT. Exceptions are made, however, for such operations as military aircraft engaged in the calibration of a radar system. Conversely, outside the airways and upper route structures OAT generally gets priority over off-route GAT.

The Initial Contact Frequencies (ICF) for each sector at what is known from its callsign as 'London Mil' are monitored permanently. LJAO is not equipped with dedicated VHF frequencies so, when a VHF service is required, use has to be made of the civil sector spare VHF frequency, subject to availability and the approval of the Chief Sector Controller. The Daventry (Mil) Sector is the busiest of the five sectors, the others being Pole Hill, Clacton, Dover/Lydd and Seaford/Hurn.

Flight Plans are vitally important for the efficient operation of the system. GAT Plans are processed in the normal way by the civil computer, while those for OAT are fed into the military *Myriad* computer by the RAF Air Movements Section. If any of the flight plans affect LJAO airspace the relevant flight progress strips are printed and distributed to the appropriate sectors.

As one military controller working in LJAO remarked, it soon becomes obvious that most of the aircraft based in the east of England want to exercise in the west, and those from the west want to exercise in the east! The problem is that to get to those areas the aircraft need to cross one of the busiest air route complexes in the world, colloquially known as 'the Ambers' after their now obsolete designation. In most cases the crossing is achieved with very little fuss due to constant co-ordination with the civil controllers on the spot.

Virtually all crossings of the airways are accomplished by means of a 'cleared level', which means that no aircraft under civil control will be allowed to occupy the negotiated level for the period that the military aircraft is crossing. When this is not possible owing to busy traffic situations, the military controller is permitted to use radar separation to achieve a safe crossing, a procedure known as 'taking five'. The name comes from the prescribed separation of at least five nautical miles or 5,000 ft vertically from any GAT aircraft in the airway. Obviously it is easier to 'take five' with a fighter aircraft than a transport owing to the higher speed and manoeuvrability.

When this method is being employed and there is a possibility of a confliction with one particular aircraft, the controller can co-ordinate with his civil opposite number. When a course of action is agreed, the military controller is able to reduce separation against that one aircraft to the standard radar separation required, depending on its flight level, ie 5 miles horizontally or 1,000 ft vertically (2,000 ft above FL245). In an emergency, when neither a radar nor procedural crossing can be obtained, an airway may be crossed at an intermediate 500 ft level, ie a level of 1,000 ft plus 500 ft. If already at a 1,000 ft level, the aircraft must climb 500 ft before entering the airway.

Further methods of crossing airways are by means of the Radar Video Corridor and the so-called Military Slot. These have been established at the points most frequently required to be crossed by military flights. The

Lichfield RVC in the north-west Midlands facilitates crossings at either FL110 or FL180, while the Scampton RVC runs through airway Bravo 1 at FL110, being controlled by Eastern Radar, formerly at RAF Watton in Norfolk but now moved to West Drayton. The Westcott Medium Level Corridor takes military traffic across the airways system just north of London at FL210 or FL220. Brize Radar at Brize Norton in Oxfordshire provides a crossing service of Golf One between KENET and ALVIN. Yeovilton Radar does the same for Alpha 25. These 'blocks' of airspace simplify crossing procedures, but the pilot must still request a prior clearance from London Mil.

Every other sector in the LJAO is similar in operation to the Daventry Sector, if not quite so busy. On the Pole Hill Sector a slight difference exists in that the Manchester Sub-Centre controls all the airspace up to and including FL 150, so requests for clearances through these levels have to be made direct to Manchester by the military controller. On the Clacton, Dover and Seaford Sectors handovers are made between LJAO and foreign military agencies, chiefly Mazout Radar in France and Belga Radar in Belgium, the aircraft being transferred to the appropriate frequency when it reaches the FIR boundary. North of 55°N, roughly an east-west line through Newcastle, Scottish Mil at Prestwick operates on the same lines as London Mil.

Most of the UK airspace at and above FL245 up to FL660 is designated as a Mandatory Radar Service Area (MRSA) with an ATC radar unit responsible for each sector. It is compulsory for pilots intending to fly in the MRSA to call the appropriate radar unit and fly under its instructions except when operating as civil air traffic or under air defence radars. Military Training Areas (MTAs) are established within MRSAs to afford freedom of operation for aircraft engaged in exercises incompatible with radar control. The MTAs which stretch upwards from FL245 to FL450 are the Lincolnshire, co-ordinated by RAF Waddington, and the North Wales, under RAF Valley. Outside the published hours of training activity MTAs revert to normal MRSA status.

Aerial Tactics Areas (ATAs) reach from FL50 up to FL245 and enable high-energy combat manoeuvres to be carried out by formations of up to six aircraft. Current examples are the Wash ATA (controlling authority Border Radar), the primary users of which are Coningsby, Cottesmore, Wittering and Alconbury, and the Bentwaters ATA (Eastern Radar), mainly used by Bentwaters, Honington and Coltishall.

Military units also offer a Lower Airspace Radar Service (LARS) outside controlled airspace up to FL100 for both military and civil aircraft, and a similar service up to FL245 within what is termed 'Middle

Airspace'. Its availability is subject to the range and cover of the particular radar in use as well as controller workload. The procedure when within approximately 30 miles of the radar unit is to establish R/T contact on the appropriate frequency using the phraseology '. . . (ATC unit) this is . . . (aircraft callsign) request Lower Airspace Radar Service'. Pilots may be asked to 'standby for controller'. When asked, they are to pass aircraft type, position and heading, flight level or altitude, intentions and type of service required. The latter may be a radar advisory or information service. (See page 89 for details.)

Military Aerodrome Traffic Zones (MATZ) normally consist of a circle of 5 nautical miles radius from the aerodrome up to 3,000 ft above aerodrome level, together with a 'stub' out to 5 miles protecting the approach path of the most used instrument runway. A MATZ Penetration Service is provided to civil aircraft, the common frequency being 122.1. Traffic information will be given along with any instructions necessary to achieve separation from known or observed traffic in the zone. In some areas MATZs may overlap to form a combined zone; in this case the altimeter pressure setting will be passed to aircraft as a 'Clutch QNH'.

The RAF Distress and Diversion Cells at West Drayton and Prestwick have already been described in Chapter 15. 'Drayton Centre', as it is known by its callsign, is currently being upgraded so that a computer-based facility can calculate and display the position of any aircraft transmitting on the military distress frequency of 243 MHz. If a crash or ditching occurs, Search and Rescue (SAR) is co-ordinated either by Plymouth Rescue Co-ordination Centre (RCC) or Edinburgh RCC at Pitreavie Castle, depending on the location. Their callsigns are *Plymouth Rescue* and *Edinburgh Rescue*, and HF frequencies are employed because of their long range. Primary Day frequency is 5680 kHZ; 3023 is used at night. They are shared by the two RCCs and, since both are world-wide common frequencies, other units such as Stavanger can be heard on them at times, as well as ground units such as Mountain Rescue Teams— callsign *Alpine*.

Of course the emergencies do not just involve aircraft; they may be ships in distress, climbing accidents, floods and a variety of other incidents. A Temporary Danger Area is established around the site so that SAR ops can be continued without interference from press aircraft and other non-essential intruders. When an aircraft is fitted with an ELT (Emergency Locator Transmitter) or a downed pilot activates a SARBE (SAR Beacon), the signals will be picked up by SARSAT (Search and Rescue Satellite Aided Tracking). The system is highly sensitive in

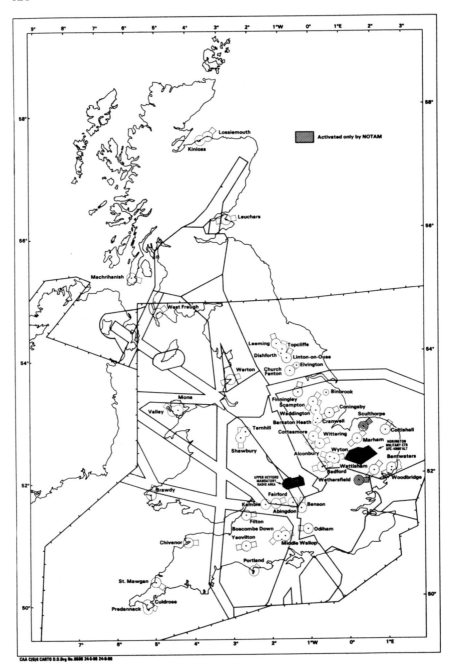

detecting transmissions on 121.5, 243 and 406 MHz and alerting the rescue services—so sensitive in fact that a stolen beacon was traced to a bedroom wardrobe. The satellite picked up the transmissions, an RAF helicopter went to the general area and homed in further with its own direction-finding equipment. A landing was made in a playing field behind the house and the culprit later said in court that he had found the beacon on a bus! He was not believed.

Operational control of The Queen's Flight is vested in the RAF. Royal Flight status is often extended to other reigning sovereigns, Prime Ministers and other Heads of State as a courtesy. Contrary to popular opinion, there are no special increased separations for Royal flights; they are treated exactly the same as any other aircraft in controlled airspace, although a higher priority is given where necessary as the Royal personage usually has to meet a tight schedule.

Royal flights in fixed wing aircraft are always provided with controlled airspace to cover the entire flight path when it is within UK airspace. This coverage is obtained by the establishment of Purple airways for the entire route and special Control Zones at the departure and destination airfields if these are not already in existence. Purple airways normally extend 5 miles either side of the route and may coincide with existing airways of the national system. The vertical dimensions, relevant radio frequencies, times and any other pertinent information will be detailed in the NOTAM concerning the flight.

The NOTAM is prepared by the Airspace Utilisation Section whenever a Royal flight is arranged. It is distributed by post to the ATCCs and airfields concerned, normally providing at least 48 hours' warning. All Purple airspace is notified as Class A, ie any aircraft within it must fly by IFR at all times. In the case of temporary Control Zones, ATC may issue Special VFR clearances to pilots unable to comply with the IFR requirements and thus ensure positive separation at all times.

Purple airspace is not normally established for Royal helicopter flights but a Royal Low Level Corridor, marked by a series of check-points, is promulgated. These check-points will be approximately 20 miles apart and will usually coincide with turning points on the route. Pilots flying near the Corridor are expected to keep a good look-out and maintain adequate separation from the Royal helicopter. The NOTAM will incorporate a list of nominated aerodromes from which pilots may obtain information on the progress of the flight.

The person on board a Royal Flight used to be readily identifiable by

Opposite *Plan of Military Aerodrome Traffic Zones* (CAA).

the callsign, eg *Kittyhawk* when HM the Queen was a passenger, *Rainbow* was the Duke of Edinburgh, *Unicorn* the Prince of Wales, and *Leopard* Prince Andrew. However, the demands of security mean that, apart from *Kittyhawk*, the other prefixes seem to have fallen out of use, although are still allocated to The Queen's Flight. Note that the prefix *Kittyhawk* does not always indicate that the Queen is on board. As before, the prefix *Kitty* and a number is employed when other members of the Royal family are being carried, and also for positioning and training flights.

US Air Force operations from British bases are handled in a similar way to those of their RAF opposite numbers. They have their own controllers in the airfield towers, but approach control may be centralised and co-ordinated by an RAF radar unit. The best example is the Honington Military Control Zone where the approach function for three airfields in close proximity—Mildenhall, Lakenheath and Honington—is combined and controlled by Eastern Radar. A similar arrangement can be found in Lincolnshire where Midland Radar operates a Combined Approach Control for Waddington, Scampton and Coningsby.

American bases make extensive use of Standard Instrument Departures (SIDs), an example being the Marston Three Departure to the north-west from Upper Heyford. One of Lakenheath's is the Thetford Two Departure to the east, associated waypoints being designated Mike Charlie One and Mike Charlie Six. One of Woodbridge's Departures is known as Sutton Three. They connect with a network of TACAN routes across Britain and mainland Europe linking TACANs, the military equivalent of the civil VOR/DME. There are a number of other US military reporting points not shown on normal charts. They include East Fix, centred over Cambridge and associated with Upper Heyford, Gate Alpha, an East Coast range exit point, and Shack, to the north-east of Alconbury.

To preserve security, some military transmissions may employ DVP (Digital Voice Protection) techniques. The speech is electronically digitised, mixed at random and then transmitted. A compatible receiver then unscrambles the sequence and restores its intelligibility. There are several code words for this secure mode; USAF AWACS aircraft, for example, refer to it as 'in the green'. Other terms are 'going tactical' and 'going crypto'. Some NATO strike aircraft are able to engage a frequency-hopping communications system *Have Quick*, which uses six channels in sequence to foil the eavesdropper. Apparently, however, a clever scanner user could still monitor the messages, but a developed version is highly secure because of its ability to race through many more frequencies right across the UHF band.

Military aviation makes considerable use of the HF bands, both the RAF and the USAF having their own networks, as does the Royal Canadian Air Force. Other foreign air forces are represented as well, but since the transmissions are made in the native language they are of little interest. The RAF's Flight Watch HF network is known as the Strike Command Integrated Communications System (STCICS). It is operated from RAF Upavon in Wiltshire with the callsign *Architect*. Its task is to handle the military equivalent of company messages, arrange telephone patches to home stations and operations centres and provide met and other information on request.

The UK Air Defence System runs a separate net providing communications between Sector Operations Centres and interceptor aircraft patrolling the UK Air Defence Regions. *Friendly, Unknown* and *Zombie* (Russian) aircraft are investigated, although the latter category would seem no longer to be a serious problem. Positions are given by the Georef system, a worldwide RAF system of grid squares, each designated by a four-letter code. They can be found on the En Route Charts published by the RAF and available to the public. Positions in latitude and longitude are converted into a code of four letters and four numbers. In the example shown, aircraft *Friendly 1234* is at 58N 02W (MKPP0000). It is thus possible to listen to interceptions and plot their progress!

An example of aircraft positioning using the Georef system.

The USAF equivalent to STCICS is GCCS, the Global Command and Control System, which divides the world into 14 Command Control Zones. The English base is at Croughton (first syllable pronounced as in 'crowd') in Northamptonshire, callsign *Croughton Global*. Its primary frequency is 11176 kHz, sometimes referred to as 'Triple One Upper'. This is a common GCCS frequency used also by Incirlik in Turkey and Ascension Island, among others, and they too can be monitored under good reception conditions. Most frequent users are the transports of Air Mobility Command giving details of loads and unserviceabilities to their destinations or ops centres. The latter are sometimes designated by a code name such as *Phantom Ops*, the European Airlift Control Centre at Ramstein, Germany, or *Falcon Ops* at Torrejon, Spain.

When an aircraft crew wish to call an Airlift Command Centre they often use the blanket callsign *Mainsail* to alert GCCS stations that a phone patch is required. The ground station will respond only if the aircraft signal is reasonably strong and clear. It is not uncommon for Croughton to have several aircraft 'queuing' for phone patches, so there are a number of back-up frequencies available. Many of the calls involve met information known as *Metro* (pronounced 'Mee-tro'). Aircrew may offer PIREPS, pilot reports of weather conditions encountered en route. This can be useful because the aircraft serial number and type are usually quoted as well as its tactical callsign if one is in use. *Capsule* messages can also be heard, periodically updating operation instructions to transport aircraft.

GCCS channels are interrupted frequently by Strategic Air Command 'Foxtrot' routine mission status broadcasts, known as *Skybird* after the blanket callsign for SAC ground stations. (SAC is soon to be absorbed by Air Combat Command, but I shall retain the familiar designation for the moment.) Part of the fail-safe system, they test communications between aircraft, ground stations and missile silos. Should the US ever have been involved in a nucelar exchange the 'go code' would have been transmitted via this network. Consisting of a string of alpha-numerics, these coded messages have been going out on HF since at least the early 1960s. The ground stations' initial call to all SAC aircraft, 'Skyking, Skyking, do not answer, do not answer', will be familiar to regular HF listeners.

The broadcasts on GCCS are repeats of those going out on SAC's own group of frequencies which is known as *Giant Talk*. SAC's primary day frequency is 11243; another is 6761, which was much used by British-based B-52s during the Gulf War. A basic form of security is the use of a channel designator such as 'Sierra 391', rather than the actual frequency.

As with many military HF frequencies, they can be 'dead' for long periods. Ground stations employ imaginative callsigns which are changed daily, examples being *Acidman*, *Chipmouse*, *Big Daddy* and *Red Cedar*. Another system is used by the US Air Force in Europe (USAFE, pronounced 'You-safe-ee'). It enables tactical aircraft such as F-111s to remain in contact with base while on practice missions as far afield as the north of Scotland.

The other major HF network is the Canadian Military Aeronautical Communication System (MACS). Easy to monitor in the UK is Lahr Military in Germany, but Trenton in Ontario and St John's in Newfoundland can also be heard at times. Not specifically aeronautical is the *Mystic Star* network which enables the US President, other VIPs and high-ranking officers to maintain contact with Washington DC. A very large number of HF frequencies are available and many of the conversations are scrambled or consist of encoded messages. The US Navy has its own HF net which often involves aircraft as well as ships. US Coast Guard aircraft can sometimes be heard over the Eastern Seaboard of the USA talking to their bases. Other miscellaneous users of the HF band include anti-drug-running aircraft and the so-called Hurricane Hunters tracking storms.

The callsigns employed by military aircraft take many forms. Most common for RAF aircraft until recently was the tri-graph, eg ABC12. However, most first-line aircraft have adopted an alpha-numeric system, examples being 7NE44, a Chinook, and F5G20, a Puma. Another style resembles the USAF tactical callsign (Carbon Two, a Tornado). One of the reasons for the change was a clash with the ICAO three-letter code allocations. On one confusing occasion in which the author was involved, an RAF Tristar, SVA14, was identified by the London computer as a Saudi Airways Tristar. The RAF decided to fall in line with the ICAO system and registered several three-letter prefixes for training units, examples being VYT and FYT (Valley and Finningley Training respectively.) More are listed in Appendix 6.

RAF Air Support Command use *Ascot* as a prefix, the aircraft type and unit or base being identified as follows, individual callsigns being numbered sequentially from the round figure quoted: 700 – Andover or BAe 125 of 32 Squadron, Northolt; 1000 – Andover or BAe 125 of 32 Squadron, Northolt; 2000 – VC10 of 10 Squadron, Brize Norton; 3000 – Tristar of 216 Squadron, Brize Norton; 4000 – Hercules from RAF Lyneham; 5000 – Hercules from RAF Lyneham; 7500 – Andover or BAe 125 of 32 Squadron, Northolt; 8000 – Andover of 60 Squadron, Northolt. Individual callsigns, eg *Ascot* 1609, are known as Task numbers.

Rafair is another prefix of long standing, although it is not heard so frequently these days. Some RAF units have special callsigns reserved for formation flights. They include *Isis* Formation (Oxford University Air Squadron) and *Liver* Formation (pronounced 'Lie-va') for Liverpool UAS. RAF Valley Hawks sometimes use *Cobra* or *Python* Formation as well as *Jester* and *Viper*, which I assume are instructors' callsigns inspired by the film *Top Gun*! Two Wessex helicopters were recently heard using *Goat* Formation, a reference to the squadron's official badge which incorporates a goat in the design.

The USAF and US Army make considerable use of so-called tactical callsigns such as *Foster* 15, the number being the pilot's personal designation, but there are frequent anomalies, *Tail Pipe Delta*, an SR-71, being an example. These prefixes are changed periodically but, having said that, there are many which have been retained for years, and some are included in Appendix 6. Air Mobility Command, formerly Military Airlift Command, transports generally use the aircraft serial, referred to as the 'tail number'. However, since Operation 'Desert Shield' alpha-numeric codes have been employed as well. The US Navy is another alpha-numeric user, *Navy* 6 Golf 086 for instance, the first two characters often referring to the code painted on the aircraft.

Other foreign air forces use self-evident prefixes such as *Danish, Saudi*, etc. *Aussie* identifies the Royal Australian Air Force and *Kiwi* the Royal New Zealand AF; the Greeks use *Hellenic Air Force* but the Spaniards hide behind *Alpha Mike Echo*. French Air Force transport aircraft often use *Cotam*, the initials of this arm of the Air Force, while the French Navy uses FMN or sometimes *France Marine*. *Mission* and up to four figures is frequently heard in use by German military aircraft and also by aircraft of other countries, including the RAF.

The tower at RAF Valley.

Chapter 17

Air band radios

In the early days of air band radios back in the 1960s, there were only two or three types available. The variety then grew steadily, prices came down and some were miniaturised to true pocket size. Manufacturers came and went, some to obscurity, others to the more lucrative field of two-way communications equipment. Today, the potential purchaser is faced with a bewildering selection of sets from around £10 up to well over £500. It is also a fact that performance is not always proportional to price.

I do not intend to give a *Which?* Magazine type of survey on the best to buy as I have not had the opportunity to test all those listed. Nor have I included all the cheap models stocked by various High Street outlets; some of these are excellent, but beware of those which purport to cover the air band but stop at 135 or even 130 MHz, thus depriving you of the upper section of the band, currently 136 but soon to be 137 MHz.

The irritating drawback with all the cheaper receivers is the absence of an accurate tuning facility, so you are never quite sure to which you are tuned until you have listened for a while. Some radios cover the entire air band with a one inch scale and if, say, 124.2 is tuned in, transmissions on the adjacent frequencies of 124.0, 124.05, 124.10 and 124.15, and 124.25, 124.30, 124.35 and so on, may be picked up as well. They are not usually as loud as the primary frequency being monitored but are annoying and confusing, particularly when a powerful transmission from a nearer source swamps the aircraft in which you are interested. A longer scale makes tuning easier but has no effect on the lack of discrimination.

Crystal-controlled receivers represent the next stage of sophistication, using pre-set crystals to tune much more quickly and accurately to a particular frequency. The selectivity is still not perfect, however, in that, for example, a 125.1 MHz crystal may also receive the channels *immediately* adjacent. Further disadvantages are the cost of the crystals (around £5 each) and the fact that the less popular frequencies may be hard to get. They can also be fiddly to change in a hurry. A large collection of them could end up costing as much as a far more expensive synthesised scanner. However, almost all of them are a combination of crystal-controlled channels and a very extensive manual tuner covering the whole air band, so they can be an advantage for those on a limited budget who only wish to monitor their local airport.

We now reach the realm of synthesised receivers controlled by microprocessors. The required frequency is keyed in and displayed digitally on an LCD display (similar to a pocket computer), overlaps with adjacent frequencies being virtually eliminated. These sets are known colloquially as scanners and specific frequencies can be stored in a memory maintained by a separate battery or an EEPROM (Electronically Erasable Read Only Memory) when the radio is switched off. In scanning mode the radio searches through them continuously, only stopping when a transmission is received. Some sets feature a delay so that the reply can be heard as well. You can also 'lock out' certain frequencies with almost continuous transmissions, such as Volmet and ATIS.

Many scanners are designed as base stations (desk-top models) and are not easily portable, whilst others are hand-held portables which tend to 'eat' batteries. Investment in rechargeable batteries and a transformer for home use is obviously desirable (they may be included in the price), but be careful that the transformer is compatible with your radio's voltage rating. The more expensive sets are advertised as communications receivers because they are able to monitor far more than merely aviation messages. It all depends on whether you wish to listen to bus and taxi drivers, the gas board and the myriad of other users of the public service bands, as well as marine and other bands.

The ideal set for the aviation enthusiast receives 108 to 137 MHz and 225 to 400 MHz and thus embraces both the civil and military air bands Some purport to do this but leave gaps, so it is essential to make a careful study of the set's capabilities before deciding which one to purchase. Advice from existing owners is also an advantage as all sets have their own little peculiarities.

There are, theoretically, 720 channels in the communications (COM) section of the air band between 118.0 and 135.975 inclusive (760 when it eventually increases to 136.975). In the UK most of the spacings are 50 kHz, ie 118.10, 118.15 etc. Many of the intervening 25 kHz frequencies, eg 118.125, 118.175 and 118.225, remain as yet unallocated.

Most of the *en route* control frequencies are transmitted from up to four remote locations to render the coverage as wide as possible. To eliminate the characteristic screech, known as a heterodyne, when more than one station transmits simultaneously, an offset carrier system is used. The offsets are ±5 kHz for a two-carrier system, ±7.5 kHz and 0 kHz for a three-carrier, and ±7.5 kHz and ±2.5 kHz for a four-carrier system. Therefore, where the sensitivity of the receiver allows, reception may be improved by tuning the set slightly higher or lower than the published frequency. Note that you cannot do this with certain scanners.

There are a great number of features on today's radios and it is important to find out exactly what is or is not included in the purchase price. Some require separate aerials, others power supplies and battery chargers. All the specialised dealers hold stocks of accessories, such as headphones, earpieces, spare crystals, chargers and assorted plugs, leads and adaptors. A number of different types of aerial are offered, including some for loft or outside mounting.

As has been stated before, VHF reception is 'quasi-line of sight' so the higher the aerial the better the result. As most air band listening will probably be done at home, it is useful to discover the best position for reception by moving the set around the house. Radio waves behave in a very peculiar fashion and marked differences will be found even in the same room. If the usual telescopic aerial or rubber antenna supplied with the set proves inadequate, a remote antenna can be purchased, or alternatively an aerial can be made very cheaply at home.

Ron Bishop of the Ulster Aviation Society has kindly supplied me with the details of how to do this. He writes: 'A simple radio aerial can be made from a piece of rod or wire a simple fraction (¼ or ½) of the wavelength you want and orientated the same way that the signal is polarised. For VHF air band, ¼ wave is 50 – 60 cm (20 – 24 ins) and the orientation is vertical. If you have a place at home where you do a lot of listening it is worth rigging up a more permanent half-wave dipole costing about 50 pence, which will substantially improve reception, particularly with the cheaper sets.

'Get two pieces of metal rod or stiff wire, each a ¼-wave long. Fix them end to end on a small block of wood or other insulator, with a gap of about 4 cm between the two ends. Attach the central core of a piece of coaxial cable to the upper element and the screening (braiding) wire to the lower element. TV aerial coaxial cable will do but UR43 cable from an electronics shop matches the impedance of the set much better. At the set end, fit the appropriate connector (BNC or mini-jack) and plug it into the aerial socket of the set. Experience shows that more sophisticated aerials are not necessarily more effective.'

The newcomer to air band listening is recommended to buy one of the more inexpensive sets first to familiarise him or herself with what is being said and its meaning. When hooked on air band (and it does not take very long!) one can move on to a more ambitious receiver. Second-hand models are often advertised in the aviation magazines, particularly the 'Freeads' column in *Aviation News*. It can be argued, however, that right from the start an investment in a proper air band scanner is desirable. This avoids the shortcomings of cheap sets already described. As ever, it all depends on money!

A further method of improving reception is a pre-amplifier (usually abbreviated to pre-amp) which fits between the antenna and the receiver on a hand-held model or inside the case of a base station. The device boosts the received signals and feeds them into the receiver. Results can vary but it may be possible to receive, say, the ground transmissions from a distant airport which were not previously audible from the same location.

The performance of some scanners can be boosted by computer control. An example is the AR 3000A which, with the aid of ACEPAC-3 software obtainable from AOR(UK) Ltd, can be run from an IBM-PC compatible computer and a standard serial lead. By exploiting the memory capabilities of the computer, more memory 'banks' can be programmed and, if required, they can be transferred to the AR 3000A's internal memory for subsequent field use without the computer. An 'activity count' mode is available where you can set the scanner searching a given bank of memory channels with the programme performing a percentage count of the activity on each. This can be for virtually any period you like and a printed report is supplied at the end! Very useful for assessing the listening possibilities of particular air band frequences. These are just a couple of useful functions—external computer control gives virtually unlimited flexibility.

A selection of air band radios currently available

NB Prices may vary as currencies fluctuate.

Price range: £10 – £25
Stewart C87; Pye TRO170; Realistic Jetstream; Steepletone SAB10; Texet HH925. All have VHF air band and AM/FM broadcast bands.

Left *The Fairmate HP-200E hand-held scanner.* (Andy Rackham, Air Supply)

Below *The Sangean ATS-803A HF set with digital tuning.* (Andy Rackham, Air Supply)

Bottom *Scanners from the Yupiteru and Alinco range.* (Andy Rackham, Air Supply)

Price range: £50 – £100
Signal R537S—VHF air band only. Tuneable dial with two selectable channels which are crystal-controlled.
Steepletone MRB7—VHF air band/AM and FM broadcast/Marine band.

Price range: around £125
Signal R528—VHF air band only. Tuneable dial with six selectable channels which are crystal-controlled.

Price range: £150 – £175
Cobra SR925—Desk-top scanner, VHF air band, etc.
WIN108—Hand-held scanner, VHF air band only.
Bearcat 175XL—Desk-top scanner, VHF air band, etc.

Price range: £190 – £200
AOR AR800E—Hand-held scanner, VHF air band/AM/FM broadcast, etc.
Black Jaguar BJ200—Hand-held scanner, VHF air band, partial UHF air band/AM/FM broadcast, etc.
Revco RS3000—Desk-top scanner, VHF air band/AM/FM broadcast, etc.

Price range: £200 – £299
AOR 900UK—Hand-held scanner, VHF and UHF air band, etc.
Realistic PRO-32A—Hand-held scanner, VHF air band, etc.
Signal R535—Desk-top scanner, VHF and UHF air band.
Sony Air 7—Hand-held scanner, VHF air band/AM/FM broadcast, etc.
Uniden Bearcat 200XLT—Hand-held scanner, VHF air band, etc.
Uniden Bearcat 800XLT—Desk-top scanner, VHF air band, etc.
Yupiteru MVT-5000—Hand-held scanner, VHF and UHF air band, etc.
Fairmate HP-1000AB—Hand-held scanner, VHF and UHF air band, etc.
Fairmate HP-100E—Hand-held scanner, VHF and UHF air band, etc.
Nevada MS-1000—Desk-top scanner, VHF and UHF air band, etc.
AR1500—Hand-held scanner, VHF and UHF air band, plus HF SSB.

Price range: £300 – £350
Realistic PRO-2005—Desk-top scanner, VHF and UHF air band, etc.

Price Range: £450 – £500
Kenwood RZ – 1—Desk-top scanner, VHF and UHF air band, etc.
AOR AR2002—Desk-top scanner, VHF and UHF air band, etc.

Price range: around £545
Standard AX700—Desk-top scanner, VHF and UHF air band, etc.

Price range: around £760
AOR AR3000—Desk-top scanner covering virtually the whole communications range from 100 Khz to 2036 Mhz with no gaps.

For some details of short wave/HF sets, see Chapter 9.

Principal air band suppliers
Air Supply, 83b High Street, Yeadon, Leeds LS19 7TA. Telephone 0532 509581
AOR (UK) Ltd, Room 2, Adam Bede High Tech Centre, Derby Road, Wirksworth, Derbyshire DE4 4BG. Telephone 0629 825926
Arrow Electronics Ltd, 5 The Street, Hatfield Peverel, Nr Chelmsford, Essex. Telephone 0245 381626; Unit 17, Six Harmony Row, Govan, Glasgow G51 38A. Telephone 041 445 3060
The Aviation Hobby Shop, Horton Parade, Horton Road, West Drayton, Middlesex, UB7 8EA. Telephone 0895 442123
Flightdeck, The Airband Shop. Telephone 061 499 9350
Javiation, Carlton Works, Carlton Street, Bradford, West Yorkshire BD7 1DA. Telephone 0274 732146
Lowe Electronics Ltd, Chesterfield Road, Matlock, Derbyshire DE4 5LE. Telephone 0629 580800; 162 High Street, Chesterton, Cambridge CB4 1NL. Telephone 0223 311230; 223 – 225 Field End Road, Eastcote, Middlesex HA5 1QZ. Telephone 01 429 3256; 27 Gillam Road, Northbourne, Bournemouth BH10 6BW. Telephone 0202 577760; 6 Ferry Steps Industrial Estate, Bristol. Telephone 0272 771770; Cumbernauld Airport Foyer, Falkirk. Telephone 0236 721004; 6 Cherwell Close, Langley, Buckinghamshire. Telephone 0753 545255; Newcastle Airport. Telephone 0661 860418
Nevada Communications, 189 London Road, North End, Portsmouth, Hants P02 9AE. Telephone 0705 662145
Raycom Communications Systems Ltd (Ham Stores), International House, 963 Wolverhampton Road, Oldbury, Warley, West Midlands B69 4RJ. Telephone 021 552 0073
SRP Trading, Unit 20, Nash Works, Forge Lane, Belbroughton, Nr Stourbridge, Worcestershire. Telephone 0562 730672
Stephens James Ltd, 47 Warrington Road, Leigh, Lancs. Telephone 0942 676790

Stewart Aviation, PO Box 7, Market Harborough, Leics LE16 8FP.
Telephone 0536 770962

Transair Pilot Shop, West Entrance, Fairoaks Airport, Chobham, Nr
Woking, Surrey GU24 8HX. Telephone 0276 858533

Waters & Stanton Electronics, Warren House, 18 – 20 Main Road, Hockley,
Essex SS5 4QS. Telephone 0702 206835; 12 North Street, Hornchurch,
Essex RM11 1QX. Telephone 04024 44765

Chapter 18

Charts and related documents

Almost as important as an air band radio itself is the acquisition of a set of radio navigation charts. These are essential to build up an overall picture of the UK airways system and the positions of its beacons and reporting points.

En route charts are published by three organisations for the United Kingdom; the Royal Air Force, British Airways Aerad and Jeppesen. The USAF produces its own charts but these are more difficult to obtain. Obviously the information on the different charts is fundamentally the same, but the presentation differs quite considerably. There is also some variation in the areas covered and only the RAF charts for the United Kingdom show the whole of the British Isles on one sheet. This is separated into two charts, 411H for high altitudes and 412S/412N for low altitudes. The low level charts are drawn to an approximate scale of 14 nautical miles to the inch, while the high level ones are about 28 nautical miles to the inch.

British Airways Aerad charts for the United Kingdom cover high altitude (H109/108) at a scale of 30 nautical miles to the inch. They feature most of Europe (except Spain and the North of Scotland). Low altitude is covered by EUR 1/2 to a scale of approximately 17 nautical miles to the inch, as far north as Edinburgh and including parts of France and Germany. Chart (EUR 3) shows the rest of Scotland.

Aerad also produce a wide range of other related documentation, including Standard Instrument Departure charts, Standard Arrival charts and airport and apron layouts. Aerad's other important publication, much prized by enthusiasts, is the Europe Supplement, a soft-backed book packed with information on airports, including their aids, runway lengths and radio frequencies.

The other chart publisher is Jeppesen Sanderson Inc, an American firm whose main distributor in the United Kingdom is CSE Aviation at Oxford Airport. Two charts cover the United Kingdom, one for high

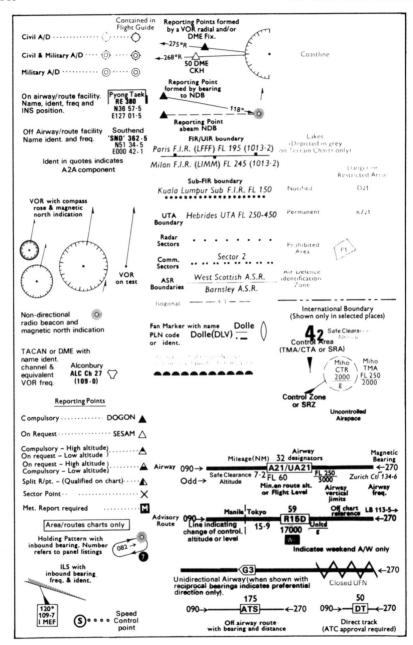

Radio navigation chart legend (British Airways Aerad).

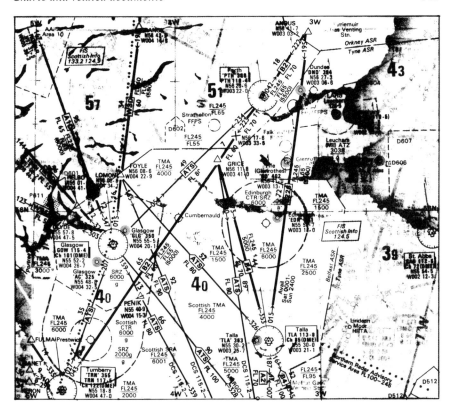

Section of an Aerad chart for Central Scotland (British Airways Aerad).

level (Ref E(HI) 3 and 4) and one for low altitudes (Ref E(LO) 1 and 2). The company also produces a variety of associated data, the most important of which are airport approach charts.

The CAA distributes a wide range of charts, including topographical maps, which are of only limited use to airband listeners, SIDS and STARs. The CAA is of course responsible for the UK Aeronautical Information Publication, known as the Air Pilot. This is really the bible for aviators in Britain's airspace but it is an extremely bulky document, divided into several volumes. Of particular interest are the AGA, COM and RAC sections, detailing aerodromes and ground aids, communications and ATC rules and procedures. It is, needless to say, very expensive and incorporates a regular updating and amendment service. All airport briefing offices have copies and you may be able to get permission to 'browse', especially if you have some *bona fide* aviation connection, such as being a flying club member.

At first sight, radio navigation charts are a perplexing welter of intersecting lines, symbols and figures, but, like any other maps, there is a key and with a few minutes' study they become logical. The radio beacons are identified by name and a three-letter abbreviation. Wallasey, for example, may be referred to by ATC and aircraft as Wallasey or Whisky Alfa Lima. The frequency of 114.1 MHz on which the beacon radiates will be adjacent to its name on the chart. Also shown on the chart are the names of the airways, their bearings in both directions, the distances in nautical miles between reporting points, the heights of their bases and upper limits and the lowest available cruising levels.

Many of the charts are stocked by air band radio suppliers but they can also be purchased direct from the publishers or their agents at the addresses listed below. Out-of-date charts are sometimes advertised in the aviation press, often at reasonably low prices. Provided they are not too old, say more than twelve months, they can still be useful.

Suppliers of Airway Charts

British Airways, Aerad Customer Services, Aerad House, PO Box 10, Heathrow Airport, Hounslow, Middlesex TW6 2JA.

CSE Aviation Ltd (Jeppesen Agents), Oxford Airport, Kidlington, Oxford, OX5 1RA.

Royal Air Force, No 1 Aeronautical Documents Unit, RAF Northolt, West End Road, Ruislip, Middlesex HA4 6NG.

Civil Aviation Authority, Printing and Publishing, Greville Air Supply, 83B High Street, Yeadon, Leeds LS19 7TA.

Airtour International, Elstree Aerodrome, Elstree, Herts WD6 3AW.

Avmail (outdated charts), 9 Hitherwood, Cranleigh, Surrey GU6 8BN.

Chapter 19

Magazines for the enthusiast and air band listener

In the 1960s spotters, as they were then known, relied entirely upon eyesight, sometimes aided by binoculars and telescopes. VHF receivers were commercially unavailable, even had we thought of this means of identifying some of the goodies which flew over in those days. Today, virtually every interesting aircraft movement in British skies is recorded by at least one of the enthusiast fraternity and is rapidly passed on through the grapevine. Thirty-odd years ago many questions went unanswered; was it an Armagnac I saw in 1957 heading out over the Irish Sea, did my friend really see a US Navy Tradewind and what were five Banshees (I think) doing on contrails over north-west England in 1958?

The only information available in those days on aircraft movements was published in *Air Pictorial* under the title 'Airport Notes— Interesting Visitors'. At first it was confined to Blackbushe, Croydon, Heathrow, Northolt and Prestwick and the selections, about a dozen each per month, were somewhat arbitrary. They were of little use to spotters in the Midlands and north who attempted to collate them with what they saw overhead. Gradually the net spread to embrace Manchester (Ringway as it then was), Birmingham (Elmdon), Liverpool (Speke) and other provincial airports.

Air Britain's *Movements Review*, a four-page news sheet available on subscription with other specialist publications, was much more useful and eventually local societies began to produce their own regional newsletters. One of the first in this field was the Merseyside Group of Aviation Enthusiasts which one day was to grow into the highly respected and successful Merseyside Aviation Society. For the time, quite comprehensive visitors lists were published for Speke, Ringway, Burtonwood and a few others. Among the features was a monthly 'Spotting Report', recording interesting overflights seen by members. With the advent of air band radios around 1961 the coverage spread even further, and at the same time other societies were printing their own magazines in a similar format.

Some were phenomenally detailed, even about military movements, hitherto veiled in mystery. Rumour had it that the air attachés of certain Eastern Bloc embassies had taken out subscriptions and it was said that the authorities had to have a quiet word with the editors asking them to be more discreet! Remember that security was much tighter in those days. In 1960 we were chased from the fence at Mildenhall by the air police at the spot where today there is a public enclosure! Nowadays the presence of a Lockheed U-2 at Lakenheath, which was discussed at length in the letters pages of contemporary aviation magazines without confirmation in 1956, would be known to all and sundry within hours, such is the enthusiasts' intelligence network.

Addresses for enthusiasts' magazines

Air Britain News and Air Britain Digest Howard Nash (Membership Secretary), 11 Thurlestone, Thundersley, Benfleet, Essex SS7 3YW.

Air Strip Midland Counties Aviation Society Honorary Registrar, 113 Ferndown Road, Solihull, West Midlands B91 2AX.

Anglia Aeronews Anglian Aviation Society Administrator, 27 Eastwoodbury Lane, Southend on Sea, Essex SS2 6UY.

Aviation Letter John R. Roach, 8 Stowe Crescent, Ruislip, Middlesex HA4 7SS.

Aviation News & Review LAAS International, M. T. Reynolds, 37 Crane Close, Dagenham, Essex RM10 8PL.

British Aviation Review and Roundel British Aviation Research Group, Paul Hewins, 8 Nightingale Road, Woodley, Berkshire RG5 3LP.

Channel Islands Aviation News Dave Bougourd, 5 Rue du Douit, Marais Lane, Vale, Guernsey, CI.

Contact Air Britain Gwent Branch, Richard Baker, 36 Brynawelan Road, Cyncoed, Cardiff CF2 6QR.

Hawkeye Gatwick Aviation Society Registrar, 11 Cray Avenue, Ashtead, Surrey KT21 1QX.

Humberside Air Review Humberside Aviation Society, Pete Wild, 4 Bleach Yard, Beverley, North Humberside.

North West Air News Air-Britain Liverpool Branch, Andrew Hulme, 65 Calthorpe Street, Garston, Liverpool L19 1RF.

Osprey Air Britain Southampton Branch, Doreen Eaves, 84 Carnation Road, Bassett, Southampton SO2 3JL.

Prestwick Airport Letter Prestwick Airport Aviation Group, D. Reid (Editor), 45 Bellesleyhill Avenue, Ayr KA8 9BJ.

Scottish Air News Central Scotland Aviation Group, 12 Pearson Drive, Renfrew PA4 0BD.

Skyward West Country Aviation Society, 54 Radcliffe Close, Southway, Plymouth PL6 6JZ.

South East Air Review West London Aviation Group, 18 Green Lawns, Ruislip, Middlesex HA4 9SP.

Southwest Aviation News Southwest Aviation Society, Richard Hodgkinson (Registrar), Marsh Farm, Salford Priors, Near Evesham, Worcestershire.

26 Threshold Air Britain Luton Branch, Chris Alton, 27 Margery Wood, Welwyn Garden City, Herts AL7 1UN.

Winged Words The Aviation Society, 6 Martin Drive, Darwen, Lancs BB3 2HW.

Ulster Air Mail Ulster Aviation Society, Kevin Johnston, 16 Ravelston Avenue, Newtonabbey BT36 6PF.

Aviation Ireland Aviation Society of Ireland, 31 Shanrath Road, Whitehall, Dublin 9, Eire.

Irish Air Letter 25 Phoenix Avenue, Pecks Lane, Castleknock, Dublin 15.

There are three commercial magazines which publish air band information in a regular column: my own *Radio Watch* in *Aviation News Magazine*, Godfrey Manning's *Airband* in *Short Wave Magazine* and Graham Duke's *Airband* in *Aircraft Illustrated*. My column serves to update this book, as I summarise relevant NOTAMs as they appear, particularly when new or revised frequencies and airspace changes are involved. I have also been able to expand such subjects as Flow Control, transponder codes and holding procedures, and list new callsign prefixes as they are allocated. Godfrey's feature is orientated differently but is no less informative. It serves chiefly as a reader forum for discussion and feedback on air band topics. The magazine also tries out new air band radios and publishes comprehensive reports backed up by a great deal of technical knowledge. Graham's column presents a similar collage of news and facts.

Appendix 1

Beacons and reporting points

The centrelines of airways are marked by navigational beacons positioned at strategic intervals, such as where the airway changes direction or where one or more of them intersect. Airway beacons are mostly VORs with an associated DME to indicate range, but some, Lichfield being a major example, are NDBs. With the aid of a radio navigation chart it is easy to find the ones nearest to your home.

Many of the reporting points are not beacons at all, but hypothetical positions formed where certain radials from two VORs intersect, and are given a standard five-letter name. It may be related to a geographical feature such as the name of a nearby town, and is often a distortion of the real name to arrive at five letters. Examples are LAMMA on Upper Red 38 south of Edinburgh (Lammermuir Hills), SAPCO at the junction of Amber 2 and White 37 (near Sapcote in Leicestershire), and SETEL north west of Pole Hill VOR on Amber 2 (Settle). Others, particularly over the sea, are purely artificial and dreamed up by the appropriate CAA department. GRICE in Scotland, by the way, is named after a retired Supervisor at Scottish ATCC!

As described in the chapter on Approach Control, each major airport has one or more terminal beacons. Well known are the LBA at Leeds, the GM and GX at Birmingham, the CA at Castle Donington and the NEW at Newcastle. Even if the destination is not mentioned in transmissions whilst on airways, such routeings as Pole Hill-LBA will immediately give a clue. 'A standard Willo Arrival Runway 26' will identify the destination as Gatwick.

Similarly, knowledge of the runway designators at various airports will be useful. Since the trend is to a single main runway with an instrument approach aid at one or both ends, with perhaps one subsidiary for light aircraft, one can soon become familiar with those in one's home area. Examples are Birmingham 15/33, Heathrow 09L & 09R/27L & 27R, Gatwick 08/26 and Manchester 06/24.

The colours previously employed for Airways have been replaced by the phonetics for the initial letters, ie A = Amber, B = Blue, G = Green, R = Red, W = White. The prefix U indicates Upper and the suffixes N, S, E and W, compass points. L is a Link Route.

Beacons and reporting points used by aircraft flying the airways

Name	Frequency	Code	Type	Approximate location
Abbey			RP	Scottish TMA
Aberdeen	114.3	ADN	VOR	Scottish East Coast
Absil			RP	UA37
Acorn			RP	London TMA
ADR	346		NDB	Belfast/Aldergrove
Agano			RP	Channel Islands CTZ
Alkin			RP	Holding pattern for London/City
Alloy			RP	East Shetland Basin
Alvin			RP	G1 E of Brecon
Alwyn			RP	East Shetland Basin
Ambel			RP	On UA2 near Dean Cross VOR
Amman			RP	On G1 in South Wales
Angel			RP	UL74, North Sea
Angla			RP	Channel Islands CTZ
Angus			RP	B2/B226 intersection
Annet			RP	UL722, London/France boundary
Arvok			RP	Eire, junction of UB2/UA38
Askey			RP	London TMA
Askil			RP	UT7
Aspen			RP	UR24, S of Bournemouth
Aspit			RP	UN582
Aston			RP	Birmingham SIDs
Astra			RP	Holding pattern for Gatwick
Bakat			RP	SL4 – SOTA
Baker			RP	B4, SE England
Bakur			RP	UA38, London/Dublin boundary
Balis			RP	Aberdeen area
Banba			RP	UB10, London/Dublin boundary
Banlo			RP	SL2 – SOTA
Barix			RP	SL3 – SL5 – SOTA
Barkway	116.25	BKY	VOR	Nuthampstead, Herts
Barra			RP	Western Isles
Bartn			RP	Manchester TMA
Baset			RP	UG1, Wiltshire
Batel			RP	London TMA
Bedfo			RP	Near Bedford on UB4
Beech			RP	SE England on G27
Beeno			RP	North Sea, junction of UB1/UB7
Begas			RP	SOTA
Beket			RP	W5D S of Sumburgh
Belfast	117.2	BEL	VOR	East of Belfast City
Benbecula	114.4	BEN	VOR	Outer Hebrides
Benbo			RP	On A1 south of Worthing
Bendy			RP	Southampton CTA
Benix			RP	Channel Islands CTZ
Benty			RP	Sumburgh Heli Routes
Berek			RP	S Midlands
Berry Head	112.7	BHD	VOR	On A25 near Torquay
Bexil			RP	Gatwick STARs
Biggin	115.1	BIG	VOR	Holding pattern for Heathrow

Name	Frequency	Code	Type	Approximate location
Birch			RP	Birmingham STARs
Biski			RP	SL1 – SL7 – SOTA
Blaca			RP	Scotland on DG27
Blufa			RP	UB1 Amsterdam/London boundary
Blusy			RP	UB29 Amsterdam/London boundary
Bolin			RP	Manchester holding pattern
Bonby			RP	W3D – Inverness
Bondy			RP	SE of London TMA
Borma			RP	UN582 – UN611
Bovingdon	113.75	BNN	VOR	Holding pattern for Heathrow
Bovva			RP	Heathrow hold when Bovingdon out of service
Bowes			RP	North Yorkshire
Boyne			RP	W911D, Irish Sea
BPL	276.5		NDB	Blackpool Airport
Brain			RP	R123 Essex
Braso			RP	R1 E of Lambourne
Bravo			RP	Cross Channel CTA
Brecon	117.45	BCN	VOR	A25/G1, South Wales
BRI	380		NDB	Bristol Airport
Brill			RP	Channel Islands CTZ
Bripo			RP	Bridport, Dorset
Brookmans Park	117.5	BPK	NDB	North of London
Bruce			RP	W910D SE of Tiree
Buken			RP	North Yorkshire
Burnham	117.1	BUR	VOR	Berkshire
Busta			RP	London TMA
Buzad			RP	A20/B3, SE Midlands
Calda			RP	NW of Manchester
Cambo			RP	UR72, London/France boundary
Carnane	366.5	CAR	NDB	Isle of Man on DG27
Caval			RP	UR168, London/France boundary
Chaly			RP	Cross Channel SRA
Chase			RP	Holding pattern for Birmingham
Chelt			RP	B39 – UA251 – UB39
Chiltern	277	CHT	NDB	North of Heathrow
Chinn			RP	NE Scotland on W3D
Chubb			RP	Channel Islands CTZ
CL	328		NDB	Carlisle Airport
Clacton	114.55	CLN	VOR	Essex coast
Cliff			RP	English Channel off SE coast
Clonmel	387	CML	NDB	Eire, junction of UB2/UG1
Clyde			RP	Scottish TMA
Codey			RP	Farnborough
Compton	114.35	CPT	VOR	Berkshire
Cork	114.6	CRK	VOR	Eire
Costa	111.8	COA	VOR	Belgian coast on B29
Cowly			RP	UA1/UW38, South Midlands
Crewe			RP	UA256/UB3, Cheshire
Croft			RP	North of Manchester TMA
Dalky			RP	B2, Shannon/Scottish boundary
Dandi			RP	UA37, Scottish/Copenhagen boundary
Daventry	116.4	DTY	VOR	South Midlands
Davot			RP	W3D, S of Inverness
Dawly			RP	UA25/UR8 off Devon coast
Dayne			RP	Holding pattern for Manchester
Dean Cross	115.2	DCS	VOR	West of Carlisle
Denby			RP	S of Pole Hill VOR
Depso			RP	East Shetland Basin
Detling	117.3	DET	VOR	Kent

Name	Frequency	Code	Type	Approximate location
Dieppe	115.8	DPE	VOR	French coast on A1E
Dikas			RP	UA25 – UB40 – UG1
Dogga			RP	UB1/UB13, North Sea
Dover	114.95	DVR	VOR	Near town
Downi			RP	Aberdeen
Drake			RP	English Channel on UA34
Drumm			RP	Manchester TMA
Dublin	114.9	DUB	VOR	North of city
Duffy			RP	N Ireland
Dumba			RP	Scottish TMA
Dundrum			RP	South of Belfast VOR on B2
Easin			RP	Southern North Sea
Eastwood			RP	Holding pattern for Gatwick
Ebony			RP	Birmingham STARs
EDN	341		NDB	Edinburgh Airport
Eider			RP	East Shetland Basin
Elder			RP	UR1W/UA34W, Isle of Wight
Eldin			RP	B5 – UB5
EMW	393		NDB	East Midlands Airport
Epsom	316	EPM	NDB	Holding pattern for Heathrow when Ockham out of service
Ering			RP	B29 – UB29
Ermin			RP	Plymouth
Ernan			RP	UN550 – UN560
Ervin			RP	UG1, Dublin/London boundary
EX	337		NDB	Exeter Airport
Exmor			RP	North Devon
Fambo			RP	North Sea on UB13
Farma			RP	London TMA
Fawbo			RP	UA34W, London/France boundary
Fawley	370	FAW	NDB	Near Southampton on UW38
Fenik			RP	Scottish TMA
Feras			RP	SE of London TMA
Fetla			RP	Unst
Finch			RP	On UW22
Findo			RP	SW of Perth
Fiwud			RP	W2D
Flame			RP	East Shetland Basin
Forty			RP	NE of Aberdeen
Foyle			RP	Scottish TMA
Frank			RP	London TMA
Fulma			RP	W958D NW of Turnberry
Gabad			RP	North Sea E of Clacton
Gapli			RP	UR8 – SOTA
Gater			RP	NE England
Gavel			RP	W5D S of Sumburgh
Gibso			RP	R8, south coast
Glasgow	115.4	GOW	VOR	Airport holding pattern
Glesk			RP	S of Aberdeen on B22
Golfy			RP	Cross Channel SRA
Goodwood	114.75	GWC	VOR	South coast on UR25
Gordo			RP	UR23, Scottish/Copenhagen boundary
Gorse			RP	Aberdeen Heli Routes
Gosta			RP	B39 in Glos
Grice			RP	North boundary of Scottish TMA
Grupa			RP	Channel Islands CTZ
Guernsey	109.4	GUR	VOR	On UR1
GX	347		NDB	Birmingham Northern Locator Beacon
GM	371		NDB	Birmingham Southern Locator Beacon
Hardy			RP	S of Seaford on A1

Name	Frequency	Code	Type	Approximate location
Hasty			RP	SE England on W8
Hazel			RP	UR8/UR1W, southern England
HB	275		NDB	Belfast/Harbour Airport
HBR	350.5		NDB	Humberside Airport
Heidi			RP	A2/W1 intersection
Helbo			RP	Scottish TMA
Hemel			RP	Herts
Henton	395	HEN	NDB	Bucks
Heron			RP	Off Ayrshire coast
Holly			RP	Gatwick STARs
Homsy			RP	Southampton
Honiley	113.65	HON	VOR	S of Birmingham airport
Indip			RP	Cross Channel CTA
Inkip			RP	Scottish TMA boundary
Inverness	109.2	INS	VOR	Inverness Airport
Isle of Man	112.2	IOM	VOR	Southern tip of island
Izack			RP	Sumburgh Heli Routes
Jacko			RP	W1/R1, North Sea
Jersey	112.2	JSY	VOR	Near airport
Karen			RP	Scottish TMA
Karil			RP	Channel Islands CTZ
Kathy			RP	UR1/UA34W, English Channel
Kenet			RP	In Wiltshire, on G1
Kilba			RP	London TMA
Killiney	378	KLY	NDB	UB2/UR14, near Dublin
Kindr			RP	Woodford
Kippa			RP	UB105
Kirby			RP	Manchester TMA
Kista			RP	W3D, SW of Sumburgh
Klonn			RP	B2D, Scottish/Stavanger boundary
Koksy	114.5	KOK	VOR	Belgian coast on G1
Koley			RP	UL7, North Sea
Komik			RP	UA37 – UB105
Konan			RP	UG1, Amsterdam/London boundary
Kulok			RP	UN582
Lager			RP	Southern North Sea
Lambourne	115.6	LAM	VOR	NE hold for Heathrow
Lamma			RP	S of Edinburgh on UR38
Lands End	114.2	LND	VOR	Land's End
Larck			RP	Gatwick STARs
Largs			RP	Ayrshire coast on B2
Lasno			RP	SOTA
LBA	402.5		NDB	Leeds/Bradford Airport
Leek			RP	NE Staffordshire
Lichfield	545	LIC	NDB	Midlands junction of A1E/W37
Liffy		LFY	RP	B1, London/Dublin boundary
Lindy			RP	UG1, W of Woodley VOR
Lirki			RP	UH71
Lisbo			RP	Lisburn, NI
Lizad			RP	UG4, France/London boundary
Logan			RP	North Sea off Essex
Lomon			RP	Scottish TMA boundary
Lonam			RP	North Sea London/Amsterdam boundary
Lorel			RP	London TMA
Lovel			RP	Manchester TMA
LPL	349.5		NDB	Liverpool Airport
Lundy			RP	UR37, Bristol Channel
Luton	345	LUT	NDB	Holding pattern for airport
Lusit			RP	Channel Islands CTZ
Lylak			RP	Alternative holding pattern for Manchester

Name	Frequency	Code	Type	Approximate location
Lynas			RP	Anglesey on B1
Lyneham	282	LA	NDB	Wiltshire
Macrihanish	116.0	MAC	VOR	Kintyre, Scotland
Magee			RP	Holding pattern for Belfast/Harbour
Malby			RP	G1 between BCN and Kenet
Maley			RP	Aberdeen area
Manchester	113.55	MCT	VOR	On the airport
Mango			RP	UR12, Essex
Manta			RP	Channel Islands CTZ
Mardi			RP	London TMA
Margo			RP	South Scotland
Match			RP	R123, Essex
Matik			RP	UN615
Mayfield	117.9	MAY	VOR	W17/A34E/A30, Sussex
Mayla			RP	London TMA
Merly			RP	UB40/UB37, Bristol Channel
Midhurst	114.0	MID	VOR	Sussex
Milde			RP	Southern North Sea
Milla			RP	London TMA
Mimbi			RP	G1 Brize inbounds
Minqi			RP	Channel Islands CTZ
Mitch			RP	Scottish TMA
Mocha			RP	W5D, S of Sumburgh
Monty			RP	Mid Wales on A25
Moody			RP	Plymouth
Moray			RP	W4D, SE of Wick
Morby			RP	Morecambe Bay
Mulit			RP	UL74, North Sea
Mulla			RP	Irish Sea on B2
Nadir			RP	B2D, North Sea
Neptu			RP	E of Great Yarmouth
Nevil			RP	London/Brest boundary on W8
Newcastle	114.25	NEW	VOR	Newcastle Airport and *en route* aid
New Galloway	399	NGY	NDB	South Scotland
Nicky	117.4	NIK	VOR	Belgian coast
Niton			RP	Mid Wales on A25
Nobal			RP	Aberdeen area
Norda			RP	Channel Islands CTZ
Norla			RP	UR37, Dublin/London boundary
Norry			RP	Berkshire
Northlight			RP	Irish Sea on W927D
Notro			RP	UT7 – SOTA
Ockham	115.3	OCK	VOR	SW holding pattern for Heathrow
Ogden			RP	Scottish TMA
Olive			RP	Birmingham STARs
Olney			RP	A20/W1 intersection
Omimi			RP	UN510 – UN520 – SOTA
Omoko			RP	SL1 – SL5 – SOTA
Orist			RP	UR24, London/France boundary
Ormer			RP	Channel Islands CTZ
Ortac			RP	UR1/UR14, France/London boundary
Orton			RP	North of Pole Hill VOR
Orvik			RP	UG11, SE of Sumburgh
Oskal			RP	UN611
Ottel			RP	Cross Channel CTA
Ottringham	113.9	OTR	VOR	Humberside on B1/UB1
Oysta			RP	Channel Islands CTZ
Pampus	117.8	PAM	VOR	Holland
Pepis			RP	R41 – W5 – UR41
Perch			RP	Channel Islands CTZ

Name	Frequency	Code	Type	Approximate location
Perth	110.4	PTH	VOR	Central Scotland
Pole Hill	112.1	POL	VOR	N of Manchester on A1
Popla			RP	Manchester TMA
Poton			RP	B4/W1, S Midlands
Radno			RP	South Wales on W39
Ranok			RP	W3D, N of Glasgow
Ratka			RP	UN510 – UN520 – SOTA
Redfa			RP	R1N, London/Amsterdam boundary
Refso			RP	Heathrow Arrivals
Rekna			RP	UR23
Rexam			RP	Wrexham on A25
Ribel			RP	N of Pole Hill VOR
Ringa			RP	Irish Sea on B2
Robbo			RP	Scottish TMA
Robin			RP	North Midlands
Ronak			RP	UN602 – UN611
Ronar			RP	A1D, NW Scotland
Rowan			RP	London TMA
Rupas			RP	Channel Islands CTZ
St Abbs	112.5	SAB	VOR	Scottish East coast on UR23
St Inglevert	387.5	ING	NDB	French coast
Salco			RP	UR1, France/London boundary
Samon			RP	UL7, North Sea
Sandy			RP	South coast on A2
Sapco			RP	A2/W37, Midlands
Sapot			RP	W3D
Seaford	117.0	SFD	VOR	South coast on A2
Selsi			RP	Gatwick STARs
Setel			RP	North west of Pole Hill VOR
Shannon	113.3	SNN	VOR	SW Eire
Shapp			RP	Cumbria on B4
Shark			RP	Holding pattern Jersey Airport
Shepy			RP	Southend SRZ
Sider			RP	UG11, Reykjavik/Scottish
Silok			RP	Sumburgh Heli Routes
Silva			RP	UR4, North Sea
Sirgo			RP	UB29 – UR12
Sitet			RP	UA34, France/London boundary
Sitko			RP	B1 – UA37 – UB1
Skate			RP	UL74, North Sea
Skery			RP	On A25 S of BHD
Skeso			RP	UA25, France/London boundary
Slany			RP	G1 Dublin/London boundary
Slyda			RP	Irish Sea on B3
Smoki			RP	NE Scotland on W4D
Sotol			RP	UR4
Southampton	113.35	SAM	VOR	On airport
Spear			RP	Kent
Spike			RP	Aberdeen area
Spijkerboor	113.3	SPY	VOR	Holland
Sprat			RP	UA37
Stafa			RP	Eccleshall, Staffs
Stansted	359	SAN	NDB	Holding pattern for airport
Stornoway	115.1	STN	VOR	Outer Hebrides
Strumble	113.1	STU	VOR	Coast of SW Wales
Sudby			RP	London TMA
Swany			RP	Bristol Channel on UB40
Takas			RP	UN490 – SOTA
Talla	113.8	TLA	VOR	South Scotland
Tanet			RP	Kent on A37

Name	Frequency	Code	Type	Approximate location
Tawny			RP	Heathrow hold when Lambourne out of service
Telba			RP	UA25E/UA34, S of Crewe
Thorn			RP	Gatwick STARs
Tilby			RP	London TMA
Tilin			RP	London TMA
Tindi			RP	W6D, SE of Benbecula
Tirik			RP	Aberdeen area
Tivli			RP	UG4, Dublin/London boundary
Tolka			RP	UW39, Dublin/London boundary
Toppa			RP	UL74, London/Amsterdam boundary
Traca			RP	Heathrow Arrivals
Trent	115.7	TNT	VOR	North Midlands
Tripo			RP	R1, Essex coast
Trout			RP	B2D NE of Aberdeen
Tubot			RP	UR23, North Sea
Tunby			RP	London TMA
Tunel			RP	London TMA
Tunit			RP	Channel Islands CTZ
Turnberry	117.5	TRN	VOR	S of Prestwick
Tysti			RP	Aberdeen area
Ullap			RP	W6D – Inverness
Upton			RP	On B1, Yorkshire
Vatry			RP	R14 – UR14
Venom			RP	Manchester Zone
Vesta	116.6	VES	VOR	Denmark
Veule			RP	A1, French coast
Wallasey	114.1	WAL	VOR	Wirral Peninsula
Weald			RP	Heathrow hold when Biggin out of service
Welin			RP	Herts
Wescott	335	WCO	NDB	South Midlands
Whitegate	368.5	WHI	NDB	Manchester TMA, SW corner
Wick	113.6	WIK	VOR	Northern Scotland
Willo			RP	Holding pattern for Gatwick
Wizad			RP	West of Dover on W17
Wobun			RP	South Midlands
Woodley	352	WOD	NDB	G1/A1E, Berkshire
Worthing		WOR	RP	South coast

The Morse Code

A	• —	J	• — — —	S	• • •
B	— • • •	K	— • —	T	—
C	— • — •	L	• — • •	U	• • —
D	— • •	M	— —	V	• • • —
E	•	N	— •	W	• — —
F	• • — •	O	— — —	X	— • • —
G	— — •	P	• — — •	Y	— • — —
H	• • • •	Q	— — • —	Z	— — • •
I	• •	R	• — •		

Appendix 2

Airways frequency allocation

AIRWAYS AREA	CALLSIGN	FREQ	REMARKS (Freq as Directed)
A1 Turnberry – N54 30	*Scottish Control*	{ 126.25 128.5	◆0700–2145 ◆2145–0700
NB54 30 – Abm Stafford			
above FL155	*London Control*	{ 131.05	129.1, 134.425
at or below FL155	*Manchester Control*	126.65	124.2
Abm Stafford – Birmingham			
above FL135	*London Control*	133.7	134.425
at or below FL135	*Manchester Control*	124.2(a)	
Birmingham – Abm Woodley	*London Control*	133.7(a)	126.825
S of Woodley – FIR Boundary	*London Control*	127.7	124.275
A2 Between Talla and N54 30	*Scottish Control*	128.5	
Between N54 30 and Abm Lichfield			
above FL155	*London Control*	131.05	134.425
at or below FL155	*Manchester Control*	126.65	124.2
Between Abm Lichfield and Abm Birmingham			
above FL135	*London Control*	121.025	133.7, 134.425
at or below FL135	*Manchester Control*	124.2	
Between Abm Birmingham and Brookmans Park	*London Control*	121.025	133.7, 126.825
S of Brookmans Park to FIR Boundary	*London Control*	127.1	132.45
A20 FIR Bdry – Biggin	*London Control*	127.1	
Biggin – Abm Birmingham	*London Control*	121.025	133.7, 126.825
Abm Birmingham – Pole Hill			
above FL155	*London Control*	131.05	
at or below FL155	*Manchester Control*	124.2	126.65
A25 Dean Cross – N54 30	*Scottish Control*	{ 126.25 128.5	◆0700–2145 ◆2145–0700
N54 30 – REXAM			
above FL155	*London Control*	128.05	129.1, 134.425
at or below FL155	*Manchester Control*	133.05	125.1
REXAM – Cardiff	*London Control*	131.2	
Cardiff – N50 00	*London Control*	132.6	135.25
N50 00 – Southern Boundary of Channel Islands Zone	*Jersey Zone*	125.2	
A30 Within London FIR	*London Control*	127.1	
A34 Within London FIR	*London Control*	127.7	124.275
A37 Entire Route	*London Control*	129.6	127.95, 133.45, 133.525

AREA		CALLSIGN	FREQ	REMARKS (Freq as Directed)
A47	Pole Hill – Lichfield			
	above FL155	*London Control*	131.05	
	at or below FL155	*Manchester Control*	126.65	124.2
	Lichfield – Abm Birmingham			
	above FL135	*London Control*	133.7	
	at or below FL135	*Manchester Control*	124.2	
	Abm Birmingham – Woodley	*London Control*	133.7	121.025, 126.825
	S of Woodley – FIR Boundary	*London Control*	122.7	135.05, 124.275
B1	W of Wallasey			
	above FL155	*London Control*	128.05	129.1, 134.425
	at or below FL155	*Manchester Control*	133.05	
	Wallasey – BARTN			
	above FL155	*London Control*	128.05	134.425
	at or below FL155	*Manchester Control*	125.1	
	BARTN – Ottringham			
	above FL155	*London Control*	131.05	134.425
	at or below FL155	*Manchester Control*	126.65	124.2
	E of Ottringham	*London Control*	134.25	127.95, 133.525
B2	N of TMA	*Scottish Control*	124.5	
	S of TMA	*Scottish Control*	135.675	
B3	BEL – W005 00	*Scottish Control*	135.675	
	W005 00 – Wallasey			
	above FL155	*London Control*	128.05	129.1
	at or below FL155	*Manchester Control*	133.05	125.1
	Wallasey – STAFA			
	above FL155	*London Control*	128.05	129.1
	at or below FL155	*Manchester Control*	125.1	124.2
	STAFA – Abm Birmingham			
	above FL135	*London Control*	133.7(a)	121.025
	at or below FL135	*Manchester Control*	125.1(a)	124.2
	Abm Birmingham – Brookmans Park	*London Control*	133.7(a)	121.025, 126.825
	S of Brookmans Park – FIR Boundary	*London Control*	127.1	134.9
B4	Detling – Brookmans Park	*London Control*	127.1	134.9
	Brookmans Park – Abm Birmingham	*London Control*	121.025	133.7, 126.825
	Abm Birmingham – ROBIN			
	above FL135	*London Control*	121.025	133.7, 134.425
	at or below FL135	*Manchester Control*	124.2	126.65
	ROBIN – Pole Hill			
	above FL155	*London Control*	131.05	134.425
	at or below FL135	*Manchester Control*	124.2	126.65
	Pole Hill – N54 30			
	above FL155	*London Control*	131.05	134.425
	at or below FL155	*Manchester Control*	126.65	124.2
	N54 30 – GRICE	*Scottish Control*	{ 128.5	◆0700–2145
			135.675	◆2145–0700
B5	Entire Route	*London Control*	{ 134.25	
			127.95	
			133.525	
B11	Within London FIR	*London Control*	134.45	127.7, 124.275
B29	Within London FIR	*London Control*	129.6	127.95
B39	MALBY – RADNO	*London Control*	131.2	
	RADNO – TOLKA	*London Control*	128.05	
B53	Entire Route			
	above FL155	*London Control*	128.05	129.1

AREA		CALLSIGN	FREQ	REMARKS (Freq as Directed)
	at or below FL155	*Manchester Control*	125.1	124.2
B226	Entire Route	*Scottish Control*	124.5	
G1	W of Brecon	*London Control*	131.2	
	Brecon – Abm Woodley	*London Control*	132.8	131.2
	E of Abm Woodley – FIR boundary	*London Control*	134.9	127.1
G27	N of N50 00	*London Control*	127.7	124.275
R1	ORTAC – Ockham	*London Control*	134.45	132.3, 127.7, 124.275
	Ockham – FIR Boundary	*London Control*	129.6	127.95, 133.45, 133.525
R3	Wallasey – ROBIN			
	above FL155	*London Control*	128.05	129.1, 134.425
	at or below FL155	*Manchester Control*	125.1	124.2
R8	DAWLY – Southampton	*London Control*	132.6	124.275
	Southampton – Midhurst	*London Control*	134.45	132.3, 127.7, 124.275
	Midhurst – Dover	*London Control*	134.9	127.1, 124.275
R12	Entire Route	*London Control*	129.6	127.95, 133.45, 133.525
R14	Within London FIR	*London Control*	131.2	
R25	Entire Route	*London Control*	127.7	
R41	ORTAC – Southampton	*London Control*	134.45	132.3, 127.7, 124.275
	Southampton – Abm Compton	*London Control*	132.8	131.2, 124.275
	Abm Compton – Westcott	*London Control*	133.7	121.025
R84	Entire Route	*London Control*	134.45	132.3, 127.7, 124.275
R126	Entire Route	*London Control*	129.6	127.95
R803	Entire Route	*London Control*	127.7	124.275
W1	Daventry – Abm Barkway	*London Control*	121.025	133.7, 126.825
	Abm Barkway – 20nm N of Dover	*London Control*	129.6	127.95, 133.45, 133.525
W5	Honiley – 5nm N of Compton	*London Control*	133.7	129.2
	5nm N of Compton – 5nm S of Compton	*London Control*	132.8	133.6
	5nm S of Compton – PEPIS	*London Control*	134.45	135.05, 127.7
	20nm N of Dover – Dover	*London Control*	134.9	127.1
W923	Entire Route			
	above FL155	*London Control*	131.05	129.1, 134.425
	at or below FL155	*Manchester Control*	126.65	124.2
W934	Within London FIR	*London Control*	127.7	124.275

(a) Birmingham Zone Control 131.325 is delegated Controlling Authority for Daventry Control Area airspace within Airway **A1** and co-incident with the boundaries of Birmingham CTA/CTZ up to and including FL80.

UPPER ATS ROUTES

AREA		CALLSIGN	FREQ	REMARKS (Freq as Directed)
UA1	N of N54 30	*Scottish Control*	135.85	
	N54 30 – Abm Lichfield	*London Control*	131.05	129.1, 134.425
	Abm Lichfield – Abm Woodley	*London Control*	133.7	
	S of Woodley – UIR Boundary	*London Control*	127.7	124.275, 127.425
UA2	Machrihanish – N54 30	*Scottish Control*	135.85	
	N54 30 – Trent	*London Control*	131.05	129.1, 134.425
	Trent – Brookmans Park	*London Control*	133.7	121.025
	S of Brookmans Park – UIR Boundary	*London Control*	127.1	132.45, 127.425

AREA		CALLSIGN	FREQ	REMARKS (Freq as Directed)
UA20	Entire Route	*London Control*	127.1	
UA25	N of N54 30	*Scottish Control*	135.85	
	N54 30 – S of Wallasey	*London Control*	128.05	129.1, 134.425
	S of Wallasey – S of Brecon	*London Control*	133.6	
	S of Brecon – UIR Boundary	*London Control*	132.6	131.05, 134.425
UA29	BAKUR – MERLY	*London Control*	133.6	
	MERLY – SALCO	*London Control*	132.6	
UA30	Entire Route	*London Control*	127.1	127.425
UA34	Wallasey – TELBA	*London Control*	128.05	129.1
	TELBA – Abm Woodley	*London Control*	133.7	
	Abm Woodley – UIR Boundary	*London Control*	127.7	124.725, 127.425
UA37	DANDI – ABSIL	*Copenhagen Control*	134.675	
	ABSIL – Gabbard	*London Control*	134.25	128.125, 133.525
	Gabbard – Detling	*London Control*	129.6	133.525, 127.425
UA47	Daventry – Woodley	*London Control*	133.7	121.025
	S of Woodley – UIR Boundary	*London Control*	127.7	135.05, 127.425
UA251	Pole Hill – TELBA	*London Control*	131.05	129.1
	TELBA – EXMOR	*London Control*	133.6	
UB1	W of Wallasey	*London Control*	128.05	134.425
	Wallasey – Ottringham	*London Control*	131.05	134.425
	E of Ottringham	*London Control*	134.25	128.125, 133.525
UB2	DALKY – Perth	*Scottish Control*	135.85	126.85
	Perth – KLONN	*Scottish Control*	124.05	
UB3	Belfast – W005 00	*Scottish Control*	135.85	126.85
	W005 00 – N53 00	*London Control*	128.05	
	N53 00 – Brookmans Park	*London Control*	133.7	121.025
	Brookmans Park – Dover	*London Control*	127.1	134.9, 127.425
UB4	FINDO – N54 30	*Scottish Control*	135.85	
	N54 30 – ROBIN	*London Control*	131.05	134.425
	ROBIN – Brookmans Park	*London Control*	121.025	133.7
	S of Brookmans Park – UIR Boundary	*London Control*	127.1	132.45, 127.425
UB5*	N of FAMBO	*Scottish Control*	135.85	
	S of FAMBO	*London Control*	134.25	128.125, 133.525
UB10	Within London UIR	*London Control*	133.6	
UB11	Within London UIR	*London Control*	134.45	127.7, 124.275, 127.425
UB29	Abm Woodley – Abm Brookmans Park	*London Control*	133.6	132.8
	E of Abm Brookmans Park – UIR Boundary	*London Control*	129.6	127.95, 133.525, 127.425
UB39	Midhurst – RADNO	*London Control*	133.6	132.6
	RADNO – TOLKA	*London Control*	128.05	127.425
UB40	Entire Route	*London Control*	133.6	132.6
UB105	Entire London UIR	*London Control*	134.25	128.125, 133.525
UG1	W of Abm Woodley – UIR Boundary	*London Control*	133.6	132.8
	E of Abm Woodley – UIR Boundary	*London Control*	134.9	127.1, 127.425
UG2	Strumble to intersection with UB39	*London Control*	133.6	132.8, 131.2
UG4	Within London UIR	*London Control*	132.6	
UG11	Within Scottish UIR	*Scottish Control*	124.05	
UG106	Within London UIR	*London Control*	134.9	127.1, 127.425
UH70	Aberdeen – Wick – GONUT	*Scottish Control*	124.05	134.775
UH71	Sumburgh – LIRKI	*Scottish Control*	124.05	134.775
UH73	GRICE – Machrihanish	*Scottish Control*	135.85	126.85
UL1	W of Abm Woodley – UIR Boundary	*London Control*	133.6	132.8
	E of Abm Woodley – UIR Boundary	*London Control*	134.9	127.1, 127.425
UL7	N of SKATE	*Scottish Control*	124.05	
	S of SKATE	*London Control*	134.25	128.125
UL74	Entire Route	*London Control*	134.25	128.125
UL722	Entire Route	*London Control*	132.6	132.95

AREA		CALLSIGN	FREQ	REMARKS (Freq as Directed)
UR1	W of or Abm Lambourne	*London Control*	134.45	127.7, 132.3, 124.275
UR12				
UR123	E of Lambourne – UIR Boundary	*London Control*	129.6	127.95, 133.45, 133.525, 127.425
UR3	Entire Route	*London Control*	128.05	134.425
UR4	IOM – Pole Hill	*London Control*	128.05	134.425
	Pole Hill – Ottringham	*London Control*	131.05	134.425
	Ottringham – SOTOL	*London Control*	134.25	12.125, 133.525
	SOTOL – DANDI	*Copenhagen Control*	134.675	
UR8	Lands End – Southampton	*London Control*	132.6	124.275
	Southampton – Midhurst	*London Control*	134.45	132.3, 127.7, 124.275, 127.425
UR14	Within London UIR	*London Control*	132.6	133.6
UR23	Glasgow – SAB	*Scottish Control*	135.85	
	SAB – REKNA	*Scottish Control*	124.05	
	REKNA – GORDO	*Copenhagen Control*	134.675	
UR24	ORIST – ASPEN	*London Control*	134.45	132.3, 127.7
UR25	Entire Route	*London Control*	127.7	124.275
UR37	W of Southampton	*London Control*	132.6	124.275
	Southampton – Abm Midhurst	*London Control*	134.45	127.7, 132.3, 124.275
	E of Abm Midhurst	*London Control*	134.9	127.1, 124.275 127.425
UR38	Newcastle – N57 15	*Scottish Control*	135.85	126.85
	N57 15 – Stornoway	*Scottish Control*	124.05	134.775
UR41	ORTAC – Southampton	*London Control*	134.45	132.3, 127.7
	Southampton – Abm Woodley	*London Control*	132.8	131.2
	Abm Woodley – Westcott	*London Control*		121.025, 133.7, 127.425
UR72	Within London UIR	*London Control*	132.6	
UR84	Entire Route	*London Control*	132.3	127.7, 127.425
UR126	Entire Route	*London Control*	129.6	127.95, 133.525
UR168	Lands End – CAVAL	*London Control*	132.6	
UT7	Lands End – NOTRO	*London Control*	132.6	
	NOTRO – ASKIL	*Brest Control*	129.5	
UW1	Daventry – Abm Barkway	*London Control*	121.025	133.7
	Abm Barkway – Clacton	*London Control*	129.6	127.95, 133.45, 133.525
UW2	Compton – Brookmans Park	*London Control*	133.6	132.6, 127.425

* On these UPPER ATS ROUTES, or portions thereof, ATC radar service is normally provided to all co-operating civil and military aircraft and is co-ordinated at the Joint Air Traffic Control Radar Units. Aircraft will normally be instructed by London or Scottish ATCCs to communicate directly with a JATCRU:-

AREA		CALLSIGN	FREQ	REMARKS (Freq as Directed)
	BUCHAN	*Highland Radar*	134.1	
A1D	FIR Boundary – Stornoway	*Scottish Control*	127.275	
	Stornoway – Glasgow	*Scottish Control*	127.275	127.275
B2D	Within Scottish FIR	*Scottish Control*	131.3	
G4D	Within London FIR	*London Control*	132.6	
N552D	Entire Route	*Scottish Control*	127.275	127.275
N562D	Entire Route	*Scottish Control*	127.275	127.275
N571D	Entire Route	*Scottish Control*	127.275	127.275

	AREA	CALLSIGN	FREQ	REMARKS (Freq as Directed)
W2D	W of Fleetwood			
	above FL155	*London Control*	128.05	129.1, 134.425
	at or below FL155	*Manchester Control*	133.05	
	E of Fleetwood			
	above FL155	*London Control*	131.05	134.425
	at or below FL155	*Manchester Control*	126.65	124.2
W3D	S of Inverness	*Scottish Control*	124.5	
	Inverness – Sumburgh	*Scottish Control*	131.3	
W4D	Within Scottish FIR	*Scottish Control*	131.3	
W5D	Within Scottish FIR	*Scottish Control*	131.3	
W6D	Glasgow – W005 00	*Scottish Control*	127.275	127.275
	W005 00 – Inverness	*Scottish Control*	131.3	
W910D	Entire Route	*Scottish Control*	127.275	127.275
W911D	N of N54 30	*Scottish Control*	124.5(a)	
	S of N54 30			
	above FL155	*London Control*	128.05	129.1, 134.425
	at or below FL155	*Manchester Control*	133.05	
W927D	W of North Light			
	above FL155	*London Control*	128.05	129.1, 134.425
	at or below FL155	*Manchester Control*	133.05	
	E of North Light			
	above FL155	*London Control*	128.05	134.425
	at or below FL155	*Manchester Control*	133.05	
W928D	Entire Route	*Scottish Control*	135.675	
W958D	Entire Route	*Scottish Control*	127.275	127.275

(a) Communications will be with *Scottish Control* on 128.5 during the hours of operation of NRASA.

NORTHERN RADAR ADVISORY SERVICE AREA

N of W911D	*Scottish Radar*	124.5	
S of W911D	*Pennine Radar*	128.675	

HEBRIDES UPPER CONTROL AREA

S of line N57 30 W010 00 – TIR – N56 36 W004 10	*Scottish Control*	135.85	126.85
N of line N57 30 W010 00 – TIR – N56 36 W004 10	*Scottish Control*	124.05	

Appendix 3

VHF air band frequencies

Frequencies of airports and airfields

Aberdeen: Tower: 118.1 GMC: 121.7 Approach: 120.4 Radar: 121.25/128.3 ATIS: 121.85/114.30
Abingdon: Tower: 130.25 Also see Benson
Aberporth: AFIS: 122.15
Alderney: Tower: 125.35
Alicante: Tower: 118.15 GMC: 121.7 Approach: 118.8
Amsterdam: Tower: 118.1 GMC: 121.7 Approach: 121.2/131.15/119.05
Andrews Field: A/G: 130.55
Anglia Radar: 125.275/128.925
Audley End: A/G: 122.35 (By arrangement)
Barcelona: Tower: 118.1 GMC: 121.7 Approach: 119.1/124.7
Barrow: A/G: (Walney Island) 123.2
Barton: A/G: 122.70
Bedford: Tower: 130.0 Approach: 130.7 Radar: 124.4/118.375
Belfast (Aldergrove): Tower: 118.3 GMC: 121.75 Approach: 120.0 Radar: 120.9
Belfast City: Tower: 130.75 Approach: 130.85 Radar: 134.8
Bembridge, Isle of Wight: A/G: 123.25
Benbecula: Tower/Approach: 119.2
Benson: Tower: 122.1 Approach: 120.9 MATZ
Beverley/Linley: A/G: 123.05
Biggin Hill: Tower: 134.8 Approach: 129.4 ATIS: 121.875
Binbrook: Binbrook Tower 125.35
Birmingham: Tower: 118.3 GMC: 121.8 Approach: 131.325 Radar: 118.05 ATIS: 120.725
Blackbushe: AFIS: 122.3
Blackpool: Tower: 118.4 Approach: 135.95 Radar: 119.95
Bodmin: A/G: 122.7
Booker (Wycombe Air Park): AFIS: 126.55 GMC: 121.6
Border Radar: 133.875
Boscombe Down: Tower: 130.0 Approach: 126.7 Radar: 130.75
Bourn: A/G: 129.8
Bournemouth: Tower: 125.6 Approach: 118.65 Radar: 119.625 ATIS: 121.95 GMC: 121.7
Brawdy: MATZ 124.4
Bristol (Filton): Tower: 124.95 Approach: 122.725/127.975 Radar: 132.35
Bristol (Lulsgate): Tower: 133.85 Approach: 132.4 Radar: 124.35
Brize Norton: Radar: 134.3/119.0 Ops: 130.075
Brough: Tower: 130.55 Approach: 118.225
Brussels: Tower: 118.6 GMC: 121.875 Approach: 118.25/122.5/127.15
Caernarfon: A/G: 122.25
Cambridge: Tower: 122.2 Approach: 123.6 Radar: 130.75
Cardiff: Tower: 125.0 Approach: 125.85 Radar: 120.05 ATIS: 119.475
Carlisle: Tower/Approach: 123.6
Chivenor: MATZ: 130.20
Chichester (Goodwood): Tower: 120.65 Approach: 122.45
Church Fenton: Tower: 122.1 Approach: 126.5

Clacton: A/G: 122.325
Coltishall: MATZ: 125.9
Compton Abbas: A/G: 122.7
Coningsby: MATZ & Approach: 120.8
Copenhagen: Tower: 118.1/119.9 GMC: 121.9 Approach: 119.8/120.25/124.975
Cottesmore: MATZ: 130.2
Coventry: Tower/Approach: 119.25/124.8 Radar: 122.0 GMC: 121.7
Cranfield: Tower: 123.2 Approach/Radar: 122.85 ATIS: 121.875
Cranwell: MATZ: 119.0
Crowfield: A/G: 122.775
Culdrose: Tower: 122.1 Approach: 134.05 Radar: 123.3
Cumbernauld: AFIS: 120.6
Denham: A/G: 130.725
Doncaster: A/G: 122.9
Dounreay (Thurso): Tower/Approach: 122.4
Dublin: Tower: 118.6 GMC: 121.8 Approach: 121.1/119.55/118.5
Dundee: Tower/Approach: 122.9
Dunsfold: Tower: 124.325 Approach: 122.55 Radar: 122.55/119.825
Dunkeswell: A/G: 123.475
Duxford: AFIS: 122.075
Eaglescott: A/G: 123.0
Earls Colne: A/G: 122.425
Eastern Radar: 128.425/133.275
East Midlands/Castle Donington: Tower: 124.0 GMC: 121.9 Approach: 119.65 Radar: 120.125
Edinburgh: Tower: 118.7 GMC: 121.75 Approach: 121.2 Radar: 128.975 ATIS: 132.075
Elstree: A/G: 122.4
Enniskillen: (St.Angelo) A/G: 123.2
Enstone: A/G: 129.875
Exeter: Tower: 119.8 Approach: 128.15 Radar: 119.05
Fairoaks: A/G: 123.425
Falmouth Radar: 122.1
Farnborough: Tower: 122.5 Approach: 134.35 Radar: 130.05 Zone: 125.25 Ops: 130.575
Fenland: AFIS/A/G: 122.925
Finningley: Tower: 122.1 Approach: 120.35 Radar: 123.3
Flotta: A/G: 122.15
Ford: A/G: 122.0
Fowlmere: A/G: 123.25
Frankfurt: Tower: 119.9 GMC: 121.9 Approach: 118.5/120.15/119.15
Geneva: Tower: 118.7 GMC: 121.9 Approach: 131.325/130.15/121.3
Glasgow: Tower: 118.8 GMC: 121.7 Approach: 119.1 Radar: 119.3/121.3 ATIS: 115.4
Glenrothes: A/G: 130.45
Gloucestershire: Tower: 122.9 Radar: 125.65 ATIS: 121.85
Great Yarmouth (North Denes): Tower: 123.4
Guernsey: Tower: 119.95 Approach: 128.65 Radar: 118.9/124.5 GMC: 121.8 ATIS: 109.4
Halfpenny Green: GMC: 121.95 AFIS: 123.0
Hatfield: Tower: 130.8 Approach/Radar: 123.35 Radar: 119.3
Haverfordwest: A/G: 122.2
Hawarden: Tower: 124.95 Approach: 123.35 Radar: 129.85
Highland Radar: 134.1 135.175
Honington: MATZ: 129.05 (Common frequency for Mildenhall and Lakenheath)
Hucknall: A/G: 130.8
Humberside: Tower: 118.55 Approach: 124.675 Radar: 123.15 ATIS: 121.775
Inverness (Dalcross): Tower/Approach: 122.6
Ipswich: A/G: 118.325
Islay (Port Ellen): AFIS: 123.15
Isle of Man (Ronaldsway): Tower: 118.9 Approach/Radar: 120.85/118.2/125.3
Isle of Wight (Sandown): A/G: 123.5
Jersey: Tower: 119.45 GMC: 121.9 Approach: 120.3 Radar: 118.55/120.3 Zone: 125.2/120.45 ATIS: 112.2
Kent Radar: 129.45
Kinloss: Tower: 122.1 Approach: 119.35 Radar: 123.3
Kirkwall: Tower/Approach: 118.3

Lakenheath: MATZ 129.05
Lands End (St Just): Tower: 130.7
Lashenden (Headcorn): A/G: 122.0
Leavesden: Tower/Approach: 122.15 Radar: 121.4
Leeds-Bradford: Tower: 120.3 Approach: 123.75 Radar: 121.05 ATIS: 118.025
Leeming: Tower: 122.1 MATZ Approach Radar: 127.75
Lee-on-Solent: Tower: 135.7
Leicester: AFIS/A/G: 122.125
Lerwick (Tingwall): A/G: 122.6
Leuchars: Tower: 122.1 Approach: 126.5 Radar: 123.3 GMC: 120.8
Linton-on-Ouse: MATZ: 129.15 PAR: 123.3
Little Gransden: A/G: 130.85
Little Snoring: A/G: 122.4
Liverpool: Tower: 118.1 Approach/Radar: 119.85 Radar: 118.45
Llanbedr: Radar: 122.5
London (City): Tower: 118.075/119.425 Approach: 132.7 Radar: 128.025
London Control: See Appendix 2
London Gatwick: Tower: 124.225 GMC: 121.8 Approach: 119.6 Radar: 125.875/118.6/129.275/134.225 ATIS:
    128.475 GMP: 121.95
London Heathrow: Tower: 118.7/118.5 GMC: 121.9/121.7 Approach/Radar: 119.2/120.4/119.5/127.55/
    119.9 ATIS: 133.075 ATIS: 113.75/115.1
London Stansted: Tower: 123.8 Approach: 125.55 Radar: 126.95/123.8 ATIS: 127.175 GMC: 121.725
London (Westland Heliport): Battersea Tower: 122.9
Londonderry (Eglinton): Tower: 122.85 Approach: 123.625
Lossiemouth: Tower: 118.9 Approach: 119.35 Radar: 123.3
Luton: Tower: 119.975 GMC: 121.75 Approach: 129.55/128.75 Radar: 127.3 ATIS: 120.575
Lydd: Tower/Approach: 120.7 Radar: 131.3
Lyneham: Tower: 118.425 Approach: 118.425 Radar: 123.3
Machrihanish: Tower: 122.1 Approach: 122.1/125.9 Radar: 123.3
Madrid: Tower: 118.15 GMC: 121.7 Approach: 119.9/120.9/127.1
Malaga: Tower: 118.15 GMC: 121.7 Approach: 118.45
Manchester International: Tower: 118.625 Approach: 119.4 Radar: 121.35 GMC: 121.7/121.85 ATIS: 128.175
Manston: Tower: 128.775/122.1 Approach: 126.35/129.45 Radar: 123.3/118.525
Marham: Tower: 122.1 Approach: 124.15 Radar: 123.3
Marston Moor: A/G: 122.975
Midland Radar (North Luffenham): 132.25
Mildenhall: Tower: 122.55 Approach: 129.05 Radar: 123.3
Mona: 122.0
Montgomeryshire/Welshpool: A/G: 123.25
Netherthorpe: A/G: 123.275
Newcastle: Tower: 119.7 Approach: 126.35 Radar: 118.5 ATIS: 114.25
Newtonards: A/G: 123.5
Northampton (Sywell): AFIS/A/G: 122.7
Northolt: Tower: 134.15 Approach: 134.15 Radar: 130.35/129.125/124.975
Norwich: Tower: 124.25 Approach: 119.35 Radar: 118.475
Nottingham: A/G: 122.8
Old Sarum: A/G: 123.575
Old Warden (Shuttleworth Collection): 123.05
Ostend: Tower: 118.7 GMC: 121.9 Approach: 120.6
Oxford: Tower: 118.875 Approach: 125.325 GMC: 121.75 ATIS: 121.95
Pailton (Rugby): Radio Test Centre 126.05 (By arrangement)
Palma: Tower: 118.3 GMC: 121.7 Approach: 119.4/119.15/118.95
Panshanger: A/G: 120.25
Paris (Charles de Gaulle): Tower: 119.25 GMC: 121.6/126.65 Approach: 121.15/119.85/118.15
Paris (Le Bourget): Tower: 119.1 GMC: 121.9 Approach: 121.15/119.85/118.15
Paris (Orly): Tower: 118.7/121.05 GMC: 121.7 Approach: 120.85/118.85/124.45
Paull: A/G: 123.0
Pennine Radar: 128.675
Penzance Heliport: A/G: 118.1
Perranporth: A/G: 119.75
Perth (Scone): Tower: 119.8 Approach: 122.3
Peterborough (Conington): A/G: 129.725

Peterborough (Sibson): A/G: 122.3
Plymouth (Roborough): Tower: 122.6 Approach: 133.55
Popham: A/G: 129.8
Portland Radar: 124.15
Prestwick: Tower: 118.15 GMC: 121.8 Approach: 120.55 Radar: 119.45 ATIS: 127.125
Redhill: AFIS: 120.275
Rome (Fiumicino): Tower: 118.7/119.3 GMC: 121.9 Approach: 119.2
St Mawgan: Tower: 123.4 Approach: 122.1/126.5 Radar: 125.55/123.3
Sandtoft: A/G: 130.425
Scatsta: Tower/Approach: 123.6 Radar: 122.4
Scilly Isles: Tower: 123.15
Scottish Control: See Appendix 2
Seething: A/G: 122.6
Shannon: Tower: 118.7 GMC: 121.8 Approach: 121.4/120.2
Shanwick Radio: 127.9/123.95/127.65/135.525/133.8
Shawbury: Tower: 122.10 Approach: 124.15
Sherburn-in-Elmet: A/G: 122.6
Shetland Radar: 118.15
Shipdham: A/G: 119.55
Shobdon: A/G: 123.5
Shoreham: Tower: 125.4 Approach: 123.15 ATIS: 121.75
Skegness: A/G: 130.45
Sleap: A/G: 122.45
Silverstone: A/G: 121.075
Southampton: Tower: 118.2 Approach: 128.85 Zone: 120.225/131.0 ATIS: 113.350
Southend: Tower: 127.725 Approach: 128.95 Radar: 125.05 ATIS: 121.8
Skegness: A/G: 130.45
Stapleford Tawney: A/G: 122.8
Stornoway: Tower/Approach: 123.5
Sturgate: A/G: 130.3
Sumburgh: Tower: 118.25 Approach: 123.15 Radar: 118.15/119.25/130.05 ATIS: 125.85
Swansea: Tower/Approach: 119.7 Radar: 120.75
Strubby Heliport, Lincolnshire: A/G: 122.375
Tatenhill: A/G: 122.2
Tees-side: Tower: 119.8 Approach: 118.85 Radar: 128.85
Thames Radar: 132.7
Thruxton: A/G: 130.45
Tiree: AFIS: 122.7
Tresco: A/G: 130.25
Turweston: A/G: 122.175
Unst: Tower/Approach: 130.35 Ops: 123.45
Upper Heyford: MATZ: 128.55
Valley: Tower: 122.1 Approach: 134.35
Waddington: Approach: 127.35 Radar: 123.3
Warton: Tower: 130.8 Approach: 124.45
Wattisham: Tower: 122.1 Approach: 135.2 Radar: 123.3
Wellesbourne Mountford: A/G: 130.45
West Freugh: Tower: 122.55 Approach/Radar: 130.05/130.725
West Malling: Tower: 130.875
Weston Super Mare: Tower: 122.5 Approach: 129.25
White Waltham: A/G: 122.6
Wick: Tower/Approach: 119.7
Wickenby: A/G: 122.45
Wigtown: A/G: 123.05
Wittering: MATZ: 130.2 (Cottesmore)
Woodford: Tower: 126.925 Approach: 130.05 Radar: 130.75
Woodvale: Tower: 119.75 Approach: 121.0
Wycombe Air Park (Booker): A/G: 126.55 GMC: 121.775
Wyton: MATZ: 134.05/123.3
Yeovil (Judwin): Tower: 125.4 Approach: 130.8
Yeovilton: MATZ: 127.35
Zurich: Tower: 118.1/119.7 GMC: 121.9 Approach: 118.0/120.75/119.7/125.95/127.75

Airband frequencies in numerical order
MHz

118.00	
118.05	Birmingham Radar
118.075	London (City) Tower
118.10	Liverpool Tower/Aberdeen Tower/Penzance Heliport/Scilly Isles
118.15	Prestwick Tower/Sumburgh Radar
118.20	Ronaldsway Radar/Southampton Tower
118.225	Brough Approach
118.25	Sumburgh Tower/Dublin ATIS
118.30	Birmingham Tower/Belfast (Aldergrove) Tower/Kirkwall Tower/Approach
118.325	Ipswich Tower & Approach
118.35	
118.40	Blackpool Tower
118.425	Biggin Hill AFIS/Lyneham Tower
118.45	Liverpool Radar
118.50	Heathrow Tower/Newcastle Radar/Dublin Radar
118.55	Jersey Tower/Humberside Tower
118.60	Gatwick Radar/Dublin Tower
118.625	Manchester Tower
118.65	Bournemouth Radar
118.70	Edinburgh Tower/Heathrow Tower/Shannon Tower
118.75	
118.80	Glasgow Tower/Cork Radar
118.825	Dunsfold Radar
118.85	Tees-side Approach
118.875	Oxford Tower
118.90	Guernsey Radar/Isle of Man Tower/Norwich Tower
118.95	Gatwick Radar
119.00	RAF Common Frequency
119.05	Exeter Radar
119.10	Glasgow Approach
119.20	Heathrow Approach/Benbecula Tower
119.25	Coventry Tower/Sumburgh Radar
119.30	Cork Tower/Hatfield Radar
119.35	Lossiemouth Approach/Norwich Approach
119.40	Manchester Approach
119.425	London (City) Tower
119.45	Jersey Tower/Prestwick Radar
119.475	Cardiff Information
119.50	Heathrow Approach
119.55	Dublin Radar
119.60	Gatwick Approach/Prestwick Approach
119.65	Castledon Approach
119.70	Swansea Tower/Approach/Wick Tower/Newcastle Tower
119.75	Perranporth A/G/Woodvale Tower
119.80	Exeter Tower/Perth Tower/Tees-side Tower
119.85	Liverpool Approach/Radar

119.875	Scottish FIS
119.90	Heathrow Radar/Cork Approach
119.95	Blackpool Radar/Guernsey Tower
119.975	Luton Tower
120.00	Belfast (Aldergrove) Approach
120.05	Cardiff Radar
120.10	Brussels Radar
120.125	Castledon Radar
120.20	Shannon Approach
120.225	Southampton Radar
120.25	Panshanger A/G
120.30	Jersey Approach/Leeds Tower
120.35	Finningley Radar
120.40	Aberdeen Approach/Heathrow Radar
120.45	Jersey Zone/North Denes
120.50	
120.55	Prestwick Approach
120.575	Luton ATIS
120.60	Cumbernauld Tower/Ostend Approach
120.65	Goodwood Tower
120.70	Lydd Approach
120.725	Birmingham ATIS
120.75	Swansea Radar
120.80	Coningsby Radar/Leuchars GMC
120.85	Ronaldsway Approach/Radar
120.90	Belfast (Aldergrove) Radar/Benson Approach
120.95	
121.00	Heathrow Tower/Woodvale Approach
121.025	London Control (Daventry sector)
121.05	Leeds Radar
121.075	Silverstone A/G
121.10	Dublin Approach
121.15	
121.20	Edinburgh Approach
121.25	Aberdeen Radar/Manston Tower
121.30	Glasgow Radar
121.35	Manchester Radar
121.40	Leavesden Radar/Shannon Radar
121.45	
121.50	DISTRESS
121.55	
121.60	Fire and Rescue Services/Wycombe GMC
121.65	
121.70	Heathrow GMC/Manchester Tower/Aberdeen GMC/Glasgow GMC/Bournemouth GMC
121.75	Luton Tower/Aldergrove GMC/Edinburgh GMC
121.775	Humberside ATIS
121.80	Birmingham GMC/Dublin GMC
121.85	Aberdeen ATIS
121.90	Jersey GMC/Heathrow GMC/Castledon GMC
121.95	Halfpenny Green GMC/Gatwick GMC GMP/Oxford ATIS/Bournemouth ATIS
122.00	Coventry Radar/Ford Tower/Lashenden Tower/Wattisham

	Tower/Baldonnel Approach/Mona AFIS
122.05	BA Ops
	Newcastle/Brymon/Heavylift/ Keenair
122.10	Benson Tower/Brize Norton Radar/Church Fenton Tower/ Culdrose Tower/Finningley Tower/ Leuchars Tower/Lyneham Radar/ Shawbury Tower
122.15	Flotta/Leavesden Tower/Approach/ Aberporth AFIS
122.20	Huddersfield (Crossland Moor)/ Tatenhill/Cambridge Tower/Haverfordwest
122.25	Leicester/Rochester/Caenarfon/Brent Oilfield, North Sea
122.30	Blackbushe/Bristol Filton Tower/ Lands End St Just A/G/Perth (Scone) Approach/Sibson
122.325	Clacton A/G
122.35	Hethel/Audley End/Airbridge Ops/Gulf Air Ops
122.375	Strubby Heliport (Lincs) Management Aviation
122.40	Little Snoring/Elstree/Dounreay Tower & Approach/Scatsta Radar
122.425	Earls Colne A/G
122.45	Belfast (City) Radar/Goodwood Approach/Sleap/Wickenby
122.50	Farnborough Tower/Weston Super Mare Tower
122.55	Dunsfold Approach/Mildenhall/West Freugh Tower
122.60	Inverness Tower/Plymouth (Roborough) Tower/Seething/ Sherburn-in-Elmet Tower/Swansea Tower/White Waltham
122.65	
122.70	Barton/Compton Abbas/Sywell/ Silverstone/Bodmin/Tiree
122.75	
122.80	Nottingham/Stapleford Tawney/ Heather Oilfield Scotland/Cranfield Approach/Eglinton Tower/ Approach
122.875	Dan-Air Lasham
122.90	Battersea Heliport/Dundee Tower/St Mawgan Tower/Staverton Tower/ Doncaster
122.925	Fenland
122.95	Stourport Heliport/Ekofisk Oilfield North Sea/BIH Aberdeen/Lasham
123.00	Halfpenny Green/Paull
123.05	Beverley A/G/Peterhead Heliport (Brittair)/Stevenage/Old Warden Shuttleworth Collection/West Sole and Viking Oilfields/Shipdham/ Wigtown A/G
123.10	Search and Rescue (Scene of Search) Frequency
123.15	Humberside Approach/Shoreham Tower/Sumburgh Approach/Port Ellen
123.20	Cranfield Tower/Barrow Tower
123.25	Isle of Wight (Bembridge)/ Bridlington/Ipswich
123.30	Culdrose Radar/Finningley Radar/ Leuchars Radar/Marham Radar/ Machrihanish Radar/Manston Radar/St Mawgan Radar/Shawbury Radar/Topcliffe Tower/Valley Radar/Wattisham Radar
123.35	Hatfield Approach/Hawarden Approach
123.40	
123.425	Fairoaks
123.45	Great Yarmouth (North Denes)/ Redhill/Bristol Helicopters
123.475	Dunkeswell A/G
123.50	Duxford/Isle of Wight Sandown/ Netherthorpe/ Newtownards/ Shobdon/Stornoway/Strathallan
123.55	Various oil rigs in the North Sea
123.575	Old Sarum A/G
123.60	Cambridge Approach/Carlisle Tower & Approach/Alderney Tower
123.65	Gamston/Coal Aston (Sheffield)/ Heathrow Executive Handling/ Wrexham/Brymon Ops
123.70	Amsterdam Radar
123.75	Leeds Approach
123.80	Stansted Tower
123.85	Amsterdam Control
123.90	London Control/Inbounds via Willo
123.95	Oceanic Clearance for Aircraft registered west of 30°W
124.00	Castledon Tower
124.05	Scottish Control
124.10	
124.15	Marham Radar/Portland Radar/ Shawbury Approach/Ternhill
124.20	Manchester Control
124.225	Gatwick Tower
124.25	Norwich Radar
124.275	London Control (Hurn Sector)
124.30	Amsterdam FIS
124.325	Dunsfold Tower
124.35	Bristol (Lulsgate) Radar
124.40	Bedford Radar/Brawdy Radar/ Topcliffe Radar
124.45	Warton Radar
124.50	Guernsey Radar/Scottish Control
124.55	Copenhagen Control
124.60	London Flight Information (East of Alpha One)
124.65	Dublin Control
124.70	Shannon Control
124.75	London Flight Information (West of Alpha One)
124.80	Coventry GMC
124.85	

124.90	Manston Tower	127.175	Stansted ATIS
124.95	Hawarden Tower/Bristol Filton Tower	127.20	Zurich Volmet
125.00	Cardiff Tower/Brussels Control South Sector	127.25	Cotswold Radar
		127.275	Scottish FIS
125.05	Southend Radar	127.30	Luton Radar
125.10	Manchester Control	127.35	Waddington Radar/Yeovilton Radar
125.15	Paris Radio (Met) (in French)	127.40	Bremen Met/Marseille Met
125.20	Jersey Zone	127.45	Milan Control
125.25	Farnborough Zone	127.50	Shannon Control
125.275	Anglia Radar	127.55	Heathrow Radar
125.30	Ronaldsway Radar	127.60	Barcelona Met/Frankfurt Met
125.35	Boscombe Down Approach/Binbrook Tower/Middle Wallop MATZ	127.65	Oceanic Clearance for Aircraft registered east of 30°W (including Australia)
125.40	Shoreham Tower/Yeovil (Judwin) Tower	127.70	London Control Southern England and Cross Channel
125.45	Paris Control		
125.50	Moscow Control	127.725	Southend Tower
125.55	St Mawgan Radar/Stansted Zone	127.75	Leeming MATZ/Air UK Ops
125.60	Bournemouth Tower	127.80	Brussels Met/Athens Met
125.65	Staverton Radar	127.85	Reims Control
125.70	Paris Information (North)	127.90	Shanwick Radio
125.725	Scottish Volmet	127.95	London Control (Clacton Sector)
125.75	Amsterdam Radar	127.975	Filton Approach
125.80	London Control Radar Departures via Brookmans Park and Clacton	128.00	Dublin Control
		128.025	London (City) Radar
125.85	Cardiff Approach	128.05	London Control Pole Hill/Irish Sea
125.875	Gatwick Radar	128.10	Paris Control
125.90	Coltishall Radar/Machrihanish Approach	128.125	London Control (North Sea)
		128.15	Exeter Approach
125.95	London Control Inbounds via Lambourne	128.175	Manchester ATIS
		128.20	Brussels East
126.00	Paris Radio (Met) (in English)	128.25	London Military
126.05	Pailton Test (Near Rugby)	128.30	Aberdeen Radar/Netheravon A/G
126.10	North Sea Radio	128.35	Dutch Military
126.15	Dusseldorf Control	128.40	London Control departures via Detling/Pisa Volmet
126.20	Amsterdam Met/Madrid Met		
126.25	Scottish Control (TMA)	128.425	Eastern Radar
126.30	London Control Inbounds via Bovingdon	128.45	Manston Approach
		128.475	Gatwick ATIS
126.35	Newcastle Approach/Manston Radar	128.50	Scottish Control (TMA)
126.40	Bordeaux Radio (Met) (in English)	128.55	Upper Heyford
126.45	London Control Inbounds via Biggin	128.60	London Volmet South/Oslo Met
126.50	Church Fenton Approach/Coningsby MATZ/Leuchars Approach/St Mawgan Approach	128.65	Guernsey Approach
		128.70	London Military Radar
		128.75	Luton Approach
126.55	Wycombe Air Park (Booker)	128.80	Brussels Control
126.60	London Volmet North/Milan Volmet	128.85	Southampton Tower/Approach/ Tees-side Director
126.65	Manchester Control		
126.70	Lydd Tower	128.90	London Control (TMA NW Outbound)
126.75	Brussels (West Sector)	128.925	Anglia Radar
126.80	Geneva Met	128.95	Southend Approach
126.825	London Control (London TMA)	128.975	Edinburgh Radar
126.85	Scottish (South West)	129.00	Brest Control
126.90	Brussels Information	129.05	Honington MATZ
126.925	Woodford Tower	129.10	London Control (Pole Hill/Irish Sea)
126.95	Stansted Approach	129.125	Northolt Radar
127.00	Dublin Volmet/Ankara Met/ Copenhagen Met	129.15	Linton-on-Ouse MATZ
		129.20	London Control (Daventry)
127.05	Frankfurt Control	129.25	
127.10	London Control Lydd Sector West	129.30	Amsterdam Control
127.15	Brussels Departures	129.35	Paris Control

129.40	Biggin Hill Tower		130.95	Marseille Control
129.45	Kent Radar		131.00	Southampton Radar
129.50	Delta Ops		131.05	London Control North East UIR (Pole Hill)
129.55	Luton Approach			
129.60	London Control (Clacton Sector)		131.10	Brussels Control (West Sector)
129.625	TWA Ops		131.15	Shannon Control (Cork Sector)
129.65	Brussels Control East Sector		131.20	London Control (Strumble Sector)
129.70	Britannia Ops/World/KLM/Fort William Heliport		131.25	Rome Control
			131.30	Lydd (Ferryfield) Radar/Scottish Control (Stornoway)
129.725	Peterborough/Conington A/G			
129.75	BMA Ops/UK Gatwick/Air Express/Filton Ops		131.35	Paris Control North
			131.40	Air India/CSA Ops
129.80	Humberside Tower/Popham/Bourn Air		131.425	Saudia Ops (Heathrow)
			131.45	Company Frequencies: Air Canada/NLM/UK/Alitalia
129.85	Hawarden Radar/West Malling			
129.875	Enstone		131.50	Aer Lingus Ops/KLM London/Air France
129.90	Hang Gliders/Balloons			
129.95	Cormorant Rigs, Scotland, North Sea		131.55	Ryanair Ops
129.975	Gliders		131.575	BMA Ops
130.00	Bedford (Thurleigh) Tower/Boscombe Down Tower		131.60	TWA Ops/Air India Ops/Field Aviation
130.05	Farnborough Radar/Sumburgh Director/Woodford Approach/West Freugh Approach		131.625	British Airways Ops
			131.65	KLM Schipol
			131.70	Swissair Ops/SAS Ops
130.075	Servisair Gatwick/Air Malta Ops		131.675	Britannia Ops
130.10	Gliders		131.75	Aer Lingus Ops
130.125	Gliders		131.775	Aeroflot Ops
130.15	Deptford Down (Salisbury Plain) Ops		131.80	British Airways Speedbird Ops (Shuttle)
130.20	Cottesmore Radar/Chivenor Radar/ Ninian Oilfield		131.85	British Airways Ops
			131.875	Dan-Air Gatwick
130.25	Abingdon Tower		131.90	British Airways Speedbird Ops (Overseas)
130.275	Henstridge			
130.30	Oxford Approach/Sturgate		131.925	Lufthansa (Heathrow)
130.35	Northolt Radar (On request)		131.95	Iberia Airlines Ops/Sabena Ops/El Al Ops
130.375	Air Hanson Ops			
130.40	Gliders		131.975	British Airways Ops (Glasgow)
130.425	Halton/Unicom for Emergency Controlling Authorities		132.00	Paris Control
			132.05	London Control TMA (Inbounds via Ockham)
130.45	Thruxton/Skegness Common Frequency/Wellesbourne			
			132.075	Edinburgh ATIS
130.475	Retford/Gamston		132.10	Paris Control
130.50	Cowes Week Heliport/Henley Regatta, etc		132.15	Shannon Control
			132.20	
130.55	Brough Tower/Andrews Field/Brands Hatch (Shawline Ops)		132.25	Midland Radar (North Luffenham)
			132.30	London Control (Hurn Sector)
130.575	Farnborough Exec		132.35	Dutch Military/Bristol (Filton) Radar
130.60	British Caledonian Ops/Servisair Ops			
130.625	BAF Ops West		132.40	Bristol Approach
130.65	Dan-Air Ops/Air 2000 Ops		132.45	London Airways (Lydd Sector)
130.70	Bedford (Thurleigh) Approach/Land's End Tower		132.50	
			132.55	Madrid Control
130.725	Freugh Radar		132.60	London Control (SW Approaches)
130.75	Belfast (City) Tower/Boscombe Down Radar/Cambridge Radar/Woodford Radar		132.65	Coastguard
			132.70	Thames Radar
			132.75	
130.80	Hatfield Tower/Hucknall/Samlesbury Tower/Warton Tower/Yeovil (Judwin) Approach		132.80	London Control (Bristol Sector)
			132.85	
			132.90	Pennine Radar
130.85	Belfast City Approach/Bristol (Filton) Approach		132.95	Moscow Control
130.90	Rome Radar		133.00	Brest Control

133.05	Manchester Control Airways Low Level Bravo 1	134.50	
133.075	Heathrow ATIS	134.55	Chelmsford Heliport/Rivenhall Heliport
133.10	Bordeaux Control	134.60	Zurich Control
133.15	Cotswold Radar	134.65	
133.20	Scottish FIS	134.70	London FIS North of Blue 1
133.25	Maastricht Control	134.75	
133.30	London Military Radar	134.80	Rhein Control
133.35		134.85	Border Radar RAF Boulmer
133.40	Manchester Control	134.90	London Control (Dover Sector)
133.45	London Control (Clacton)	134.95	
133.50	Paris Control North	135.00	
133.525	London Control (North Sea)	135.05	London Control (Hurn Sector)
133.55	Plymouth Approach	135.10	
133.60	London Control (Strumble)	135.15	London Military Radar
133.65	Rhein Control	135.175	Highland Radar
133.70	London Control (Daventry West Sector)	135.20	Wattisham Approach
		135.25	London Control (Cardiff Sector)
133.75	Madrid Control	135.275	Eastern Radar
133.80	Oceanic Tracks Broadcast	135.30	Paris Control North
133.85	Maastricht Control/Bristol Tower	135.35	Dusseldorf Information
133.875	Border Radar	135.375	London Volmet Main
133.90	London Military Radar	135.40	
133.95	Maastricht Control	135.45	Maastricht Control
133.975	Luton Arr ATIS	135.50	Reims Control
134.00	Scottish FIS	135.525	Shanwick Oceanic (Clearances)
134.05	Wyton Radar/Culdrose Approach	135.55	
134.10	Highland Radar	135.60	Shannon Control
134.15	Northolt Approach	135.65	Brest Control
134.20	Rome Control	135.675	Scottish Control
134.225	Gatwick Radar	135.70	Lee on Solent Tower
134.25	London Control North East Bravo 1 East of Ottringham	135.75	
		135.80	Paris Control
134.30	Brize Radar/Highland Radar	135.85	Scottish Control
134.35	Valley Radar/Farnborough Radar	135.90	Paris Control
134.40	Reims Control	135.95	Blackpool Approach
134.425	London Control (Pole Hill/Irish Sea)	136.80	Airtours Ops
134.45	London Control (Hurn Sector)		

Appendix 4

UHF air band frequencies

This listing has been compiled from official sources available to the general public. There are of course many other allocations, including air-to-air refuelling, TADs, Ops and satellite communications. The information reflects a major change during 1992 right across the NATO air forces. The spacing between channels has been reduced to 25 kHz, effectively doubling the number of frequencies available.

Frequencies of Military Airfields

Aberdeen: Approach/Radar: 353.55
Aberporth: AFIS: 259.0
Abingdon: Tower: 344.6 Approach/Radar: 358.8/315.75/344.0
Alconbury: Tower: 383.45 GMC: 259.825 Approach (Wyton): 362.375/375.525 Ops: 342.225/364.675/284.925
Aldergrove: Tower/Approach: 310.0 Ops: 241.825
Barkston Heath: Tower: 342.075 Approach: 340.525
Bedford: Tower: 337.925 Approach: 383.625/362.2 PAR: 386.725
Benson: Tower: 279.35 Approach/Radar: 268.825/361.875/358.8
Bentwaters: Tower: 264.925 GMC: 244.775 Approach: 362.075/258.975 PAR: 368.325 OPS: 356.825/282.15 ATIS: 341.65
Binbrook: Tower: 311.4
Border Radar: 275.625
Boscombe Down: Tower: 370.1 Approach/Radar: 291.65/380.025/276.85 PAR: 381.125 ATIS: 279.325
Boulmer: A/G: 299.1/282.8
Brawdy: Tower: 249.95 GMC: 259.95 Approach/Radar: 367.95/254.75/358.5 PAR: 340.15/268.4
Bristol Filton: Tower: 342.025 Approach/Radar: 256.125/336.475
Brize Norton: Tower: 381.2 GMC: 370.3 Approach/Radar 342.45/356.875 PAR: 338.65/385.4 Ops: 357.475 ATIS: 254.475
Brough: Tower: 310.35 Approach/Radar: 379.775
Cambridge: Tower/Radar: 372.425
Cardiff: Approach/Radar: 277.225
Chivenor: Tower: 362.45 GMC: 379.925 Approach/Radar: 364.775/340.0/376.675/312.425 PAR: 356.175
Church Fenton: Tower: 262.7 GMC: 340.2 Approach/Radar: 300.775/282.075/381.075/292.8/358.85 PAR: 366.725/385.4
Coltishall: Tower: 339.95/142.29 GMC: 296.725 Approach/Radar: 379.275/342.25/293.425 PAR: 275.975/254.25 Ops: 364.8
Coningsby: Tower: 275.875 GMC: 358.55 Approach/Radar: 312.225/344.625/262.95 PAR: 300.925/337.975
Cosford: Tower: 357.125 Approach: 276.125
Cottesmore: Tower: 370.05 GMC: 336.375 Approach/Radar: 312.075/340.575/358.725/376.575 PAR: 262.9/337.875
Cowden Range: 241.775/260.0
Cranfield: Tower: 341.8 Approach/Radar: 362.15

Cranwell: Tower: 379.525 GMC: 297.9 Approach/Radar: 340.475/250.05/282.0 PAR: 383.475/285.15
Croughton: A/G: 343.6
Culdrose: Tower: 380.225 GMC: 299.4 Approach/Radar: 241.95/339.95/379.5 PAR: 358.7/259.75 ATIS:
    372.3
Dishforth: Tower: 259.825 Approach: 379.675 Ops: 252.9
Donna Nook Range: 232.075/342.175
Dunsfold: Tower: 375.4 Approach/Radar: 367.375/312.625
Eastern Radar: 229.975
Edinburgh: Tower: 257.8 Radar: 362.3
Fairford: Tower: 337.575/142.225 GMC: 259.975 Approach/Radar (Brize): 342.45/376.625 Ops:
    379.475/307.8/371.2/259.4
Farnborough: Tower: 357.4 Approach/Radar: 336.275/315.525 PAR: 259.0 Ops: 379.975
Finningley: Tower: 379.55 GMC: 340.175 Approach/Radar: 358.775/285.125/315.5 PAR: 383.5/385.4
Garvie Range: 337.95
Glasgow: Radar: 362.3
Halton: Aero Club: 356.275
Hatfield: Tower: 359.45 Approach/Radar: 343.7
Hawarden: Tower: 336.325
Holbeach Range: 343.375/360.45
Honington: Tower: 282.275 GMC: 241.975 Approach/Radar: 338.975/254.875/315.575/309.95 PAR: 358.75
Inverness: Approach: 362.3
Jurby Range: 337.6/376.6
Kinloss: Tower: 336.35 Approach/Radar: 259.975/311.325 PAR: 370.05/376.525 Ops: 259.825
Lakenheath: Tower: 358.675 GMC: 397.975 Approach/Radar: 315.575/398.35 PAR:
    243.6/309.075/290.825/262.925/338.675/149.65 Ops: 300.825/398.2/259.4
Leconfield: A/G: 244.875/282.8
Leeming: Tower: 344.575 GMC: 338.85 Approach/Radar: 337.825/292.7/358.65 PAR: 336.35/309.875 Ops:
    356.725
Lee-on-Solent: Tower: 315.65
Leuchars: Tower: 258.925 GMC: 259.85 Approach/Radar: 262.7/292.475/PAR: 370.075/268.775 Ops:
    285.025
Linton-on-Ouse: Tower: 300.425 GMC: 340.025 Approach/Radar: 362.675/292.8/344.475/381.075
    PAR: 358.525/259.875
Llanbedr: Tower: 380.175 Approach/Radar: 386.675 PAR: 370.3
London Military: Initial Contact Frequency: North: 292.525 South: 275.475 Pole Hill/Irish Sea: 231.625
    Daventry: 291.8 Clacton: 264.475 Dover/Lydd: 277.95 Seaford/Hurn: 255.4 London Upper: 235.05
Lossiemouth: Tower: 337.75 GMC: 299.4 Approach/Radar: 376.65/398.1/259.975/311.325
    PAR: 250.05/312.4
Luton: Approach: 259.875
Lyneham: Tower: 386.825 GMC: 340.175 Approach/Radar: 359.5/345.025/300.475 PAR: 375.2 Ops: 254.65
    ATIS: 381.0
Machrihanish: Tower: 358.6 Approach/Radar: 344.525/259.925 PAR: 337.975
Manston: Tower: 344.35 Approach/Radar: 379.025/338.625 PAR: 312.325
Marham: Tower: 337.9 Approach/Radar: 291.95/293.775 PAR: 379.65 Ops: 312.55
Merryfield: Tower: 312.7
Middle Wallop: Tower: 372.625 Approach/Radar: 312.0/312.675/364.825
Mildenhall: Tower: 258.825 GMC: 340.125 Approach/Radar: 254.875/315.575 Ops: 365.1/307.8/344.8
    Metro: 259.4
Mona: Tower: 358.75 Approach: 379.7
Netheravon: Tower: 290.95 Approach: 362.225 A/G: 253.5
Newcastle: Approach/Radar: 284.6
Newton: Tower: 375.425 Approach: 251.725
Northolt: Tower: 312.35 Approach/Radar: 344.975/379.425 PAR: 375.5 Ops: 244.425 ATIS: 300.35
Odiham: Tower: 309.625 Approach/Radar: 315.975/386.775 PAR: 300.45 ATIS: 276.175
Portland: Tower: 337.75 Approach/Radar: 300.175 PAR: 312.4 A/G: 282.8
Predannack: Tower: 338.975/370.0 Approach (Culdrose): 241.95
Prestwick: Tower: 257.8 Approach/Radar: 362.3 Navy Prestwick: 337.75
Rosehearty Range: 337.7
St Athan: Tower: 336.525 Approach/Radar: 357.175/380.125/340.1
St Mawgan: Tower: 241.825 Approach/Radar: 357.2/360.55 PAR: 336.55 Ops: 260.0
Salisbury Plain: A/G: 282.25

Scampton: Tower: 282.4 GMC: 372.5 Approach/Radar: 357.05/249.85 PAR: 357.1/341.925
Scottish Mil: 249.475
Sculthorpe: Tower: 340.825 GMC: 309.5 Approach/Radar: 246.7/275.65/277.075/359.525/378.3
Shawbury: Tower: 269.1 GMC: 337.9 Approach/Radar: 276.075/254.2/ 386.875 PAR: 356.975
Spadeadam: 369.15
Stanford: A/G: 307.8
Stornoway: Tower: 362.3
Swinderby: Tower: 375.3 Approach: 283.425
Tees-side: Tower: 379.8 Approach/Radar: 296.725/259.025
Ternhill: Tower: 338.825 Approach: 276.825/365.075 Chetwynd Traffic: 309.55
Topcliffe: Tower: 309.725 Approach/Radar: 357.375/344.35
Upavon: Tower: 275.8
Upper Heyford: Tower: 316.0 GMC: 375.175 Approach/Radar: 364.875 PAR: 283.625/343.625/264.125/
    398.05 Ops: 277.175/357.9 Metro: 358.6 ATIS: 242.125
Valley: Tower: 340.175 GMC: 386.9 Approach/Radar: 372.325/268.775/337.725 PAR: 358.675 SAR: 282.8
Waddington: Tower: 285.05 GMC: 342.125 Approach/Radar: 312.5/296.75/300.575/249.85 PAR: 309.675
    Ops: 244.275
Wainfleet Range: 340.05/356.8
Warton: Tower: 311.3 Approach/Radar: 336.475/311.3/343.7
Wattisham: Tower: 343.425 Approach/Radar: 291.125/283.575/277.475 PAR: 356.175/359.825
West Freugh: Tower: 337.925 Approach/Radar: 383.525/259.0
Wittering: Tower: 357.15 GMC: 311.95 Approach/Radar: 380.95/376.575 PAR: 383.225/337.95
Woodbridge: Tower: 291.35 GMC: 383.275 Approach/Radar: 362.075/258.975 Ops: 356.825/282.15 Metro:
    259.4 ATIS: 341.65
Woodford: Tower: 358.575/269.125 Approach/Radar: 269.125/358.575
Woodvale: Tower: 259.95 Approach: 312.8
Wyton: Tower: 312.275 GMC:.293.65 Approach/Radar: 362.375/375.525/249.55 PAR: 292.9
Yeovil: Tower: 372.425 Approach/Radar: 369.975
Yeovilton: Tower: 372.65 GMC: 311.325 Approach/Radar: 369.875/338.875 PAR: 339.975 ATIS: 379.75

Miscellaneous

NATO Common Frequencies: Tower: 257.8 Approach: 362.3 Radar: 344.0 PAR: 385.4 Low Flying: 273.9
    Distress: 243.0 Scene of Search: 282.8

UHF air band frequencies in numerical order

MHz

142.225	Fairford Tower	251.725	Newton Approach
142.29	Coltishall Tower	252.90	Dishforth Ops
149.65	Lakenheath PAR	253.50	Netheravon A/G
231.625	London Mil Pole Hill/Irish Sea	254.20	Shawbury Radar
232.075	Donna Nook Range	254.25	Coltishall PAR
235.05	London Mil Upper	254.475	Brize ATIS
241.775	Cowden Range	254.65	Lyneham Ops
241.825	Aldergrove Ops/St Mawgan Tower	254.75	Brawdy Radar
241.95	Culdrose Radar/Predannack Approach	254.875	Honington Radar
241.975	Honington GMC	255.40	London Mil Seaford/Hurn
242.125	Upper Heyford Metro	256.125	Filton Radar
243.00	Distress	257.80	Nato Common Tower
243.60	Lakenheath PAR	258.825	Mildenhall Tower
244.275	Waddington Ops	258.925	Leuchars Tower
244.425	Northolt Ops	258.975	Bentwaters Approach/Woodbridge
244.775	Bentwaters GMC		Approach
244.875	Leconfield A/G	259.00	Aberporth AFIS/Farnborough
246.70	Sculthorpe Radar		PAR/West Freugh Radar
249.475	Scottish Mil	259.025	Tees-side Radar
249.55	Wyton Radar	259.40	Fairford Metro/Lakenheath Metro/
249.85	Scampton Radar		Mildenhall Metro/Woodbridge
249.95	Brawdy Tower		Metro
250.05	Cranwell Radar/Lossiemouth PAR	259.75	Culdrose PAR

259.825	Alconbury GMC/Dishforth Tower/
	Kinloss Ops
259.85	Leuchars GMC
259.875	Linton-on-Ouse PAR/Luton Approach
259.925	Machrihanish Radar
259.95	Brawdy GMC/Woodvale Tower
259.975	Fairford GMC/Kinloss Radar/
	Lossiemouth Radar
260.00	Cowden Range/St Mawgan Ops
262.70	Church Fenton Tower/Leuchars Radar
262.90	Cottesmore PAR
262.925	Lakenheath PAR
262.95	Coningsby Radar
264.125	Upper Heyford PAR
264.475	London Mil Clacton
264.925	Bentwaters Tower
268.4	Brawdy PAR
268.775	Leuchars PAR/Valley Radar
268.825	Benson Radar
269.10	Shawbury Tower
269.125	Woodford Radar
275.475	London Mil South
275.625	Border Radar
275.65	Sculthorpe Radar
275.80	Upavon Tower
275.875	Coningsby Tower
275.975	Coltishall PAR
276.075	Shawbury Radar
276.125	Cosford Approach
276.175	Odiham ATIS
276.825	Ternhill Approach
276.85	Boscombe Radar
277.075	Sculthorpe Radar
277.175	Upper Heyford Ops
277.225	Cardiff Approach
277.475	Wattisham Radar
277.95	London Mil Dover/Lydd
279.325	Boscombe ATIS
279.35	Benson Tower
282.00	Cranwell Radar
282.075	Church Fenton Radar
282.15	Bentwaters Ops/Woodbridge Ops
282.25	Salisbury Plain A/G
282.275	Honington Radar
282.40	Scampton Tower
282.80	Boulmer A/G/Leconfield A/G/
	Portland A/G/Valley SAR Ops
283.425	Swinderby Approach
283.575	Wattisham Radar
283.625	Upper Heyford PAR
284.60	Newcastle Radar
284.925	Alconbury Ops
285.025	Leuchars Ops
285.05	Waddington Tower
285.125	Finningley Radar
285.15	Cranwell PAR
290.825	Lakenheath PAR
290.95	Netheravon Tower
291.125	Wattisham Radar
291.35	Woodbridge Tower
291.65	Boscombe Radar

291.80	London Mil Daventry
291.95	Marham Radar
292.475	Leuchars Radar
292.525	London Mil North
292.70	Leeming Radar
292.80	Church Fenton Radar
292.90	Wyton PAR
293.425	Coltishall Radar
293.65	Wyton GMC
293.775	Marham Radar
296.725	Coltishall GMC/Tees-side Radar
296.75	Waddington Radar
297.90	Cranwell GMC
299.10	Boulmer A/G
299.40	Culdrose GMC/Lossiemouth GMC
299.975	Eastern Radar
300.175	Portland Radar
300.35	Northolt ATIS
300.425	Linton-on-Ouse Tower
300.45	Odiham PAR
300.475	Lyneham Radar
300.575	Waddington Radar
300.775	Church Fenton Radar
300.825	Lakenheath Ops
300.925	Coningsby PAR
307.80	Fairford Ops/Mildenhall Ops/
	Stanford A/G
309.075	Lakenheath PAR
309.50	Sculthorpe GMC
309.55	Ternhill (Chetwynd Traffic)
309.625	Odiham Tower
309.675	Waddington PAR
309.725	Topcliffe Tower
309.875	Leeming PAR
309.95	Honington Radar
310.00	Aldergrove Tower/Approach
310.35	Brough Tower
311.30	Warton Tower
311.40	Binbrook Tower
311.325	Kinloss Radar/Lossiemouth
	Radar/Yeovilton GMC
311.95	Wittering GMC
312.00	Middle Wallop Radar
312.075	Cottesmore Radar
312.225	Coningsby Radar
312.275	Wyton Tower
312.325	Manston PAR
312.35	Northolt Tower
312.40	Lossiemouth PAR/Portland PAR
312.425	Chivenor Radar
312.50	Waddington Radar
312.55	Marham Ops
312.625	Dunsfold Radar
312.675	Middle Wallop Radar
312.70	Merryfield Tower
312.80	Woodvale Approach
315.50	Finningley Radar
315.525	Farnborough Radar
315.575	Honington Radar
315.65	Lee-on-Solent Tower
315.75	Abingdon Radar

315.975	Odiham Radar
316.00	Upper Heyford Tower
336.275	Farnborough Radar
336.325	Hawarden Tower
336.35	Kinloss Tower/Leeming PAR
336.375	Cottesmore GMC
336.475	Filton Radar/Warton Radar
336.525	St Athan Tower
336.55	St Mawgan PAR
337.575	Fairford Tower
337.60	Jurby Range
337.70	Rosehearty Range
337.725	Valley Radar
337.75	Lossiemouth Tower/Portland Tower/Navy Prestwick
337.825	Leeming Radar
337.875	Cottesmore PAR
337.90	Marham Tower/Shawbury GMC
337.925	Bedford Tower/West Freugh Tower
337.95	Garvie Range/Wittering PAR
337.975	Coningsby PAR
338.625	Manston Radar
338.65	Brize PAR
338.675	Lakenheath PAR
338.825	Ternhill Tower
338.85	Leeming GMC
338.875	Yeovilton Radar
338.975	Honington Radar/Machrihanish PAR/Predannack Tower
339.95	Coltishall Tower/Culdrose Radar
339.975	Yeovilton PAR
340.00	Chivenor Radar
340.025	Linton-on-Ouse GMC
340.05	Wainfleet Range
340.10	St Athan Radar
340.125	Middle Wallop GMC
340.15	Brawdy PAR
340.175	Finningley GMC/Lyneham GMC/Valley Tower
340.20	Church Fenton GMC
340.475	Cranwell Radar
340.525	Barkston Heath Approach
340.575	Cottesmore Radar
340.825	Sculthorpe Tower
341.65	Bentwaters ATIS/Woodbridge ATIS
341.80	Cranfield Tower
341.925	Scampton PAR
342.025	Filton Tower
342.075	Barkston Heath Tower
342.125	Waddington GMC
342.175	Donna Nook Range
342.225	Alconbury Ops
342.25	Coltishall Radar
342.45	Brize Radar
343.375	Holbeach Range
343.425	Wattisham Tower
343.60	Croughton A/G
343.625	Upper Heyford PAR
343.70	Hatfield Radar/Warton Radar
344.00	Nato Common Radar
344.35	Manston Tower/Topcliffe Radar
344.475	Linton-on-Ouse Radar
344.525	Machrihanish Radar
344.575	Leeming Tower
344.60	Abingdon Tower
344.625	Coningsby Radar
344.80	Mildenhall Command Post
344.975	Northolt Radar
345.025	Lyneham Radar
353.55	Aberdeen Approach
356.175	Chivenor PAR/Wattisham PAR
356.275	Halton Aero Club
356.725	Leeming Ops
356.80	Wainfleet Range
356.825	Bentwaters Ops/Woodbridge Ops
356.875	Brize Radar
356.975	Shawbury PAR
357.05	Scampton Radar
357.10	Scampton PAR
357.125	Cosford Tower
357.15	Wittering Tower
357.175	St Athan Radar
357.20	St Mawgan Radar
357.375	Topcliffe Radar
357.40	Farnborough Tower
357.475	Brize Ops
357.90	Upper Heyford Command Post
358.50	Brawdy Radar
358.525	Linton-on-Ouse PAR
358.55	Coningsby GMC
358.575	Woodford Tower
358.60	Machrihanish Tower/Upper Heyford Metro
358.65	Leeming Radar
358.675	Lakenheath Tower/Valley PAR
358.70	Culdrose PAR
358.725	Cottesmore Radar
358.75	Honington PAR/Mona Tower
358.775	Finningley Radar
358.80	Abingdon Radar/Benson Radar
358.85	Church Fenton Radar
359.45	Hatfield Tower
359.50	Lyneham Radar
359.525	Sculthorpe Radar
359.825	Wattisham PAR
360.45	Holbeach Range
360.55	St Mawgan Radar
361.875	Benson Radar
362.075	Bentwaters Approach/Woodbridge Approach
362.15	Cranfield Radar
362.20	Bedford Approach
362.225	Netheravon Approach
362.30	Nato Common Approach
362.375	Wyton Radar
362.45	Chivenor Tower
362.675	Linton-on-Ouse Radar
364.675	Alconbury Ops
364.775	Chivenor Radar
364.80	Coltishall Ops
364.825	Middle Wallop Radar
364.875	Upper Heyford Radar

365.075	Ternhill Approach		379.50	Culdrose Radar
365.10	Mildenhall Ops		379.525	Cranwell Tower
366.725	Church Fenton PAR		379.55	Finningley Tower
367.375	Dunsfold Radar		379.65	Marham PAR
367.95	Brawdy Radar		379.675	Dishforth Approach
368.325	Bentwaters PAR		379.70	Mona Approach
369.15	Spadeadam		379.75	Yeovilton ATIS
369.875	Yeovilton Radar		379.775	Brough Radar
369.975	Yeovil Radar		379.80	Tees-side Tower
370.00	Predannack Tower		379.925	Chivenor GMC
370.05	Cottesmore Tower/Kinloss PAR		379.975	Farnborough Ops
370.075	Leuchars PAR		380.025	Boscombe Radar
370.10	Boscombe Tower		380.125	St Athan Radar
370.30	Brize GMC/Llanbedr PAR		380.175	Llanbedr Tower
371.20	Fairford Ops		380.225	Culdrose Tower
372.30	Culdrose ATIS		380.95	Wittering Radar
372.325	Valley Radar		381.00	Lyneham ATIS
372.425	Cambridge Tower/Radar/Yeovil Tower		381.075	Church Fenton Radar
			381.125	Boscombe PAR
372.50	Scampton GMC		381.20	Brize Tower
372.625	Middle Wallop Tower		383.225	Wittering PAR
372.65	Yeovilton Tower		383.275	Woodbridge GMC
375.175	Upper Heyford GMC		383.45	Alconbury Tower
375.20	Lyneham PAR		383.475	Cranwell PAR
375.30	Swinderby Tower		383.50	Finningley PAR
375.40	Dunsfold Tower		383.525	West Freugh Radar
375.425	Newton Tower		383.625	Bedford Approach
375.50	Northolt PAR		385.40	Nato Common PAR
375.525	Alconbury Approach/Wyton Radar		386.675	Llanbedr Radar
376.525	Kinloss PAR		386.725	Bedford PAR
376.575	Cottesmore Radar/Wittering Radar		386.775	Odiham Radar
376.60	Jurby Range		386.825	Lyneham Tower
376.625	Fairford Radar		386.875	Shawbury Radar
376.65	Lossiemouth Radar		386.90	Valley GMC
376.675	Chivenor Radar		397.975	Lakenheath GMC
378.30	Sculthorpe Radar		398.05	Upper Heyford PAR
379.025	Manston Radar		398.10	Lossiemouth Radar
379.275	Coltishall Radar		398.20	Lakenheath Ops
379.425	Northolt Radar		398.35	Lakenheath Radar
379.475	Fairford Ops			

Appendix 5

ICAO Aircraft type designators

The designators listed below are used for flight planning purposes and also by ATC on flight progress strips. The aircraft name or designation in full is normally used on the R/T but many of the abbreviated versions may also be heard. This list is a sample of the most common ones.

AA5	Grumman AA5	C172	Cessna 172	L188	Lockheed Electra
AC6T	Turbo Commander	C310	Cessna 310	LR24	Learjet 24
AC12	Rockwell 112	C401	Cessna 401	LR35	Learjet 35
AC14	Rockwell 114	C421	Cessna 421	ND16	C160 Transall
AP2S	Super Guppy	C500	Cessna Citation	ND26	Nord 262
B73F	Boeing 737 – 400	C550	Citation II	PA28	Cherokee
B73S	Boeing 737 – 300	CNBR	Canberra	PA31	Navajo
B74S	Boeing 747SP	CV58	Convair 580	PAZT	Aztec
B707	Boeing 707	D228	Dornier 228	PN68	Partenavia P68
B727	Boeing 727	DA20	Falcon 20	S210	Caravelle
B737	Boeing 737	DA50	Falcon 50	S601	Corvette
B747	Boeing 747	DH6	DHC-6 Twin Otter	S880	Rallye
B757	Boeing 757	DH7	DHC-7 Dash 7	SC3	Bulldog
B767	Boeing 767	E110	Bandeirante	SC4	Jetsream
BA11	BAe 111	E121	Xingu	SF34	SAAB-Fairchild SF340
BA31	Jetsream	EA30	Airbus A300	SH5	Belfast
BA46	BAe 146	FK27	Friendship	SH33	Shorts SD3-30
BATP	BAe ATP	FK28	Fellowship	SH36	Shorts SD3-60
BE10	Beech King Air 100	G2	Gulfstream II	SW2	Merlin IIA
BE20	Super King Air 200	G159	Gulfstream I	SW3	Merlin III
BE40	Beechjet 400	GA7	Grumman Cougar	SW4	Merlin IV/Metro
BE55	Beech Baron	HAR	Harrier	TB09	TB-09 Tampico
BE60	Beech Duke	HP7	Herald	TB10	TB-10 Tobago
BE90	Beech King Air 90	HS04	Dove	TU34	Tupolev TU-134
BE95	Beech Travelair	HS25	BAe 125	TU54	Tupolev TU-154
BH06	Bell Jet Ranger	HS74	BAe 748	VC7	Viscount 700
BN2	BN-2 Islander	IL18	Ilyushin IL-18	VC8	Viscount 800
BN3	BN-3 Trislander	IL62	Ilyushin IL-62	VC9	Vanguard/Merchantman
BT12	Pup	JAGR	Jaguar		
C150	Cessna 150	L101	Tristar		

Appendix 6

Aircraft radio callsigns

The callsign prefixes below include many officially allocated to various British operators, although in practice some are rarely used. A few military callsigns to be heard over Britain have been incorporated as they have remained unchanged for many years.

Due to the limited number of combinations available in two-letter designators, it was agreed by participating states of ICAO to convert to a three-letter system and this has now been fully implemented.

The three-letter codes are listed separately as many operators use them rather than the allocated company designator, for example ESY instead of *Exco Air*, either being permissible. There are now so many of them to be heard over Britain that the computer at London Air Traffic Control Centre has been programmed to print the spoken callsign as well as the three-letter code on the controllers' flight progress strips, to make things easier for them. Unfortunately, new operators are appearing so fast that confusion still occurs at times, particularly when a callsign is spoken in a foreign accent. Military callsigns are further explained in Chapter 16, many being changed frequently for security reasons. This is not a problem for training aircraft and many three-letter prefixes reflect their bases, examples being VYT and FYT for Valley and Finningley Training respectively. They have been assimilated into the ICAO three-letter system.

I have endeavoured to include as many as possible of the civil prefixes heard over Britain and further afield on HF, but the list is not claimed to be exhaustive. Indeed, it can never be so as companies come and go, and foreign operators make rare visits or overfly the UK.

R/T callsign	Operator	R/T callsign	Operator
ABG	Abelag	Adria	Adria Airways
Abingdon	Abingdon MU	Aer Arann	Aer Arann
Aceforce	Allied Command Europe	Aerial	Aerial Enterprises
Actair	Air Charter Scotland	Aerocarga	Carga Mexicana

R/T callsign	Operator	R/T callsign	Operator
Aerocaribbean	Aerocaribbean	Airwork	Airwork Services
Aerocentre	Birmingham Aero Centre	Air Zaire	Air Zaire
Aerocharter	Aero Charter Midlands	Air Zimbabwe	Air Zimbabwe
Aeroflot	Aeroflot	Albion	Albion Aviation
Aero Lloyd	Aero Lloyd	Alderney	Channel Air Services
Aeromar	Aeromaritime	Alitalia	Alitalia
Aeromexico	Aeromexico	All Charter	All Charter
Aeronaut	Cranfield	All Nippon	All Nippon
Aeropool	Turbo Pool	Aly Aviation	Aly Aviation
Aeroservice	Europe Aero Service	Alyemda	Yemen Airlines
Aerostar	Mann Aviation	Amber	Amber Airways
Aer Turas	Aer Turas	American	American Airlines
African Express	African Express	Amtran	American Trans Air
African West	African West (Senegal)	Aravco	Aravco
Afro	Affretair	Argentina	Aerolineas Argentinas
Aigle Azur	Aigle Azur	Arkia	Arkia (Israel)
Airafric	Air Afrique	Armyair	Army Air Corps
Air Atlantis	Air Atlantis	Ascot	RAF No 1 Group
Air Belgium	Air Belgium	Aspro	Intereuropean Airways
Air Berlin	Air Berlin	Astel	Air Service Training
Airbridge	Air Bridge Carriers	Atas	Air Gambia
Air Cadet	RAF Air Cadet Schools	ATI	Aero Transport Italiani
Air Canada	Air Canada	Atlantic	Air Atlantique
Air Charter	Air Charter (France)	ATS	ATS Air Charter
Aircontinental	Air Continental	Auctions	ADT Aviation
Airevac	USAF Ambulance	Austrian	Austrian Airlines
Air Experience	Air Experience Flight	Aviaco	Aviaco (Spain)
Air Ferry	British Air Ferries	Avianca	Avianca (Columbia)
Air Force One	US President	Avonair	Avon Air Services
Air Force Two	US Vice-President	Avro	BAe Woodford
Air France	Air France	Ayline	Aurigny Air Services
Airgo	Airgo Ltd	Backer	British Charter
Air Hanson	Air Hanson	Bafjet	BAF Business Jets
Air Hong Kong	Air Hong Kong	Balair	Balair (Switzerland)
Air India	Air India	Balkan	Balkan-Bulgarian
Air Inter	Air Inter	Bandit	BAC Charter
Air Jet	Air Jet (France)	Bangladesh	Bangladesh Biman
Air Lanka	Air Lanka	Barons	Barons (UK)
Airlease	Aero Leasing France	Batman	Ratioflug Frankfurt
Air Liberté	Air Liberté	Beatours	British Airtours
Air Limousin	Air Limousin	Beaupair	Aviation Beauport
Air Littoral	Air Littoral	Beeline	Biggin Hill Executive
Air London	Air London	Belgair	Trans European Airways
Air Malta	Air Malta	Belgian Carriers	Belgian International
Air Mauritius	Air Mauritius	Birmex	Birmingham Executive
Airmed	Air Medical Ltd	Bizair	Business A/C Users
Air Mil	Spanish Air Force	Bizjet	Hamlin Jet
Air Nantes	Air Nantes	Biztravel	Business Air Travel
Air Nav	Air Navigation & Trading	Blackbox	RAE Bedford
Air Portugal	Air Portugal	Blackburn	BAe Scampton
Air Rwanda	Air Rwanda	Black Magic	Black Magic Project
Air Service	Europe Aero Service (France)	Blue Eagle	Eagle Flying Services
		Blue Jet	LTE International (Spain)
Airstar	Airstar Ltd	Bobfly	MLP Aviation
Air Sweden	Air Sweden	Bodensee	Delta Air (Germany)
Airswift	Air Swift	Bohemia	Bohemian Air Transport
Airtax	Birmingham Aviation	Bond	Bond Helicopters
Air Truck	Air Truck (Spain)	Braathens	Braathens (Norway)
Air Vendée	Air Vendée	Bristow	Bristow Helicopters

R/T callsign	Operator	R/T callsign	Operator
Britannia	Britannia Airways	Cranwell	Cranwell FTU
Brittany	Brit Air	Croatia	Croatian Airlines
Broadway	Fleet Requirements Unit	Cross Air	Cross Air
Brunei	Royal Brunei Airlines	Crusader	Firebird Aerobatics
Bryanair	Bryan Aviation	CSA Lines	Czech Airlines
Brymon	Brymon Airways	CTA	CTA (Switzerland)
Buffalo Air	Buffalo Airways (USA)	Cubana	Cubana
Bul Air Cargo	Bulgarian Air Cargo	Cygnet	BAe Flying College
Busy Bee	Busy Bee of Norway	Cyprus	Cyprus Airways
Cabair	Cabair Air Taxis	Dairair	Dairo Air Services (Uganda)
Caledonian	Caledonian	Danair	Dan Air
Calibrator	CAA Calibration Flight	Dantrans	Danish Air Transport
Cam-Air	Cameroon Airlines	Delta	Delta Airlines
Cambrian	Cardiff Aviation	Deltair	Delta Air Transport
Camelot	Excalibur Airways	Diamond	Diamond Airways
Cameo	Cam Air	Direct Flight	Air Direct
Canada	Worldways Canada	Dollar	Dollar Air Services
Canadian	Canadian Airlines	Dravidian	Dravidian Air Services
Canforce	Canadian Armed Forces	Dynamite	Dynamic Air (Holland)
Carbon	SM Exports Ltd	Eagle Air	Eagle Air (Iceland)
Cargo	Safair Freighters (S Africa)	Eastex	Eastern Executive
Cargolux	Cargolux Airlines	Egyptair	Egyptair
Catbird	US Navy Naples	El Al	El Al
Cathay	Cathay Pacific	Electricity	SWEB Helicopter Unit
Cecil	Cecil Aviation	Elite	Air 3000 (Canada)
Cedarjet	Middle East Airlines	Elmair	Elmdon Aviation
Ceebee	CB Executive Helicopters	Emery	Emery Worldwide
Cega	Cega Aviation	EMA	East Midland Aviation
Celtic	Celtic Airways	Emirates	Emirates
Centurion	Cumbernauld Flight Centre	Empress	CP-Air
Cessnair	Westair Flying Services	Ethiopian	Ethiopian Airlines
Chad	Chad Air Services	Euralair	Euralair (France)
Challair	Challeng'air (France)	Euroair	Euroair
Channex	Channel Express	Eurobelgian	Eurobelgian Airlines
Chartair	Chartair Ltd	Eurocommuter	Regionair
Charter Express	Air Charter Express	Eurojet	Eurojet (Spain)
Cheshair	Cheshire Air Training	Europa	Europe Air
Cheyne	Cheyne Motors Ltd	Eurotrans	European Air Transport
China	CAAC	Eurowest	Euroflight (Sweden)
China Eastern	China Eastern Airlines	Evergreen	Evergreen International
Church Fenton	Church Fenton FTU	Exam	CAA Flight Examiner
Cimber	Cimber Air	Excalibur	Air Excel (UK)
City	NLM City Hopper	Executive	Extra Executive (Germany)
Clan King	Air Sinclair	Express	Federal Express
Clansman	Airwork	Fairflight	Fairflight
Classic Air	Classic Air	Falcon	Falcon Cargo (Sweden)
Club	Club Air Europe	Falcon Jet	Falcon Jet Centre
Clue	7005th Air Base Sqn	Fanum	Automobile Association
Clyde	Clyde Surveys	Ferranti	Ferranti
Commuterbird	National Commuter	Fieldair	Field Aircraft Services
Compass	Compass Aviation	Finnair	Finnair
Conair	Conair (Canada)	Finningley	Finningley FTU
Condor	Condor Flugdienst	Flagship	Express Airlines
Consort	Consort Aviation	Flamingo	Nurnburger Flugdienst
Contactair	Contactair Flugdienst	Flash	Flash Airlines (Nigeria)
Continental	Continental Airlines	Flint	Flight Services Intl
Corsair	Corse Air	Flyer	Cityflyer Express
Cotam	French AF Transport	Food	Food Brokers Ltd
County	County Air Services	Fordair	Ford Motor Co

R/T callsign	Operator	R/T callsign	Operator
Foxair	Foxair Ltd	JAT	Jugoslovenski
Foxclub	Leicester Aero Club		Aerotransport
Foxtrot Mike	French Air Force	Jayceebee	JCB Excavators
Foyle	Air Foyle (TNT)	Jersey	Jersey European
Frans Air Force	French Air Force	Jes Air	Jes Air (Bulgaria)
Fred Olsen	Fred Olsen (Norway)	Jet Fret	Jet Fret
Frevag	Frevag (Belgium)	Jetplan	Memrykord Ltd
Gama	Gama Aviation	Jetset	Air 2000
Gamair	Gamair (Gambia)	Jolly	USAF HH-53 Rescue
Gauntlet	Boscombe Down MoD/PE		Helicopters
Genex	Aviogenex	Jordanian	Royal Jordanian
German Air Force	German Air Force	Kabo	Kabo Air Travels (Nigeria)
German Cargo	German Cargo	Karair	Kar-Air (Finland)
Germania	Germania	Karpat	Karpatair (Bulgaria)
German Wings	German Wings	Keenair	Keenair Services
Ghana	Ghana Airways	Kentair	Surrey and Kent Flying
Gibair	GB Airways		Club
Gillair	Gill Aviation	Kent Exec	Kent Executive
Gojet	Eurojet Aviation	Kenya	Kenya Airways
Gram Air	Grampian Helicopters	Key Air	Key Airlines (USA)
Grampian	Aberdeen Airways	Kilro	Air Kilroe
Granite	Business Air	King	67th Rescue Sqn, USAF
Green Air	Green Air (Turkey)	Kittyhawk	Queen's Flight (HM the
Greenlandair	Greenlandair		Queen on board or certain
Grid	National Grid Co		other members of the Royal
Grosvenor	Grosvenor Aviation		Family)
Guernsey	Guernsey Airlines	Kiwi	Royal New Zealand Air
Gulf Air	Gulf Air		Force
Hambrair	Hambrair Ltd	KLM	KLM
Hamburg Air	Hamburg Airlines	Knightway	Knightway Air Charter
Hamlin	Hamlin Aviation	Koreanair	Korean Airlines
Hapag Lloyd	Hapag-Lloyd	Kuwaiti	Kuwait Airways
Harvest	Harvest Aviation	Lair	Lionair (Luxembourg)
Hatair	Hatfield Executive	LAN	LAN Chile
Havelet	Havelet Leasing	Lark	55th Weather Recce Sqn,
Hawker	BAe Dunsfold		USAF
Heavylift	Heavylift Cargo	Lauda	Lauda Air
Heli Hire	Helicopter Hire	LCN	Lineas Aereas Canarias
Heritage	Jet Heritage	Leud Air	Leud Air (France)
Hot Air	Baltic Airlines	Leck	Lec Refrigeration
Hunting	Hunting Hivolt	Leisure	Air UK (Leisure)
Hyde	Hyde Helicopters	Leopard	Queen's Flight (Prince
Iberia	Iberia		Andrew)
Iceair	Icelandair	Libair	Libyan Arab
IDS	IDS Aircraft	Lifeline	Aeromedicaire Ltd
Indonesian	Garuda Indonesian	Linton on Ouse	Linton on Ouse FTU
Info	Independent Nuclear Forces	Lion	British International
	Observers		Helicopters
Instone	Instone Airlines	Logan	Loganair
Interflight	Interflight Ltd	Lord	207th Aviation Coy, US
Invicta	Kentair International		Army
Iona	Iona Airways	Lovo	Lovaux Ltd
Iranair	Iran Air	LTS	LTU Sud
Iraqi	Iraqi Airways	LTU	Lufttransport
Irish Club	Club Air	Lufthansa	Lufthansa
Isle Avia	Island Aviation	Luxair	Luxair
Italjet	Italjet	Lynton	Lynton Aviation
Janes	Janes Aviation	MAC	Military Airlift Command
Japanair	Japan Airlines	MacDonald	MacDonald Aviation

R/T callsign	Operator	R/T callsign	Operator
Macline	McAlpine	Oasis	Oasis International
Maerskair	Maerskair (Denmark)	Octavia	Octavia Air
Magec	Magec Aviation	Odiham	Odiham FTU
Majan	Royal Omani AF	Okada Air	Okada Airlines (Nigeria)
Malawi	Air Malawi	Olympic	Olympic Airways
Malaysian	Malaysian Airlines	Oman	Oman Royal Flight
Malev	Malev (Hungary)	Orange	Air Holland
Mamair	MAM Aviation	Orion	Orion Airways
Mann	Alan Mann Helicopters	Orkney	Air Orkney
Manta	Woodford Flight Test	Outremer	Air Outre Mer
Manx	Manx Airlines	Oxford	CSE Aviation
March	March Helicopters	Pakistan	Pakistan International
Marocair	Royal Air Maroc	Para	Army Parachute Centre
Marshall	Marshall of Cambridge	Parachute	UK Parachute Centre
Martin	Martin-Baker	Paraguaya	Lineas Aereas Paraguayas
Medic	Medical Air Services	Peacock	H.E. Peacock & Sons
Medivac	London Helicopter Emergency Medical Service	Pearl	Oriental Pearl Airways
		Peregrine	Peregrine Air Services
Merlin	Rolls Royce (Military)	Philippine	Philippine Airlines
Merrix	Merrix Air	Pirol	Bundesgrenschutz
Metman	Met Research Flight	Plum	PLM Helicopters
Metpol	Metropolitan Police Flying Club	Poachers	Poachers Team
		Pointscall	Points of Call Airlines
Midas	Milford Docks Air Service	Police	Police Aviation Services
Midfly	Midtfly (Denmark)	Pollot	LOT (Poland)
Midland	British Midland	Port	Skyworld Airlines (USA)
Mike Romeo	Air Mauritanie	Proteus	Proteus (France)
Minair	CAA Flying Unit	Provost	Bearing Supplies Ltd
Minerve	Minerve (France)	Puma	Phoenix Aviation
Monarch	Monarch Airlines	Qantas	Qantas
Moonrun	Benelux Falcon (Belgium)	Racal	Racal Avionics
Morefly	Morefly (Norway)	Rafair	Royal Air Force
Moth	Tiger Fly	Rainbow	Queen's Flight (Prince Philip)
Mountlee	Mountleigh Air Services		
Mozambique	LAM-Mozambique	Rangemile	Rangemile Ltd
Multi	Air Transport Schipol	Ranger	Defence Products Ltd
Myson	Myson Group	Raven	Raven Air
Nacar	Air Sur (Spain)	Raymond	RSJ Aviation
Nationair	Nation Air (Canada)	Reach	USAF Air Mobility Command
Navy	Royal or US Navy	Rega	Swiss Air Ambulance
Navco	Navco Airways	Regal	Crown Air (Canada)
Neatax	Northern Executive	Relief	Relief Transport Services
Netherlands Air Force	RNAF	Rescue	RAF Rescue
Netherlands Navy	Netherlands Navy	RFG	RFG Regionalflug
Netherlines	Netherlines	Richair	Rich International
Newdan	Newair (Denmark)	Rogav	Rogers Aviation
Newpin	BAe Hawarden	Rolls	Rolls Royce (Bristol)
New Zealand	Air New Zealand	Roman	R.M. Aviation Ltd
Nightflight	Night Flight Ltd	Rosenbalm	Rosenbalm Aviation (USA)
Nile Safaris	Nile Safaris	Rushton	Flight Refuelling
Nordic	Nordic Air Services	Ryanair	Ryanair
Northair	Northern Air Taxis	Ryburn	Ryburn Air
Northwest	Northwest Orient	Sabena	Sabena
Norlink	Norlink Air Ltd	Saint Athan	St Athan MU
Norspeed	Norway Airlines	Saltair	Saltair Ltd
Nortel	Northern Airlines	Sam	Special Air Mission (USAF)
Norving	A/S Norving (Norway)	Sapphire	Bristol BAe
Norwegian	Royal Norwegian Air Force	Sarnair	Channel Aviation
Nugget	RAe Farnborough	Saudi	Saudi-Arabian Airlines

R/T callsign	Operator	R/T callsign	Operator
Scampton	Scampton FTU	Swedair	Swedair
Scandinavian	Scandinavian Airlines System	Swedic	Swedish Airforce
		Swedline	Linjeflyg
Scanwings	Malmo Aviation	Swinderby	Swinderby FTU
Schreiner	Schreiner Airways	Swissair	Swissair
Seafly	South East Air	Syrianair	Syrian Arab Airlines
Seagreen	Seagreen Air Transport	Tango Lima	Trans Mediterranean
Secoat	South East College of Air Training	Tarmac	Tarmac PLC
		Tarnish	BAe Warton
Selair	Sierra Leone Airways	Tarom	Tarom (Rumania)
Seychelles	Air Seychelles	Tat	Tat France
Shamrock	Aer Lingus	Tayflight	Tayflight
Shawbury	Shawbury FTU	Tayside	Tayside Aviation
Shell	Shell Aircraft	Tee Air	Tower Air
Short	Short Brothers	Tennant	BAe Prestwick
Shuttle	British Airways Shuttle	Tester	Empire Test Pilot School
Silverline	Sterling Helicopters	Thai Inter	Thai International
Simflight	Simulated Flight Training	Thurston	Thurston Aviation
Singapore	Singapore Airlines	Tibbet	BAe Hatfield
Skegair	Skegair	Tiger	Flying Tiger
Sky Bird	Anywair Travel (UK)	Time Air	Time Air (Canada)
Skye Line	West Highland Aviation	Tomcat	Cologne Commercial Flight
Skyfame	Skyfame Ltd	Topcliffe	Topcliffe FTU
Skyguard	Skyguard Ltd	Torair	Toros Airlines (Turkey)
Skyjet	Panair Spain	Touchstone	Touchstone Aviation
Skylane	Skylane Air Charter	Transamerica	Transamerica Airlines
Skyman	Air Foyle (Executive)	Trans Arabian	Trans Arabian
Skyrover	Skyrover Ltd	Transat	Air Transat
Sky Service	Sky Service (Belgium)	Transatlantic	Transatlantic (Gambia)
Skyship	Skyship Industries	Transavia	Transavia (Holland)
Sloane	Sloane Aviation	Transcon	Trans Continental
Snoopy	Air Traffic GMBH	Transcorp	Transcorp Airways
Sobelair	Sobelair	Trans Europe	Trans Europe Air Charter
Solo	Solo Flying School	Transwede	Transwede
Somalair	Somali Airlines	Transworld	Trans World
Southern Air	Southern Air Transport	Trehaven	Crest Aviation
Spar	58th Mil Airlift Sqn, USAF	Trent	Trent Air Services
Sparrowhawk	Edinburgh Air Centre	Triangle	Atlantic Island Air (Iceland)
Special	Metropolitan Police Air Support Unit	Tropic	Tropair
		Tunair	Tunis Air
Speedbird	British Airways	Turkair	Turkish Airlines
Speedfox	Jet Air (Denmark)	Tutor	G & B Air Academy
Spider	Ibis (Belgium)	Tyrolean	Tyrolean Airways
Spooner	Spooner Aviation	Uganda	Uganda Airlines
Springbok	South African Airways	Ukay	Air UK
Stampede	Holidair (Canada)	Uni Air	Uni Air (France)
Standards	CAA Training Standards	Unicorn	Queen's Flight (Prince Charles)
Star	Star Aviation		
Stellair	Stellair (France)	United	United Airlines
Sterling	Sterling Airways	Universair	Universair (Spain)
Streamline	Streamline Aviation	US Air	US Air
Suckling	Suckling Airways	UTA	UTA (France)
Sudanair	Sudan Airways	Varig	Varig Brazil
Sudavia	Sudavia (West Germany)	Vectis	Pilatus Britten Norman
Sunshine	Sunshine Aviation	Veritair	Veritair Ltd
Sunturk	Pegasus (Turkey)	Viasa	VIASA (Venezuela)
Sunwing	Spanair	Vickers	Vickers Shipbuilding
Surewings	Sure Wings Ltd	Viking	Scanair (Denmark)
Surinam	Surinam Airways	Virgin	Virgin Atlantic

R/T callsign	Operator	R/T callsign	Operator
Viva	Viva Air	Woodair	Woodgate Air Services
Watchdog	Ministry of Fisheries	Woodpecker	Howarth Timber
Wayne Air	BW Air Services	World	World Airways
WDL	WDL Flugdienst	Yemeni	Yemen Airways
Wessex	Wessex Airlines	Yeoman	Foster Yeoman
West Indian	BWIA	Yoobee	United Biscuits
Westland	Westland Helicopters	Yorkair	Yorkshire Flying Services
West London	West London Aero Services	Yugair	Air Yugoslavia
Whitbread	Whitbread Ltd	Zambia	Zambia Airways
Wickom	Wycombe Air Centre	Zap	Titan Airways
Wingwork	Wingwork Aviation	ZAS Airlines	ZAS Airlines Egypt
Witchcraft	Flugdienst Fehlhaber	Zebra	African Safari
Wizard	Merlin Air Services	Zimex	Zimex (Switzerland)

Suffixes to the flight number have various meanings:

A Extra flight on the same route. If more than one B, C etc may be used

F Freight

P Positioning flight

T Training flight

X Allocated by ATC when two aircraft from different companies but with the same flight number are on the same frequency and there is a likelihood of confusion.

Heavy Reminds ATC that aircraft is wide-bodied with a strong turbulent wake.

Note that British Airways Shuttle callsigns, for example Shuttle 6Z, are unique to this operation.

Some operators have their own system of suffixes. An example is Gillair of Newcastle, one of whose flights, GIL04L, indicates a *L*iverpool mail run; an M suffix would signify Manchester. Britannia Airways uses the suffixes A and C, and B and D, signify outbound and inbound flights respectively, eg

BAL220A   Luton to Milan   BAL462C   Cardiff to Palma
BAL220B   Milan to Luton   BAL462D   Palma to Cardiff

British Airways' domestic flights now employ a two or three-digit number denoting the route and a suffix letter identifying the particular service. It is a development of the Shuttle callsigns which have been in use for many years as follows: Shuttle 2 — London to Manchester; Shuttle 3 — Manchester to London; Shuttle 4 — London to Belfast; Shuttle 5 — Belfast to London; Shuttle 6 — London to Glasgow; Shuttle 7 — Glasgow to London; Shuttle 8 — London to Edinburgh; Shuttle 9 — Edinburgh to London. The letter suffixes change alphabetically for each service throughout the day.

ICAO company designators

3-letter code	Operator	3-letter code	Operator
AAB	Abelag Aviation	AZR	Air Zaire
AAC	Army Air Corps	AZW	Air Zimbabwe
AAF	Aigle Azur	BAC	BAC Leasing
AAG	Atlantic Aviation	BAF	British Air Ferries
AAL	American Airlines	BAL	Britannia Airways
AAN	Oasis International	BAT	Bohemian Air Transport
ABB	Air Belgium	BBB	Balair
ABN	Abingdon MU	BBC	Bangladesh Biman
ACF	Air Charter International	BBN	BAe Scampton
ACW	RAF Air Cadet Schools	BCR	British Charter
ADB	Antonov Design Bureau	BCS	European Air Transport
ADR	Adria Airways	BDN	Boscombe Down MoD/PE
AEA	Air Europa	BEE	Busy Bee of Norway
AED	Air Experience Flight	BER	Air Berlin
AEF	Aero Lloyd	BEX	Benin Air Express
AEK	African Express Airways	BGS	Bundesgrenschutz
AFB	Belgian Air Force	BHE	Biggin Hill Executive Aviation
AFC	African West	BHL	Bristow Helicopters Group
AFM	Affretair	BIC	Belgian International Air Carriers
AFN	African International	BIH	British International Helicopters
AFP	Portuguese Air Force	BLM	The Black Magic Project
AGL	Air Angouleme	BMA	British Midland
AGS	Air Gambia	BOB	MLP Aviation
AGX	Aviogenex	BRA	Braathens
AHD	Air Holland	BRY	Brymon Airways
AHK	Air Hong Kong	BVA	Buffalo Airways
AIA	Air Atlantis	BWA	BWIA International
AIJ	Air Jet	BWO	BW Air Services
AIZ	Arkia Israel	BWY	Fleet Requirements Air Direction Unit
ALK	Air Lanka	BZH	Brit Air
AMC	Air Malta	CCA	Air China
AME	Spanish Air Force	CCF	Cologne Commercial Flight
AML	Air Malawi	CDN	Canadian Airlines International
AMM	Air 2000	CEG	Cega Aviation
AMR	Air America	CFD	Cranfield Institute of Technology
AMT	American Trans Air	CFG	Condor Flugdienst
AMX	Aeronaves De Mexico	CFN	Church Fenton FTU
ANA	All Nippon Airways	CFU	CAA Flying Unit
ANZ	Air New Zealand	CHX	Air Charter Express
AOL	Aero Leasing France	CKS	Connie Kalitta Services (USA)
APR	Air Provence	CKT	Caledonian Airways
ARG	Aerolineas Argentinas	CLC	Classic Air (Switzerland)
ASN	Air Service Nantes	CLG	Challeng' Air (France)
ATI	Aero Transport Italiani	CLS	Club Air (Eire)
ATJ	Air Traffic GMBH	CLU	Club Air Europe
ATQ	Air Transport Schiphol	CLX	Cargolux Airlines
ATT	Aer Turas Teoranta	CMM	Air 3000 (Canada)
AUA	Austrian Airlines	COA	Continental Airlines
AVA	Avianca	CPA	Cathay Pacific
AVB	Aviation Beauport	CRL	Corse Air International
AVD	Air Vendée	CRN	Aero Caribbean
AVT	ATS Charter	CRX	Cross Air
AVZ	Avon Air Services	CSA	Czech Airlines
AWC	Titan Airways	CTA	Compagnie De Transport Aerien
AYC	Aviaco	CTN	Croatia Airlines
AYR	British Aerospace Flying College	CUB	Cubana

3-letter code	Operator	3-letter code	Operator
CUL	Culdrose SAR Training Unit	GMI	Germania
CWL	Cranwell FTU	GMP	Transwede
CWS	Air Swazi Cargo	GRL	Gronlandsfly
CYP	Cyprus Airways	GRN	Green Air (Turkey)
DAH	Air Algerie	HAF	Greek Air Force
DAL	Delta Airlines	HAS	Hamburg Airlines
DAN	Danair Services	HAV	Hamlin Aviation
DAT	Delta Air Transport	HHL	Helicopter Hire
DEL	Delta Air	HLA	Heavylift Cargo
DMA	Maersk Air	HLF	Hapag-Lloyd
DMD	Diamond Airways	HOT	Baltic Airlines
DNX	Donoghue Aviation	HRN	Airwork
DQI	Cimber Air	IAW	Iraqi Airways
DSR	Dairo Air Services (Uganda)	ICE	Icelandair
DUN	BAe Dunsfold	ICG	Icelandic Coastguard
DYA	Alyemda Democratic Yemen Airlines	IDS	IDS Aircraft
EAX	Eastern Executive Travel	IEA	Intereuropean Airways
EEB	Euroberlin	IFT	Interflight
EEX	Euro Express Cargo Airlines	IMX	Zimex Aviation (Switzerland)
EIA	Evergreen International Airlines	IND	Iona National Airways
EIN	Aer Lingus	IRA	Iran Air
ESA	Seagreen Air Transport	ISL	Eagle Air
ESY	Executive Aviation (Nigeria)	ITF	Air Inter
ETH	Ethiopian Airline Corp	ITJ	Italjet
ETP	Empire Test Pilots School	IYE	Yemen Airways
EUA	Europe Air	JAL	Japan Air Lines
EUL	Euralair International	JAT	Jugoslovenski Aerotransport
EUX	European Expedite (Belgium)	JES	Jes Air (Bulgaria)
EWW	Emery Worldwide	JFT	Jet Fret
EXS	Channel Express	KAC	Kuwait Airways
EXT	Extra Executive Transport	KAL	Korean Airlines
EYT	Europe Aero Service	KAR	Kar-Air (Finland)
FAF	French Air Force	KBS	Gamair
FCN	Falcon Cargo (Sweden)	KEY	Key Airlines (USA)
FDX	Federal Express	KFK	German Wings
FFG	Flugdienst Fehlhaber	KIS	Contactair Flugdienst
FFU	Ferranti	KQA	Kenya Airways
FGN	Gendarmerie Nationale	LAA	Libyan Arab Airlines
FIN	Finnair	LAM	Linhas Aereas Mocambique
FJC	Falcon Jet Centre	LAN	LAN Chile
FLR	Flight Refuelling	LAP	Lineas Aereas Paraguayas
FOF	Fred Olsen	LAZ	Balkan-Bulgarian Airlines
FOX	Jetair (Denmark)	LCN	Lineas Aereas Canarias
FSB	Flight Services International	LDA	Lauda Air
FSH	Flash Airlines (Nigeria)	LEA	Lead Air (France)
FVG	Frevag (Belgium)	LGL	Luxair
FWC	Freeway Air (Holland)	LIB	Air Liberté
FXR	Foxair	LIN	Linjeflyg (Sweden)
FYY	Finningley	LIR	Lionair (Luxembourg)
GAF	German Air Force	LIT	Air Littoral
GAL	Gemini Airlines	LOP	Linton on Ouse FTU
GBL	GB Airways	LOT	Lot Polskie
GEC	German Cargo Services	LTE	LTE International Airways
GEM	BAe Bristol	LTS	LTU Sud
GFA	Gulf Air	LTU	Lufttransport
GHA	Ghana Airways Corp	LWA	Liberian World
GHW	Airstar	LYD	World Executive Airways
GIA	Garuda Indonesian Airlines	MAH	Malev

3-letter code	Operator	3-letter code	Operator
MAS	Malaysian Airline System	RFR	Royal Air Force
MAU	Air Mauritius	RGA	Regency Air Services
MDF	Midtfly (Denmark)	RGN	Berlin European UK
MEA	Middle East Airlines	RIA	Rich International
MET	Meteorological Research Flight	RJA	Royal Jordanian
MIN	Minerve	RKA	Air Afrique
MKA	MK Air Cargo	ROT	Tarom
MOH	Tigerfly	RRL	Rolls Royce (Military Aviation)
MON	Monarch Airlines	RRR	RAF – 1 Group (Air Transport)
MOR	A/S Morefly	RRS	Bedford RAE
MPH	Martinair Holland	RTS	Relief Transport Services
MRT	Air Mauritanie	RWD	Air Rwanda
MSR	Egyptair	RYR	Ryanair
MUK	Muk Air Taxi (Denmark)	SAP	Scampton FTU
NAF	Royal Netherlands Air Force	SAW	Sterling Airways
NAN	National Airlines	SAY	Suckling Airways
NCA	Nippon Cargo	SAZ	Swiss Air Ambulance
NCL	National Commuter Airways	SCH	Schreiner Airways
NCR	Air Sur	SCW	Malmo Aviation
NDC	Nordic Air Services	SDC	Swedish Air Force
NET	Netherlines	SEI	Scottish Express International
NFD	Nurnberger Flugdienst	SEU	Scottish European Airways
NGA	Nigerian Airways	SEY	Air Seychelles
NLM	NLM City Hopper	SFR	Safair Freighters
NOR	A/S Norving (Norway)	SHF	Support Helicopter Flight NI
NOS	Norway Airlines	SHS	Sunshine Aviation
NOW	Royal Norwegian Air Force	SIA	Singapore Airlines
NRN	Royal Netherlands Navy	SJM	Southern Air Transport
NSA	Nile Safaris	SKK	Skylane Air Charter
NTL	Northair Aviation	SKR	Skyrover
NVY	Royal Navy	SKS	Sky Service
NWA	Northwest Orient	SLK	Silkair (Singapore)
NXA	Nationair (Canada)	SLM	Surinam Airways
OAL	Olympic Airways	SLR	Sobelair
OCT	Octavia Air Ltd	SOM	Somali Airlines
OJA	Oriental Pearl Airways	SPC	Skyworld Airlines (USA)
OKJ	Okada Airlines (Nigeria)	SPP	Spanair
OPT	Optica Industries	STM	Streamline Aviation
OYC	Conair (Denmark)	STN	St Athan MU
PAL	Philippine Airlines	STP	Holidair
PBU	Air Burundi	STR	Stellair
PGT	Pegasus (Turkey)	SUD	Sudan Airways
PIA	Pakistan International	SVA	Saudi Arabian Airlines
PJS	Jet Aviation (Switzerland)	SWB	Sure-Wings
PLC	Police Aviation Services	SWD	Swinderby FTU
PNR	Panair (Spain)	SWE	Swedair
PRB	Proteus (France)	SWR	Swissair
PTS	Points of Call Airlines	SYR	Syrian Arab Airlines
QKL	Aeromaritime	SYS	Shawbury FTU
QNK	Kabo Air Travels (Nigeria)	TAF	Time Air (Canada)
QSC	African Safari Airways	TAP	TAP (Portugal)
RAM	Royal Air Maroc	TAR	Tunis Air
RAN	Defence Products	TAT	TAT
RAX	Rosenbalm Aviation	TAU	Toros Airlines (Turkey)
RAZ	Rijnmond (Holland)	TCN	Trans Continental
RBA	Royal Brunei Airlines	TCP	Transcorp Airways
RCC	Racal Avionics	TEA	Trans European Airways
RFG	RFG Regionalflug	TEU	Trans Europe Air Charter

3-letter code	Operator	3-letter code	Operator
TFL	Tayflight	UTA	Union Des Transports Aeriennes
THA	Thai Airways	UYC	Cameroon Airlines
THY	Turk Hava Yollari	VIA	Viasa (Venezuela)
TMA	Trans Mediterranean Airlines	VIR	Virgin Atlantic
TOF	Topcliffe FTU	VKG	Scanair
TOW	Tower Air	VLL	Valley SAR Training
TPL	Turbo Pool	VNR	Viennair
TRA	Transavia (Holland)	VRG	Varig
TRT	Trans Arabian Air Transport	VYT	Valley FTU
TSC	Air Transat (Canada)	WDL	WDL Flugdienst
TSV	Tropair Air Services	WFD	BAe Woodford
TWA	Transworld Airlines	WHA	West Highland Aviation
TWE	Transwede	WHE	Westland Helicopters
TYR	Tyrolean Airways	WLA	West London Aero Services
UAE	Emirates	WOA	World Airways
UAI	Uni Air International	WSX	Wessex Air Services
UGA	Uganda Airlines	WTN	BAe Warton
UKA	Air UK	WWC	Worldways Canada
UKL	Air UK (Leisure)	YRG	Air Yugoslavia
UNA	Universair	ZAC	Zambia Airways
UPA	Air Foyle	ZAS	ZAS Airlines of Egypt
URO	Euroair		

Appendix 7

UK SSR Code Allotment Plan

Codes/Series	Controlling Authority/Function
0000	SSR data unreliable
0001 — 0017	Allotted to France and Denmark
0020	Medivac – London Helicopter Emergency
0021	Fixed-wing aircraft (Receiving service from a ship)
0022	Helicopter(s) (Receiving service from a ship)
0023	Aircraft engaged in actual SAR Operations
0024	Radar Flight Evaluation/Calibration
0025	MET research flight – DRA Farnborough
0033	Aircraft Paradropping
0040	Civil Helicopters North Sea
0041 — 0057	Allotted to Belgium
0060 — 0077	Allotted to Ireland, Netherlands and Norway
0101 — 0137	ORCAM Brussels
0140 — 0177	ORCAM Amsterdam
0201 — 0277	Aberdeen Approach, RNAS Portland , RAF Woodbridge, RAF Upper Heyford
0201 — 0227	RAF Finningley
0301 — 0305	ORCAM Heathrow
0306 — 0377	ORCAM London
0401 — 0437	Eire Domestic Military
0401 — 0476	RAE Farnborough
0477	RAF Odiham
0401 — 0467	RAF Lakenheath
0440 — 0467	ACMI (NSAR)
0470 — 0477	RN South West Approaches, RAF Sculthorpe
0501 — 0577	ORCAM London
0601 — 0677	ORCAM Frankfurt
0701 — 0777	ORCAM Maastricht
1000	Autonomous FTR Ops
1001 — 1077	ORCAM Paris
1100	Autonomous FTR Ops
1101 — 1137	ORCAM Frankfurt
1140 — 1177	ORCAM Scottish
1200	Autonomous FTR Ops
1201 — 1277	Channel Islands Domestic
1300 — 1317	Aircraft receiving service from AEW aircraft
1320 — 1327	Autonomous FTR Ops
1330 — 1377	ORCAM Bremen/Dusseldorf
1400	Autonomous FTR Ops

Codes/Series	Controlling Authority/Function
1401 — 1407	Scottish Domestic
1410 — 1417	RAF Coltishall/Norwich Approach
1420 — 1457	Shannon inbound UK Domestic
1460 — 1477	Pennine Radar, Guernsey Approach, RAF Coltishall, Bristol Approach
1500 — 1557/67/77	RAF Buchan
1560 — 1566	RAF Saxa Vord
1570 — 1576	RAF Benbecula
1600 — 1657	RAF Boulmer
1660 — 1667	RAF Tycroes
1670 — 1677	RAF Portreath
1700 — 1727	RAF Staxton Wold
1730 — 1733	RNAS Lee-on-Solent
1730 — 1753	RAF Valley
1730 — 1757	RAF Waddington/Scampton, RAF Lossiemouth/Kinloss
1740 — 1757	RAF Benson
1760 — 1777	RAF Wattisham, RAF Chivenor
2000	Aircraft from non SSR environment
2001 — 2077	ORCAM Shannon
2100	Autonomous FTR Ops
2101 — 2177	ORCAM Amsterdam
2200	Autonomous FTR Ops
2201 — 2210	ORCAM Manchester
2211 — 2215	ORCAM Gatwick
2216 — 2277	ORCAM London
2300	Autonomous FTR Ops
2301 — 2327	ORCAM Brest
2330 — 2377	ORCAM Reims
2400 — 2457	RAF Neatishead
2460 — 2477	RAF Ash
2500	Autonomous FTR Ops
2501 — 2577	ORCAM Rhein (Karlsruhe)
2600	Autonomous FTR Ops
2601 — 2637	Highland Radar Civil
2640	Highland Radar Helicopters
2601 — 2627	RAF Linton-on-Ouse
2644 — 2657	RAF Leuchars
2650 — 2677	Sumburgh Domestic
2660 — 2677	BAe Warton, RAF Lyneham, RAF Marham
2700	Autonomous FTR Ops
2701 — 2737	ORCAM Shannon
2740 — 2777	ORCAM Zurich
3000	Autonomous FTR Ops
3001 — 3077	ORCAM Zurich
3100	Autonomous FTR Ops
3101 — 3177	ORCAM Rhein (Karlsruhe)

Codes/Series	Controlling Authority/Function	Codes/Series	Controlling Authority/Function
3200	Autonomous FTR Ops	5701 — 5777	ORCAM Geneva
3201 — 3277	LJAO	6001 — 6007	Eastern Radar (Sector 8)
3300	Autonomous FTR Ops	6010 — 6077	Eastern Radar (Sectors 1-7)
3301 — 3377	RNAS Yeovilton	6001 — 6027	Guernsey Approach
3301 — 3324	RAF Wyton	6030 — 6077	Jersey Approach
3400	Autonomous FTR Ops	6101 — 6177	Eastern Radar (Sectors 10-17)
3401 — 3477	Scottish Domestic (Within Scottish FIR)	6201 — 6207	Eastern Radar (Sector 20)
		6210 — 6237	London Radar (Sectors 21-23)
3410 — 3427	RAF Leeming, Stansted Approach (3421 permanently allocated Essex police Helo), RAF Brawdy	6240 — 6267	Eastern Radar (Sectors 24-26)
		6270 — 6277	Not allocated
		6301 — 6307	London Radar Special Tasks (Sector 38)
3430 — 3477	Anglia Radar	6310 — 6377	London Radar (Sectors 31-37)
3500	Autonomous FTR Ops	6401 — 6477	London Domestic
3501 — 3507	ORCAM Berlin	6501 — 6577	Scottish Military, A & AEE Boscombe Down
3510 — 3537	ORCAM Maastricht		
3540 — 3577	ORCAM Berlin	6501 — 6507	RAF Wittering/RAF Cottesmore
3601 — 3677	Sumburgh Domestic	6510 — 6546	RAF Honington
3601 — 3644	Border Radar	6547	Cambridge Approach
3651 — 3654	Border Radar	6550 — 6577	RAF Cottesmore
3660	Border Radar	6601 — 6627	ORCAM Frankfurt
3670	Border Radar	6630 — 6677	ORCAM Dusseldorf
3671 — 3677	DRA Aberporth	6701 — 6777	ORCAM Marseille
3701 — 3717	RAF Coningsby	7000	Conspicuity code
3701 — 3717	A & AEE Boscombe Down	7001	Military Low Level Climbout/Conspicuity
3720 — 3727	RAF Northolt		
3720 — 3733	RAF Church Fenton	7002	Danger Areas General
3730 — 3767	RAE Bedford	7003	Red Arrows Transit/Display
3770 — 3777	RAF Mildenhall	7010 — 7043	RAF Spadeadam
4001 — 4047	ORCAM Brest	7010 — 7023	RAF Cranwell
4050 — 4077	ORCAM Bordeaux	7010 — 7077	RAF Bentwaters
4101 — 4177	ORCAM Frankfurt/Dusseldorf	7010 — 7057	RNAS Yeovilton
4201 — 4214	Heathrow Domestic	7060 — 7067	BAe Dunsfold, BAe Brough, BAe Warton
4215 — 4245	Dublin inbound UK Domestic		
4246 — 4253	CCF Special Tasks	7100 — 7177	ORCAM Brussels
4254 — 4625	Gatwick Domestic	7200 — 7217	Aberdeen Approach, Exeter Approach, Gatwick Approach, East Midlands Approach, Prestwick Approach
4266 — 4277	London Domestic		
4301	RSRE Malvern, ARE Portsdown		
4302	Blackpool Approach		
4303	RSRE Malvern	7220 — 7237	Manchester Approach
4304	Marconi, Rivenhall	7230 — 7247	Luton Approach, Cardiff Approach
4305	Royal Flights – Helicopters	7250	FIR Lost
4306	Selected Flights – Helicopters	7251 — 7257	London Special Tasks
4307	Not allocated	7251 — 7267	Edinburgh Approach
4310	Not allocated	7260 — 7277	Heathrow Approach, Birmingham Approach
4311	Antenna trailing/target towing		
4312	MATO Special Tasks	7270 — 7277	Scottish Special Tasks
4313/4314	Coventry Approach	7300 — 7307	London D & D Cell
4315	RAF Kemble	7310 — 7317	Eastern Radar (Allocator)
4316 — 4322	Not allocated	7320 — 7327	London Radar (Allocator North)
4323 — 4377	Manchester Domestic	7330 — 7337	London Radar (Allocator South)
4401 — 4477	London Domestic	7340 — 7377	Newcastle Approach
4510 — 4527	Westland Helicopters Yeovil	7400 — 7437	Scottish Domestic
4530 — 4537	BAe Filton	7440 — 7477	London Domestic
4540 — 4547	BAe Hatfield	7500	Hi-jacking
4560 — 4567	BAe Woodford	7501 — 7537	ORCAM Geneva
4560 — 4577	LONDON City Airport Approach	7540 — 7547	ORCAM Rhein
4570 — 4577	Filton Special Tasks	7550 — 7577	ORCAM Paris
4570	Humberside Approach	7600	Radio Failure
4571 — 4577	Humberside Approach	7601 — 7617	ORCAM Reims
4601 — 4677	Brize Radar, RAF Alconbury	7620 — 7647	ORCAM Paris
4701 — 4777	RNAS Culdrose	7650 — 7677	ORCAM Marseille
4740 — 4777	Scottish Domestic	7700	Emergency
5001 — 5077	Scottish Domestic	7701 — 7710	Not allocated
5101 — 5177	Scottish Domestic	7711 — 7717	SAR Operations
5201 — 5277	ORCAM London	7720	Not allocated
5301 — 5377	ORCAM Barcelona	7721 — 7727	SAR Operations
5401 — 5477	London Domestic	7730 — 7776	Not allocated
5501 — 5577	ORCAM Barcelona	7777	SSR Monitors
5601 — 5637	ORCAM Bordeaux		
5640 — 5677	ORCAM Paris		

Index

Mach Number 15
Microwave Landing
  System (MLS) 40
Military Aerodrome
  Traffic Zones
  (MATZ) 123-4
Military callsigns 129-
  30
Military Slots 121-2
Military Training
  Areas 34, 122
Minimum Descent
  Height 51
Minimum Noise
  Routes 106
Morse Code 153

Non-Directional
  Beacons (NDB) 36

Obstacle Clearance
  Height 51
Oceanic Control 79-87
Omega 41
ORCAM 66-7

PAPI 96-7
Phonetic Alphabet 18-9
Prohibited Areas 35
Purple airspace 125

Q-Code 19-20
QFE 14, 54, 90
QGH 59
QNH 14, 54, 91
Quadrantal Rule 17

Radar Advisory
  Service 88
Radar Information
  Service 89
Radar Video Corridor
  121-2
Radio failure 117-8
Readability scale 21
Royal Flights 125-6
RTTY 86
Runway markings 99
Runway Visual Range
  (RVR) 92

Satellite navigation 41
Secondary
  Surveillance Radar
  (SSR) 44-5, 49
SELCAL 82
Separation standards
  29
SIGMET 92
SNOWTAMS 93
Special VFR 17, 75

Speed control 52, 108
Squawks 15, 66-7
Standard Instrument
  Departures (SIDs)
  108, 126
Studs 119
Surveillance Radar
  Approach (SRA) 53-4
  phraseology 54-6

TACAN 126
TCAS 42
Transition altitude 14
Transponders 15, 41-2

Upper airspace 30-1
UTC 15
VASI 96-7
Visual Flight Rules
  (VFR) 16
Visual Meteorological
  Conditions (VMC)
  16
VOR 36
VOR/DME holding
  procedures 108
Vortex wake 63, 101
  separations 101-4

Wind shear 92-3